TELLING
TENNANT'S
STORY

I0022403

TELLING TENNANT'S STORY

The strange career of the
great Australian silence

DEAN ASHENDEN

Black Inc.

Published by Black Inc.,
an imprint of Schwartz Books Pty Ltd
22-24 Northumberland Street
Collingwood VIC 3066, Australia
enquiries@blackincbooks.com
www.blackincbooks.com

Copyright © Dean Ashenden 2022
Dean Ashenden asserts his right to be known as the author of this work.

ALL RIGHTS RESERVED.
No part of this publication may be reproduced, stored in a retrieval system,
or transmitted in any form by any means electronic, mechanical, photocopying,
recording or otherwise without the prior consent of the publishers.

9781760641757 (paperback)
9781743822258 (ebook)

A catalogue record for this
book is available from the
NATIONAL LIBRARY OF AUSTRALIA
National Library of Australia

Cover and text design by Tristan Main
Typesetting by Typography Studio
Cover image: Ingo Oeland / Alamy Stock Photo
Maps by Alan Laver

Aboriginal and Torres Strait Islander readers are advised that this publication contains names and images of people who have passed away.

'... the other side of a story over which the great Australian silence reigns, the story, in short, of the unacknowledged relations between two racial groups within a single field of life'

W.E.H. Stanner, 1968

CONTENTS

PART TWO

THE STRUGGLE TO DISMANTLE THE SILENCE

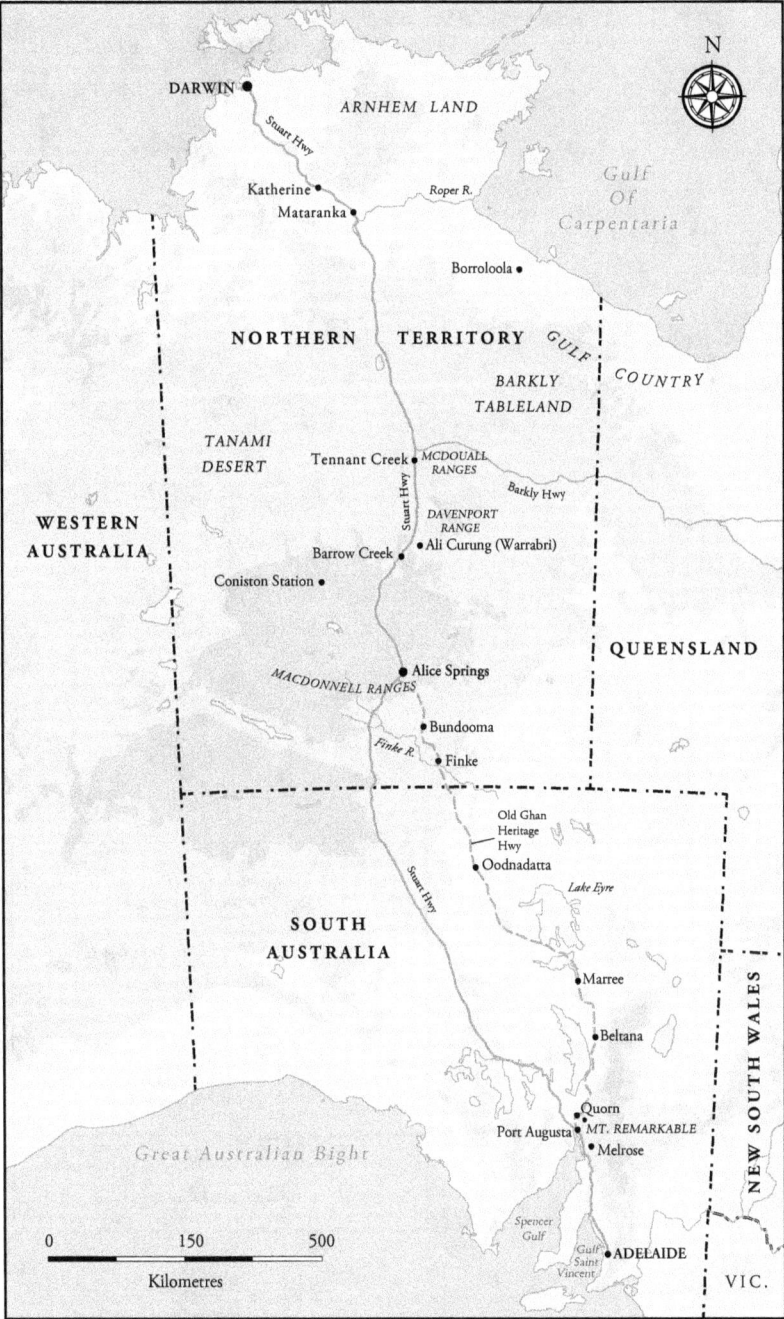

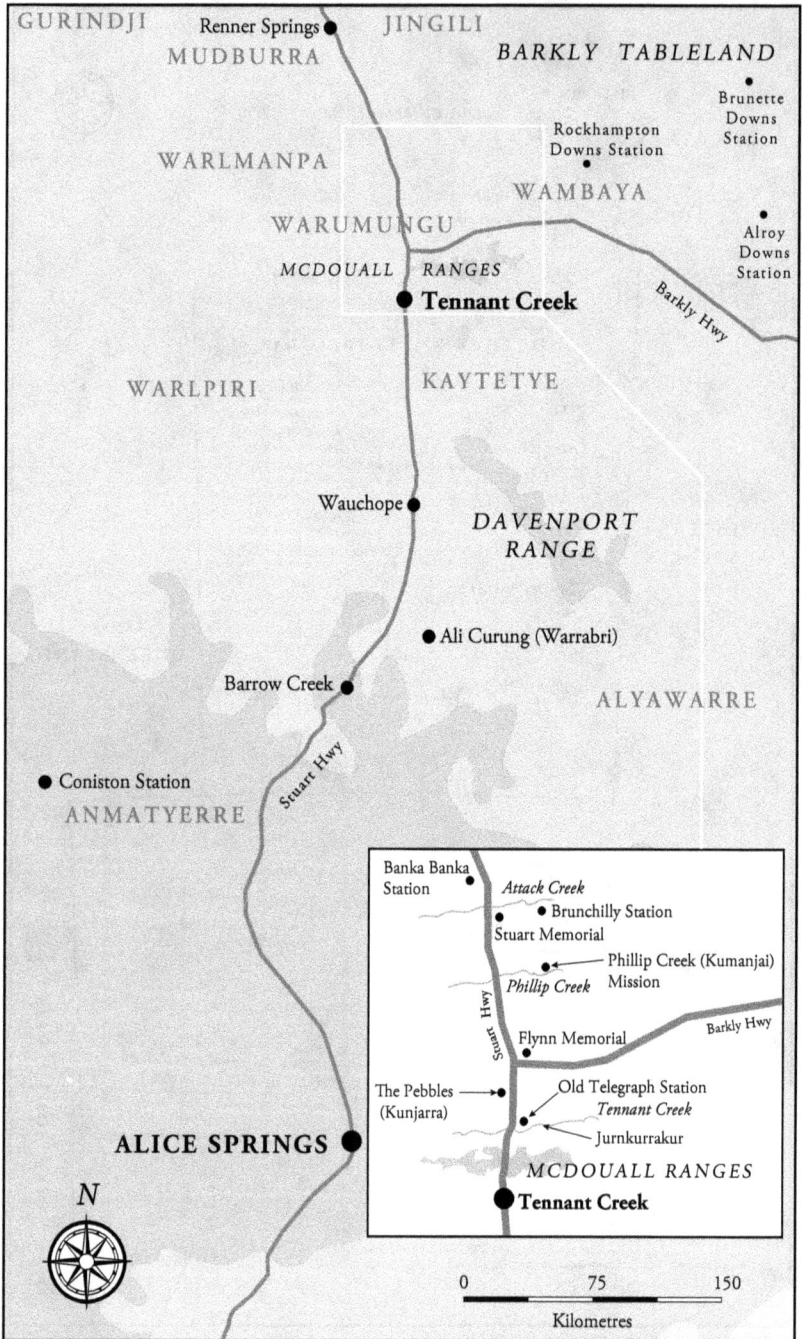

GURINDJI

Renner Springs

JINGILI

MUDBURRA

BARKLY TABLELAND

Brunette
Downs
Station

Rockhampton
Downs Station

WARLMANPA

WAMBAYA

WARUMUNGU

Alroy
Downs
Station

MCDOUALL   RANGES

Tennant Creek

Barkly Hwy

WARLPIRI

KAYTETYE

Wauchope

DAVENPORT
RANGE

Ali Curung (Warrabri)

Barrow Creek

ALYAWARRE

Coniston Station

ANMATYERRE

Stuart Hwy

ALICE SPRINGS

N

Banka Banka
Station

Attack Creek

Brunchilly Station

Stuart Memorial

Phillip Creek (Kumanjai)

Phillip Creek   Mission

Stuart Hwy

Flynn Memorial

Barkly Hwy

The Pebbles
(Kunjarra)

Old Telegraph Station
Tennant Creek

Jurnkurrakur

MCDOUALL RANGES

Tennant Creek

0   75   150

Kilometres

NOTE ON USAGE

There is still no agreed or non-contentious way for people like me, a fourth-generation Australian of English and Scottish extraction, to refer to those who were here before 'us', and their descendants. In the course of my lifetime, struggles for respect and against stigma have shifted usage from 'natives' or 'blacks' or 'aborigines' to 'Aborigines' to 'Aboriginal' and 'Indigenous' to 'First Australians', 'First Peoples' and, most recently, to specific 'nations' and groups. The term 'black' (or 'Black') has made a limited comeback; 'natives' is irretrievably derogatory. The recently introduced generics have been used only occasionally in this book; in the context of a story stretching over more than two centuries, they would read as self-conscious retrofits. The general rule I have tried to follow is that where 'Aboriginal' or 'Aboriginal Australian' or 'black' or 'blackfella' or '*wumparrani*' (a Warumungu word) have been used, then 'European' or 'white' or 'whitefella' or '*papulanyi*' are also used or clearly implied. The terms 'us' and 'them' refer to common practices of identity and affiliation, not to wholly exclusive categories. The many derogatory and demeaning terms applied by 'us' to 'them' – 'niggers', 'Abos', 'half-caste', 'lubra' and all the rest – are treated as historical artefacts and relics, indicated by inverted commas, except where it is obvious that the past is speaking in its own voice. Some terms used to refer to earlier generations of white Australians – 'settler', 'explorer' and 'pioneer', for example – are likewise framed by inverted commas or questioned directly. These precepts have no doubt been imperfectly followed, and are inherently provisional anyway. Struggles over and learning about language are central parts of the continuing story of the 'relations between two racial groups within a single field of life',[1] the subject matter of this book.

PROLOGUE

By lunchtime on the first day we were in Melrose, a pretty town tucked up against Mt Remarkable, in the lower Flinders Ranges. Lunch was a sandwich in the municipal park, and in the park was a billboard. 'Paradise Square,' it announced, perhaps with dry humour. 'The following is a list of known burials that took place here in the Old Melrose Cemetery between 1846 and 1872.' And there they were, scores of names in alpha order, each with date and age of death and a crisp descriptor. NOTT, Thomas Freedman, a surveyor of Melrose, died aged sixty-five on 5.12.1865. NOTT, Mildred, a widow of Melrose, followed her husband on 12.11.1869, aged fifty-five. Jesse Jones, a bushman of Melrose, went aged fifty in 1861. William Jones, storekeeper, went later (1868) but younger (thirty-four). The dead of Melrose included carpenters, shepherds, a hawker, carriers and teamsters, a corporal of police, a bailiff, a surgeon, all men. The women were daughters, mothers, wives, widows. Then there were the children, so many children, aged three months or six weeks, or five years or nine years, an 'unnamed son of Richard Saunders' who died on 3.1.1863 after just four hours of life. It was a touching record of another age. In a reverie as I read the names, the dates, the lives summed up in a few numerals and a word or a phrase, I struggled to recognise a feeling that refused to surface. And then, it did: where are the Aboriginal dead?

The first of the burials in the Old Melrose Cemetery was in 1846, just ten years after the colony of South Australia was declared in Adelaide, 270 miles south of here. Melrose in 1846 would have been on the frontier. Where were the Aboriginal dead?

It was the same in Quorn, less than an hour up the road, lots of info about the Ghan and the movies that had been made in the district but nothing about Aboriginal people, who they were or how they fared when the inexorable frontier arrived. Beltana, a scattering of houses and ruins further on, dwelt on its overland telegraph station, long since passed from use. Nothing about the Aboriginal people there either.

I'd begun to take photos of the many markers of the past, the monuments, the plaques, the info boards, the billboards and museums, and to puzzle over them. What was going on? Some of what was going on was obvious. 'History' was a boom industry fed by tourism. Melrose announced itself as 'historic', chiefly on the ground that it had been base camp for John McDouall Stuart on his many attempts to cross the continent from south to north and back again. Quorn was 'historic'

'Many markers of the past'

because on the old line it used to be the last stop for the Ghan before it headed out into the desert for Alice Springs, a couple of days away. Beltana was 'historic' by virtue of its telegraph station and by being not much more than a collection of ruins. The old road, which followed the old railway line that followed the old Overland Telegraph Line that followed Stuart's epic plod, was itself historic. It was now 'The Old Ghan Heritage Trail'. The first of these many markers of History had been installed in the 1960s but most were of more recent date. They were about an implied 'us', our Pioneers, our Settlers, our Explorers, our feats of endurance, engineering, discovery. This was winners' history. Where were the losers?

The losers made their first appearance near Lake Eyre, 400-odd kilometres on from Melrose. An info board there detailed the many traditional and contemporary uses of ochre, mined nearby. This was the equal and opposite of the markers in which the Aborigines didn't appear; there was no mention of *us*. Neither the markers about us nor the markers about them reported when or where or what happened when we encountered them, and they us. The ochre info board and many to follow did a jump cut: one moment we're in Traditional Times, the next, in the present. How did they get from then to now? Just don't mention the war.

That remained the overwhelming rule for a thousand kilometres or more, although there were exceptions, reports of the terror provoked by the huge four-legged, hard-footed animals that appeared without warning in the 1860s, references to the disruption of Indigenous land 'since the Europeans first permanently arrived/invaded', info boards about police operations 'to control cattle spearing by Aborigines on newly established pastoral properties', an info board that dispensed with evasions about 'arrival/invasion' and just called the spade a spade, even an angry denunciation of the 'transnationals and colonialist governments … defying the natural order of things in their quest for material wealth'.

I photographed every one of these many markers and kept on puzzling. Eventually I realised what should have been obvious: the history wars then raging in newspapers and scholarly articles and books and on the airwaves had been going on out here for decades. We'd won the country and then set out to win the story as well. The struggle over what the story would and would not tell was as much a part of the story as the events themselves. By the time I reached Tennant Creek, a couple of weeks after lunch in Paradise Square, the telling of the story had been added to my list of things to find out about. Eventually, it worked its way to the top.

•

I left Tennant Creek in 1955, aged thirteen. I had never been back and never wanted to go back. In fact, I'd wanted to not go back. I didn't like it when we lived there and ached to leave, despite the fact that it was a kind of kids' paradise. We'd thread our way through the spinifex to old mine shafts and chuck beer bottles down to see how deep they were, or lie on our backs inside the fence around the aerodrome and scare ourselves stupid as the DC-3, feeling for the runway, roared over us just a few feet above. Out the back of our place was the Works and Housing depot, surrounded by piles of junk from the war, then only seven years away, including, inexplicably, an old Rolls-Royce limo complete with a screened-off passenger compartment and a speaking tube through which we'd issue instructions in what we took to be toffy tones. There were topknot pigeons to be shot at with air rifles and old tins and jars to be blown up with miners' lamp carbide. We stood at the dam behind the pub where the night before a bloke had bet he could swim across, but drowned, and we pedalled out to the bend in the Peko road where

Mr Archer had killed himself when he rolled his Fargo ute. We swam in the waterhole under redgums at Seven Mile, and every Saturday night there were the pictures at the open-air theatre, westerns mostly, in my memory anyway. Sometimes even a kid could see the magic in the desert, the sunsets, the fresh and vivid world after rain, the brilliant stars that would light our way home after the pictures. But mostly it wasn't like that at all, just the blinding light that flattened and bleached, and the heat, and the incessant moaning of the wind and the ugly cawing of the crows.

I now suspect that in developing something close to loathing for Tennant, I had been taking my mother's part. She suffered in the heat and despaired at the red-brown dust that was forever blowing through the flyscreened verandas onto furniture, floors, ledges, shelves, everywhere. She became anaemic, teary and homesick. She missed her family and the soft green Adelaide Hills where they worked their orchards and market gardens, and where she'd grown up, and she missed her eldest son, who'd been sent to Alice Springs for high school. She wanted to leave, and so did I, but couldn't. She fretted that her husband would apply for a transfer rather than wait for another promotion, and it would be her fault.

Her husband, my father, was in his element. For fifteen years he'd been a teacher. Now he was the head teacher, a member of Tennant's public service elite. Our house was one of five or six identical government houses lined up along with the police station, the post office and the school at the southern end of town. At the other end were two general stores, the bakery-cum-café, the cool drink factory, the picture theatre, and the pubs, the Goldfields and the Tennant. It was only half a mile or so to the other end of town and we went down there just about every day. We'd ride our bikes along the narrow bitumen strip between expanses of gravelly red dirt, the Alice–Darwin highway that doubled as Tennant's main street, lined by dusty shanties with stamped earthen floors and push-out galvanised-iron windows, which looked as though

Grades I–VII Tennant Creek Primary School, 1952

they had slumped in the heat. I'd visit Mum at the general store where she worked behind the counter or go to mates' places or ride past the stinky din of the front bar of the pub and see inside as the door swung open or just hang around. It was wholly familiar, but mysterious. We knew that this was the real Tennant to which teetotal public service blow-ins had no access, but we caught glimpses and heard echoes in the stories Tennant told about itself.

These were the stories we told back in Adelaide three years later as reports from another planet, stories about gold that went missing after a couple of fellas came up on the Tuesday plane and went back down again on Wednesday, about cattle rustling or bar-room brawls, about mysterious deaths and fortunes won and lost, and of course the one about how Tennant Creek the town was seven miles south of Tennant Creek the creek because that's where the beer truck had broken down. To these we added stories of our own, about 100 days in a row over the 100 mark, the dust storms, the weekly bath in a few inches of increasingly brown water, a diet strong on meat but light on fruit and veg, the Barcoo Rot and the conjunctivitis from the diet and the flies, about Dad asking the police sergeant whether bush turkeys were protected and being told that they were and how to cook them, and about the New Year's Day when Danny Brookes' Rolls-Royce limo – he'd tracked down the owner and bought it for sixty quid, apparently – trundled past our place, draped with men and women in various states of undress, still carousing, did a stately U-turn then headed back to the other end of town.

What I couldn't understand then was that we had returned from the frontier, the place that all of Australia has been at one time or another. Some of it still is.

•

We'd hardly arrived in Tennant before we found out about the kids from the mission. We saw them every Saturday night at the open-air pictures. We all sat in a deck-chair sort of arrangement, rows and rows of long horizontal poles with canvas strips slung between them. It paid to get there early because the canvas strips, permanently exposed to the elements, often ripped to cheers and whistles in the middle of a film and the strips got shorter and tauter every time they were repaired. Anyway, we'd all be settled under our blankets against the cold desert nights and waiting for 'God Save the Queen' when the kids from the mission would file in between us and the screen, crossing to the far side to the benches reserved for them. After the pictures they'd climb onto the mission truck and head off up the road into the darkness while we walked home under that vast, glittering sky, in the other direction.

Apart from Saturday nights you could never tell when you might see them. Sometimes there was a black tracker at the back of the police station. Once I saw four or five Aborigines a bit of a distance out in the spinifex that stretched away from our back fence to a distant horizon. I got close enough to see them squatting in the sandy dirt behind a low humpy, playing cards. Then one day they were gone. Sometimes when I visited Mum at the general store there would be several old Aboriginal men sitting, cross-legged, on the veranda. Perhaps it was them I saw one day on a truck rigged up to carry cattle, the mission truck I suppose. They were in army greatcoats, standing motionless and silent as the truck went slowly past.

There was a sports day at the creek. We all drove out from the town and they came down from the mission. We spread ourselves under the gums by the waterhole. They were across the other side of a dusty clearing where the races were run, adults as well as children. We were invited to Sunday lunch at Banka Banka, the nearest station to Tennant Creek. Seated at a long table, we were served by Aboriginal women who padded silently across the cool concrete floor. One September holidays Dad loaded up his single-spinner V8 Ford Custom with camping gear and off we went to Darwin, where we saw the wrecks in the harbour and neat rows of bullet holes in the walls of the old post office, and gawked at the Aborigines who hung around the back streets. They were *really* black, we observed, not just dark like ours. On the way back we stayed a night at the Mataranka Station homestead, already operating as a guest house. We swam in the warm bubbling spring at the head of the Roper River, clear as crystal. In the morning, at breakfast, the room was dominated by a noisy group a couple of tables away. They're making a film, Dad told us. Among them, quite still, and very beautiful, was a young Aboriginal woman.

These were encounters as in a tableau. So far as I can recall I never spoke to any of these Aborigines, nor they to me. The only exceptions to this rule, and even more puzzling because of it, were three Aboriginal kids at school, the brothers Roy, Rex and Rennie Hare. How come they lived in the town and not out on the mission? Was it because they weren't real Aborigines? Their father, Mr Hare, was the nightsoil man who collected the tubs slopping with shit and phenol and sodden strips of newspaper from the back of the drop dunnies. Mr Hare was white, but Roy and Rex and Rennie's mother was Aboriginal. The Hares lived in one of those tin shanties, the very last one right up the other end of town.

The Aborigines were nearly invisible yet somehow always there somewhere; sometimes referred to, even discussed, but never explained. Our Grade VI Social Studies text recorded the feats of John McDouall Stuart, whose explorations prepared the way for the Overland Telegraph Line, which I could see just by looking out the schoolroom window. I was in awe of Stuart. How *could* he have walked all that way from Adelaide? More than a thousand miles! Five times! I designed a kind of palanquin supported by poles carried by a horse at each corner that he could have used to stroll along in permanent shade. The Social Studies textbook told us about Stuart's encounter with fierce Aborigines just a bit further on from Tennant Creek the creek. When we crossed Attack Creek at the beginning of our big camping trip to Darwin, there was a small thrill of excitement. Shots were fired, and spears thrown, *here!*

The space between that day in June 1860 and ours was filled by a vague sense of a vanished world. On one of our Sunday drives along bush tracks, we passed close to the bluffs of the gap in the range just north of the town. That's Gins' Lookout, Mum said, pointing to one of the bluffs. That's where the 'lubras' used to keep a lookout for the men coming back from the hunt. She told us that one of the old men who sat on the veranda of the general store was their king. Such a dignified old man, she said.

•

In the early 1960s I went to uni in Adelaide, to what was then generally regarded as the hottest history department in the country. In four years my cohort did no Australian history at all, let alone the history of relations between black and white. It was the fag end of the mental world of the Grade VI Social Studies textbook. Elsewhere on campus, however, were signs of what was to come, including meetings and protests in support of 'rights for Aborigines'. Scrappy little events like the two or three I went to turned into an uproar that subsequently rose and fell but never really went away – a freedom ride, a tent embassy, speeches and tracts and posters beyond counting, strikes, investigations, legislation and litigation, movies, books and docos, then *Mabo*, a semi-official accusation of genocide, and the ferocious history wars.

All that provided the means by which people of my generation and demographic learned what we hadn't been told and unlearned some of what we had. For reasons that I can't really explain but suspect don't do me much credit, it was a long time before I started to connect all that national uproar with the one time and place at which my life had intersected so directly with the lives of Aboriginal people – and the people who kept them out on the mission, over to one side at the movies, out of our school and town, out of mind. It wasn't just that I didn't know; I hadn't realised how much I didn't know. Thanks to all those Westerns, I could reel off a long list of 'Indian' tribes, the Cheyenne, the Comanche, the Apache and the rest, but I did not even know that we had been living among the Warumungu and the Warlpiri. I didn't know what the 'mission' was or how the Warumungu and the Warlpiri got to be there or even where it was.

I began finding out, partly out of embarrassment, but also curiosity. Who *were* they? Where on earth had a full-on policed and regulated apartheid regime come from? Where did it go? The more I read the more there was to know and the more I wanted to know it. That was a puzzle in itself. After a pretty slow start, why the obsession? No doubt it was the usual thing, the further you get from childhood the more fascinating it becomes, but it wasn't just that. I was being carried along by a deep emotional undertow. The Aboriginal people and their relationship with the rest of us have become sites of proxy political warfare and synthetic emotions but there's real stuff there too, ranging from just feeling *bad* (in my case, whenever I think about those kids crossing in front of the screen at the Pioneer Picture Theatre) through to how *everyone* felt when Cathy Freeman won the big race. Against any expectation and all intentions, and with very mixed feelings, I decided to go back.

It was in part just a standard grey-nomad kind of thing to do, and a chance to revisit what had been, after all, a burst of the vivid in an otherwise sepia-toned boyhood, but there were offsets too – the old aversions and a new one, the fact that Tennant had turned into Australia's most notoriously dysfunctional town, something I had no wish to see. But I did want to find out where the Tennant Creek I'd lived in had come from, and gone, and thought (correctly, as it turned out) that I couldn't unless I went there.

So, I set out for Tennant Creek to find out about relations between two racial groups in that particular field of life but didn't get far – to Paradise Square in Melrose, at lunchtime on Day One to be exact – before there was something else to find out about: how the story of those relations had been told, and not told. All the stories that the Tennant Creek of my boyhood had told about itself and the stories we took back to tell our uncles and aunts and grandparents, they weren't Tennant's big story at all. By the time I'd made the last of three trips back to Tennant I'd learned that the struggles over whether and how to tell Tennant's story were for a century and a half Australia's struggles writ small, and intense. I found that among the protagonists were several of Australia's intellectual luminaries and that not once but twice poor beaten-down smashed-up Tennant Creek had managed to make it onto the national stage, not in a starring role but a big enough part to earn a place in the credits. Tennant, with and like Australia, had tried to tell the story.

PART ONE

CONSTRUCTING THE SILENCE

Mt Liebig, Central Australia, 1932

CHAPTER ONE

1860

The vague sense of a vanished world that I carried with me from Tennant Creek became less vague in a single moment. I'm not sure when I first saw Norman Tindale's map 'Tribal Boundaries in Aboriginal Australia', but it was certainly long before it became available on the internet and was probably soon after it was published in its final form in 1974.[1] It wasn't just a map of tribal boundaries. It was an assertion that on 26 January 1788 there existed on this continent a social order of elaborate scale. In Tindale's map, Australia looked like medieval Europe but only more so: hundreds of little republics, between them covering every square kilometre of the continent and many of its offshore islands as well.[2] And there – surrounded by the Bingongina, the Tjingil (Jingili), the Wambaia (Wambaya), the Indjilandji, the Wakaja, the Kaititja (Kaytetye) and the Walpiri (Warlpiri) – were the people of Tennant Creek, the Waramanga (Warumungu).[3] They had once belonged to an entire civilisation.

The Aborigines and their ways had fascinated European diarists, keepers of journals, artists and authors from the moment they arrived (the first book featuring the Aborigines was published in London less than two years after the First Fleet dropped anchor), but when Tindale took an interest in them in the late 1920s, he joined a select few. When he submitted the first version of his map for publication in 1940 it was

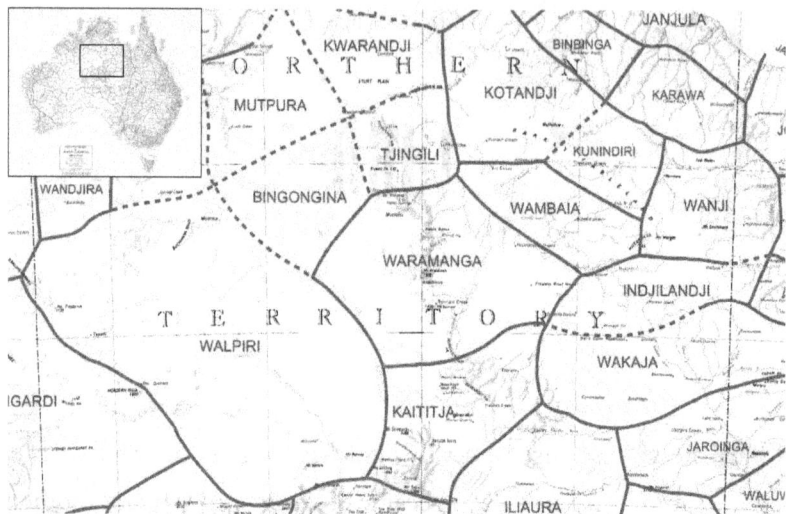

'And there ... were the Waramanga'

queried on the grounds that, as everyone knew, the Aborigines were simply wanderers, roaming over the country at will. Soon after realising that the Aboriginal world was geographically, socially and culturally highly organised, Tindale assembled evidence to show that it was long-established as well. The Aborigines were not recent arrivals, he argued, but had inhabited Australia for several thousand years. That assertion too was greeted with disbelief.[4]

Tindale was an early rider of the second great wave of fascination with the Aborigines. By the time he at last put down his pen and camera in 1993, his interest was the reverse of eccentric. It was no longer pastoralists, explorers, missionaries and government officials who were recording what they saw but linguists, anthropologists and archaeologists, professionals in the business of recovering what was, a few rapidly disappearing remnants excepted, no longer there to be seen. This they did in extraordinary detail. A digest of what was known about the world of the First Australians by the late 1990s encompassed Aboriginal social groupings, relations and structures, economic life, relationships with the land, growing up and the life cycle, religious beliefs and practices, magic and sorcery, law and order, politics, art and aesthetic expression, and death and the afterlife.[5]

Tindale's early estimate of several thousand years of Aboriginal occupation was pushed out to ten then twenty then forty and is now sixty thousand years or more, a span difficult and perhaps impossible to comprehend.[6] Ancient Greece and Rome? Two or three. The first cities and states in the Middle East and India? Five or six. Early agriculture: seven or eight. The end of the last Ice Age: ten or eleven. Humans reaching the north and then the south American continents: around twenty. And that still leaves forty-plus millennia to go. When Governor Phillip landed there were between three-quarters of a million and a million or more people living in 'Australia'. One estimate was that the continent had been home to a thousand generations, a total of something like 400 million people. But that was when it was thought that people had been here for 20,000 years. At 50,000 years, Australia's most eminent archaeologist suggested a billion or so; how many might be added by yet more thousands of years and hundreds of generations?

As remarkable is the fact that, with some notable exceptions (including perhaps the unfortunate megafauna), these people found ways to live within their ecological means.[7] They developed powerful combinations of expertise and technique to sustain and use the land transmitted through stories, dance, instruction, injunction and cosmology.[8] 'Australia,' one anthropologist has written, 'was groomed by people who dedicated their lives to the task of life's priests.' Aboriginal peoples included every significant topographical feature of the entire continent in their imaginative world and made their material world into 'the biggest estate on earth'. It gave them diets of grains, fruit, nuts, honey, insects, meats and, for many, the bounty of lakes, streams and oceans vastly superior to that of the Europeans of the First Fleet. People living in what is now known as the Little Sandy Desert in Western Australia used eighty-nine species of food plants (including roots, tubers and twelve species of fruit), as well as birds, animals, moths and larvae.[9] In most circumstances they enjoyed a working day that we could envy, with ample time for a rich cultural life that included painting, carving, and drawing on the walls of caves, in the sand, on implements, weapons, jewellery and bodies; song, dance and storytelling; making tools and weapons from stone, wood, skins, wax and resin; and many combinations of these in ceremonies and rituals. They had worked out complex forms of social organisation and an equally complex political order; relationships between tribal groups included multi-layered rights to land and water access and use. (The last of these complications, by the way, makes the boundaries on Tindale's map and my use of the term 'republics' risky simplifications). They had taken 'the Zen road to affluence', their millennia of isolation perhaps accounting for the intricacy and variety of cultural rather than technological development.[10]

Thus equipped, Aboriginal peoples were capable of extraordinary continuity but also substantial change, including coping with major fluctuations in rainfall and temperature and the end of the ice age, which reduced the landmass by about a third. They developed trade routes which took ochre, axe heads and other goods over many hundreds of miles. Stories and ceremonies, often remembered with remarkable fidelity over centuries, travelled from one end of the continent to another along the 'songlines' given contemporary currency by Bruce Chatwin's 1987 book. They had an enviable sense of the oneness of the world and of its endlessness. They succeeded in matters where we have not: bringing up kids, integrating young men into the social order, looking after old people (although few were old by our standards), knowing how to grieve and, of course, knowing how to run sustainable economic, political and social systems. They were multilingual. They were fit and lean. They lived in a world of certainties and of magic. In 1975 Geoffrey Blainey was the first to use a burgeoning mass of scholarly evidence to complement Tindale's satellite view, creating a detailed portrait of a vanished world. He called it *Triumph of the Nomads*.

I was awed particularly by the desert people, perhaps because the frontier left them to survive longest to become a common image of 'the Aborigine', perhaps because these were the people I saw, remembered and eventually met, perhaps because of their austere, disciplined lives.[11] The anthropologist Baldwin Spencer, of whom much more will be heard, listed the possessions of a man who died during Spencer's time with the Warumungu: one tomahawk (got from the whitefellas), one adze, one club, six pitchis (his wife's property, really) and six head and neck bands.[12] The desert Aborigines were able to flourish in country that Europeans could scarcely cross (witness John McDouall Stuart) let alone live in.

'Do not sentimentalise these people,' an old hand warned a colleague new to learning about Aboriginal worlds, past and present. Much in the present is miserable; much in the past was harsh. There was plenty to be unsentimental about. A male-dominated gerontocracy[13] was maintained by methods that sometimes included the kind of violence by men against women that so shocked Arthur Phillip.[14] (Aboriginal people, it should be noted, were as shocked by his kind of violence – hanging and whipping, for example – as he was by theirs.) Brutal raids on neighbours and sorcery created an undercurrent of fear. Anthropologist Ted Strehlow, brought up by his missionary parents with the Arrernte people of central Australia, once claimed that an outbreak of inter-group violence there was so costly that many were relieved to have it ended by the arrival of the Europeans.[15] Pain and discomfort were familiar parts of everyday life. Drought often made a bountiful world hostile. Their lives were much shorter than ours. But in the most important sense this kind of audit doesn't matter.[16] Better? Worse? Some of each? All beside the point. The point is that it was theirs. They had no wish or need to be saved from it. They fought hard to keep it and to go on being themselves. If 'we' – by which I mean those who, like me, are of British descent – if we set aside for a moment our feelings about the fact that it was us whom they had to fight against and who made their world vanish, and the fact that it was them not us who suffered from its loss, it is still possible to feel a simple sadness that a world made by hundreds of millions of people over tens of millennia disappeared in a blink, that what has been recovered in our imaginations is in fact gone, irretrievably.

•

The frontier that got under way in Sydney in January 1788 was the first of many and the model for most. First came a beachhead – Hobart, Perth, Adelaide, Melbourne, Brisbane and others – then movement inland, usually along a snail-trail traced on the map by an explorer, sometimes preceded by sealers or whalers and, in the early stages particularly, often accompanied by devastating diseases. Contact sometimes began in hesitant curiosity or an effort at comprehension by each side of the other. It often degenerated into violence and sooner or later arrived at elimination or an 'accommodation' on grossly unequal terms. Sometimes the frontier was driven by timber-getting or mining, rarely by agriculture or horticulture, mostly by pastoralism, sheep at first then later, and further inland, cattle.

The Warumungu were unusual in confronting two of these violent frontiers in quick succession and just about unique in surviving both. The first made its tentative appearance in June 1860, a mere lifetime after the first of the frontiers began in Sydney, in a form that scarcely hinted at what was to come. The explorer in the Warumungu case was

John McDouall Stuart. He turned up four months after setting out from his base north of Adelaide, the modest capital of the infant colony of South Australia. He got the impression that the Warumungu had some awareness of the whites, but a Warumungu man later recalled thinking that Stuart and his little party had come out of the ground.[17] At all events, the Warumungu got a good look at massive, hard-hooved animals, and in the death of a young man at Attack Creek from gunshot wounds an inkling of a new and baffling kind of power.[18] But Stuart went away. He reappeared twice over the next couple of years, but each time disappeared again.

Stuart was not just a passing visitor, however. He was a land prospector.[19] (He named Tennant Creek after one of his many pastoralist backers.) Unbeknown to the Warumungu, their Country soon appeared on maps, neatly divided into lots by men in Adelaide who dreamed of new fortunes from selling land and of making South Australia the first colony in history to found a colony of its own, the Northern Territory of South Australia.[20] Stuart was followed by several groups of men with more strange animals and another skirmish, but these men too disappeared and did not return. The Warumungu were sometimes referred to by their neighbours as *bata aurinnia*, 'people who dwell on hard ground'.[21] Much of their Country was too poor (and too far from markets) to support cattle or sheep. In fact, it wasn't even good enough to sustain flocks and herds in transit.

Just what the Warumungu made of this sequence of strange events is impossible to know, but it seems likely that they didn't realise what they were up against until more of the white men came and did not go away again. To the contrary, those white men put up a building and there they remained. It was only then that the Warumungu gave these strange people a name: they were the *papulanyi*, 'denizens of buildings', people who, extraordinarily, stayed in one place.

We used to pass the old telegraph station whenever we went out to the creek for a swim. We'd head north through the town and then the gap in the range where, my mother had said, 'the lubras' kept a look-out for the men coming back from the hunt. Another two or three miles along we'd turn right off the highway onto a bumpy track. A few hundred yards in, just before the waterhole, was the old station, its galvanised-iron roof sloping close to the ground to make a deeply shaded veranda around stone walls. Thanks to Social Studies and the misfortune of living with the Social Studies teacher, we – my two brothers and I – knew all about the telegraph station. It was one of twelve strung out along the 2000 miles of the Overland Telegraph Line, which ran between Adelaide and Darwin.[22] That line connected with others to put Australia in instantaneous touch with London and therefore the world. The line, we were taught, was a marvel of technology and construction, completed in just two years by engineer Charles Todd. Todd was second in esteem only to Stuart, whose intrepid path the line had followed. (Todd got his knighthood but Stuart, on account of his 'habits of intemperance', missed out.)[23]

Todd preferred conciliation to confrontation and his crews were under strict orders to avoid provoking the Aboriginal people, but since they brought with them hundreds of horses, cattle and sheep that consumed phenomenal quantities of water and trammelled the pristine edges of waterholes, and since they had come into tribal lands without waiting at the border for permission to proceed, and since they often committed offences like stumbling into secret ceremonies – some have suggested that this provoked the violence at Attack Creek – provocation was part and parcel of the entire project. The line's stations were built in the form of a square with a central courtyard and just one entrance, barred windows, and firing loopholes in thick stone walls, a tacit admission that Todd and his men knew what they were doing.

They might have expected that if an attack was coming it would come first from the Warumungu; of all the tribes encountered by Stuart and the others who had followed, only the Warumungu had opted for violent resistance, first and famously at 'Attack' Creek and then in two more fatal skirmishes a decade or so later.[24] It was not the Warumungu who snapped, however, but their southern neighbours, the Kaytetye.

Aboriginal peoples were entirely familiar with violence, but what they were not used to – in fact, what none had ever seen, attempted or imagined – was conquest. Did the Kaytetye realise that the previously unimaginable was happening, that the white men were trying to take their Country? That and other explanations have been advanced; all remain speculative. For whatever reason or combination of reasons, in 1874, less than two years after the line was put through their Country, the Kaytetye attacked. It was a dramatic episode played out over and again in colonial imaginations: sunset, the men of the Barrow Creek station gathered on the front veranda to enjoy the cool of the evening and the violin of the stationmaster, oblivious to twenty-odd Kaytetye men descending the hill behind the station, apparently unarmed but

'Descending the hill behind the station'

in fact dragging spears between their toes.[25] The sudden assault left a linesman dead and the stationmaster dying before the survivors could grab their guns and repel the attack.

Poignancy was now added to drama. The stationmaster's wife, more than a thousand miles away in Adelaide, was brought to the General Post Office by the carriage of Todd himself. There a young telegraph officer by the name of Francis Gillen transmitted to and fro the last words between man and wife. He recorded the scene forty years later as one half of the celebrated anthropologist duo Spencer and Gillen.[26] 'In the crowded and busy room of the General Post Office … with dozens of machines incessantly ticking messages … the wife spoke to her husband far away in the centre. In the Barrow Creek station, where he lay dying, there was perfect silence save for the ticking of the one machine as it received the message from Adelaide and sent back the last farewell of the expiring man.'

Meanwhile, news of the attack went up and down the line. Men from stations to the north and the south, Tennant Creek and Alice Springs, rode to join the survivors at Barrow Creek and to prepare to teach the 'natives' a lesson they would never forget, as the currency of the day had it, and they did. Just how many people were killed is unknown, but it is known that a posse led by Constable Gason was in the saddle for six weeks, roaming far beyond Kaytetye Country to deliver the lesson to any who might need it. Gason reported eleven deaths, but evidence subsequently given to anthropologists and others suggests that the actual number was several multiples of that figure.[27] The Warumungu learned the lesson inflicted on their unfortunate neighbours and never repeated their earlier use of violence against the *papulanyi*. With a lot of luck and a certain amount of judgement, they had survived their first violent frontier. Their second would be very different, and much more dangerous. It came not in the form of tentative pastoralism and a relatively benign telegraph line but as a massive invasion of cattle, horses and guns. And it came not from the south or the north but from the east, from Queensland. It was not the last armed assault by white on black, but it was a climactic spasm of the last of the violent Australian frontiers.

•

By 1850 the vast area now known as Queensland was the last expanse of 'good' country still available to be 'opened up'. Much of it was densely populated, its quarter of a million or more inhabitants representing around a third of the Aboriginal population of the continent when the Europeans arrived. Much of the country was defendable as well as rich and desirable, much like the south, where Aboriginal resistance had often held up the frontier for years or even pushed it back. But now the white men were better prepared and better equipped. When Queensland was hived off from New South Wales as a separate entity in 1859, it inherited a paramilitary force that became known as the Queensland Native Police (QNP).[28] The nub of the idea was to set Aborigines to work on hunting Aborigines. It was by no means the first or the last such relationship between white and black, but it was far and away the most lethal.[29]

The QNP comprised around a hundred Aboriginal troopers and a handful of white officers. They operated from forty-odd semi-permanent campsites to conduct both regular and ad hoc mounted patrols. Their firepower increased over four decades of operation, from muzzle-loaders to breech-loading Snyders that fired huge .522 calibre soft-nosed bullets over hundreds of yards to Martini-Henry rifles accurate over half a mile or more. If ever an antidote to sentimentalising the Aborigines were needed, the QNP provides it. Historians and others have agonised over what to make of the behaviour of the 'native troopers'.[30] In explanation and/or exculpation, it can be said that the troopers were themselves brutalised survivors of dreadful experience, or that they wanted power among their own people by associating with the powerful newcomers, or that they were recruited, paid and directed by the invaders, or that 'Aboriginal' is our concept not theirs and the people shot down were foreigners at war, but the fact remains that the Aboriginal troopers were brutal killers on a massive scale in a grossly lopsided conflict. Permitted to operate without direct supervision or accountability but well supplied with arms, equipment and ammunition, the QNP eschewed mere reprisal for pre-emptive elimination and intimidation.

The activities of the QNP and the Queensland frontier in general have been researched by many historians over several decades, yielding steadily rising estimates of casualties.[31] The most recent of these estimates – 'cautious [and] minimal', the researchers insist – is a total of 66,000 deaths in Queensland: about two-thirds of them down to the QNP, the rest to the settlers, with a black:white death ratio of 44:1. Deaths from frontier violence elsewhere would make a total well in excess of Australian casualties in the First World War (around 63,000) and close to double the number lost in the Second World War. The frontier wars were the most catastrophic in Australian history, even if it were only a matter of numbers killed.

The mayhem of the Queensland frontier swept in ragged order over the Great Dividing Range and across vast plains to the Northern Territory. It was amplified by the Kimberley gold rush of 1885, which took hundreds of prospectors along the gulf track from Queensland through the Territory to Western Australia. (Among the blazers of that trail were the Durack brothers, whose epic 1879 cattle drive entered legend with the publication in 1959 of *Kings in Grass Castles*, a family saga authored by one of the third generation of Duracks.)[32]

Seeing opportunity for a pastoral bonanza at last, the South Australian government gazetted fourteen leases in the 'Gulf country', a rectangle of land the size of Victoria stretching down from the Gulf of Carpentaria across the Barkly Tableland to the northern fringes of Warumungu Country.[33] It was a condition of the leases that they be stocked within three years. By 1885, 200,000 cattle and 10,000 horses had passed from Queensland into the Territory.[34] The Gulf frontier, an extension of Queensland's and suffused with the brutality and contempt generated by a century's conflict between black and white, far from government, missionaries, journalists and other nosy parkers, adopted what was referred to as 'the Queensland method'. Grossly disproportionate reprisals by white pastoralists were reinforced by 'pacification'. Two of the fourteen new cattle stations maintained a 'no shooting' policy, which suggests that twelve didn't. A historian of the Gulf country in these years cites participants, witnesses and even official reports as recording that 'the blacks' were shot down like crows, like kangaroos, or hunted for sport, or to take women.[35] Some of the captured women were sold for five or ten pounds. The grandmother of one of my Tennant Creek contemporaries was a Garrwa woman brought to Banka Banka station, just north of Tennant Creek, by one cattleman as a gift to another. Girls as young as seven were raped by syphilitics. Fleeing groups were hunted over weeks. Raids on campsites involved slaughtering everyone in the camp then burning bodies, dwellings, weapons and canoes. At one point in the Abner Range, now known as Massacre Hill, people were driven over a cliff. One station manager had forty pairs of Aboriginal ears nailed to the walls of his hut. And the children? 'Gottem stick, knockem in the head or neck. Some kid, piccanin', that small one, like a goanna, hittem longa tree.'[36]

The people of the southern half of the Gulf country, the Barkly, were just about wiped out.[37] I drove through that country on one of my several trips north. Now, as then, it is a landscape apart. 'The country opened out suddenly, as if a veil of timber had been drawn aside,' a Territory official rhapsodised.[38] 'As far as the eye could see there were miles of

land covered with waving green grass, the very best of natural feed.'
There was nowhere to hide from the Snyders and the Martini-Henrys.
By the time the Northern Territory passed from South Australian to
Commonwealth control in 1911, its Aboriginal population had shrunk
from around 50,000 to less than half that number.[39]

Violent dispossession was a fundamental of the relationship between
black and white but not the whole. It included curiosity, friendship and
incomprehension as well as efforts to comprehend and to reach an
understanding, as is suggested by the remarkable experience of a young
Warumungu man known as Dick Cubadgee.[40] Soon after the cattle
had stampeded across the Barkly, Cubadgee met a cattleman, David
Lindsay. They got on famously. Cubadgee arranged for Lindsay to be
treated by the Warumungu as his brother, and Lindsay asked Cubadgee
if he would like to return with him to Adelaide, which he did. There,
Cubadgee lived with and worked for the Lindsay family, who showed
him off and took him to Government House and to the theatre. They
had Cubadgee photographed in guises ranging from a bowler-hatted

Cubadgee as gentleman, c. 1888

gentleman to splendid Native Specimen, unclothed but for a small but tactfully placed apron.

Whatever was going on in that young man's mind seems to have included a plan, perhaps already in gestation when he agreed to travel to Adelaide. By Lindsay's account, Cubadgee told him that 'the white people had no right to take away the tribal lands of his people. They should pay for them in cattle [and] leave the tribe with sufficient land for a cattle station of their own.' Cubadgee's thinking was not altogether different from that of the Europeans. Under the terms of pastoral leases offered by the South Australian government, the Aborigines were to be allowed 'full and free access to the entire leased area ... as if the lease had not been granted'. Unfortunately – or perhaps not – Cubadgee never found out whether his hosts would come to terms. He was operated upon for a tumour on his neck but died soon after. The surgeons had an interest in 'physical anthropology', a search for definitive differences in the physiology and anatomy of racial groups. They filleted Cubadgee's body and put the skeleton on display in the South Australian Museum, where it stayed for sixty years. My parents often took us kids to the museum, so I expect that I saw it there.

The people who had hosted an Aboriginal man and had inserted an enlightened clause into their pastoral leases were also driven to take what they wanted. It is often said that frontier barbarisms were committed by the dregs of European society because the frontier attracted the dregs, and that is so, but they worked hand in glove with colonial grandees.[41] Tony Roberts published his history of the Gulf country in 2005 then set himself another task, to find out how no fewer than fifty massacres over a period of forty-odd years could have been committed with very few charges laid and no convictions, ever. What Roberts found shocked him. A son of South Australia, he had grown up (as I had) taking it for granted that South Australia was different, a paradise of Dissent – no convicts, a bastion of right-thinking Protestant Christianity and liberal humanism. In fact, Roberts discovered, governments – including and sometimes led by men bearing the names of old and powerful Adelaide families, names known to him from childhood, had variously supported, supplied, commissioned and concealed activities commanded or abetted by police designed to instil fear and dread. These right-thinking Christian gentlemen were also leaders of the property-owning classes, pastoralists particularly, desperate to find a way out of the debt and derision which their mad Territory caper had brought them. The subduing of 'the natives' is not a matter of law, said one attorney-general, 'but essentially one of policy'.[42]

What to call this? Atrocity? War crime? Murder? Perhaps all of these, but for the Warumungu it was terrorism, state-sponsored terrorism. We know now that they were relatively fortunate in their location, particularly in being on land of no use to cattle, but they didn't know that. Everything the *papulanyi* did was unprecedented, unimaginable and often, even after the event, inexplicable. Over three or four decades, the Warumungu saw people to their north, east and south attacked, driven from their Country, or exterminated. They had no way of knowing whether or when it would be their turn. There were no missionaries to protect them, as the Arrernte had been protected at Hermannsburg, 300 miles away, and no government-appointed protector of the kind that had in some times and places managed to shield Aboriginal people to some degree at least. The police were more likely to be a source of terror than of protection. 'It was one word *fear* all through,' wrote one of the rare exceptions to the policing rule 'No matter what it is these poor creatures have to submit to it is simply through *fear*.'[43]

It would be three or four decades before the Warumungu could be reasonably sure that the killers weren't coming for them. By then they had worked out an understanding with the *papulanyi*. Some of the little republics had been destroyed in favour of cattle stations that didn't work; five of the fourteen had been abandoned within a decade, while others were downsized or sold. The cattlemen were forced to conclude that cheap Aboriginal labour was the difference between viability and failure. For the Warumungu, being useful to the *papulanyi* was the difference between staying on Country and not. The young people, Cubadgee's contemporaries, worked 'in the cattle' as stockmen (and sometimes stockwomen) and as domestics on what was now known as the Barkly Tableland: as Banka Banka, Brunette Downs, Alroy Downs, Munkaderry, Rockhampton Downs. My age-mates who as kids had stolen across in front of the screen of the Pioneer Picture Theatre told me that the old people didn't go to the pictures on Saturday nights because they were frightened of the guns in the Westerns.[44]

The Queensland–Northern Territory frontier petered out because there was no more good country. There would be aftershocks of violence, including several in the north-west of Western Australia and another that brought more difficulties for the Warumungu, as well as what might be called casual violence – whippings, beatings, shooting of individuals, kidnapping – that continued for decades, but organised violence, more or less continuous since the 1790s, had reached a terrible climax. What had been done could not be undone. What should be thought, felt and said?

•

That problem came with the First Fleet. It had sailed from Portsmouth just over a decade after the Americans had declared independence (*We hold these truths to be self-evident, that all men are created equal*) and arrived in Port Jackson the year before the Bastille was stormed (*Liberty, Equality, Fraternity*). Its departure from England coincided almost exactly with the beginnings of a British anti-slavery movement driven by the conviction that all are equal in the sight of God.[45] Those who had dispatched the First Fleet and its commanders thought of themselves as humane Christians, as representatives of an advanced and enlightened civilisation, as tribunes of the rule of law. The difficulty lay in the fact that the First Fleet also belonged to a rising imperial power. Arthur Phillip, commander of the fleet and the colony's governor, found himself in a jam. On the one hand, his instructions (and his Protestant, enlightened, civilised conscience) enjoined him to live 'in peace and amity' with the 'natives'. On the other, he was also required to take active possession of 'Our Territory called New South Wales', to become self-sufficient as soon as possible and to hand out extensive land grants.[46]

Phillips' efforts to 'conciliate the Natives', however deluded, were also close to saintly, even after one of them speared him in what could easily have been a fatal encounter, but several years later he and his tiny colony were facing starvation. Inner conflict flickered and flared then exploded in the most famous and consequential tantrum in Australian history. In retaliation for the spearing of his gamekeeper, Phillip ordered that ten Aboriginal men in the Botany Bay area be captured and killed and that their severed heads be brought back in bags provided for the purpose. His instructions were softened under pressure from the officer detailed to do the job, and anyway vengeance was not wreaked – the troops came back empty-handed – but it was the attempt that mattered. The frontier would do whatever had to be done.

In this, as in most areas of frontier history, Henry Reynolds was early on the scene, uncovering the foundational conflict between wants and conscience and its consequences. In his 1987 book *The Law of the Land*, Reynolds showed how the British and then the colonists claimed sovereignty over much of the Australian continent *and* ownership of the land – all the while knowing perfectly well that the latter was contrary to international and British law. The fig leaf? The natives didn't really occupy the land, they merely roamed over it – a legal fiction which lasted for 200 years. In *This Whispering in Our Hearts* (1998), Reynolds showed that the consequences of these offences against conscience were morally and psychologically damaging as well as corrupting of the law.

Reynolds' representative figure was Richard Windeyer, a Sydney barrister and landowner prominent in the fierce debates of the 1840s.[47] By then the frontier that began at Sydney Cove was past the Blue Mountains and far into the rich western plains. Speaking in 1842, Windeyer asserted the entitlement of the colonists (himself included) to all this on the usual grounds: the Aborigines 'have never tilled the soil, or enclosed it, or cleared any portion of it, or planted a single tree, or grain or root', so they didn't actually inhabit the land, they merely ranged over it. Having made what he reckoned was a watertight case, Windeyer paused, realising that he hadn't even convinced himself. 'How is it our minds are not satisfied?' he asked. 'What means this whispering in the bottom of our hearts?'

Windeyer was one of tens, perhaps hundreds or thousands, of colonists to be bothered by a whispering that just wouldn't go away. It was made worse by another self-deception. In the absence of any wish by Aboriginal people to give up their land or any inclination by the insurgents to negotiate with them, the matter was settled by increasingly widespread and systematic violence. It was warfare, and often referred to by participants and observers as a war, but officially it wasn't. It was an undeclared war. There were 'no agreed rules of engagement ... no conventions for the treatment of prisoners, no armistice, no surrender, no treaties, no indemnities or reparations and, afterwards, no recognition of a gallant foe'.[48] But if it wasn't war, then – as Henry Reynolds has pointed out – it was murder, and the murder, what's more, of people who were supposed to be under British protection. But that was principle, not practice. The law followed the pastoralists and others into

Aboriginal territory and then operated to punish Aboriginal people who took white lives and property, all the while protecting whites who were taking Aboriginal lives and property.

In flouting their own rules and conventions, the frontiers rotted the Europeans' sense of themselves. Consciences twisted and turned in search of a way out. Some brave or foolish souls became saints, a number of whom are honoured by Reynolds in *This Whispering*, campaigners who appealed to Christianity and human feeling, to governments, to the Colonial Office in far-off London, to Queen Victoria, to the Vatican, to anyone or anything that might at least moderate what was happening.[49] Others became genuine villains, truculent haters, contemptuous of do-gooders and Aboriginal people alike, men (they were almost always men) who vilified the campaigners as mad or disloyal knockers, who urged extermination, who nailed ears to walls or bashed babies' brains out. The language of contention over the frontier was often as violent as the frontier itself.[50] 'Is there room for both of us here?' asked one opponent of the humanitarian case. 'No. Then the sooner the weaker is wiped out the better, as we may save some valuable lives in the process.'

Most were neither saints nor villains. They avoided, equivocated, rationalised and projected. They deplored gratuitous violence rather than confront the fact that the frontier was 'taking possession' of what was already possessed, or they regretted events as unfortunate costs of inevitable progress, or they accused the 'natives' of 'outrages' or 'treachery'. They flipped and flopped. News of white deaths at Aboriginal hands provoked demands for revenge; reprisals provoked demands for investigation and punishment. The colonists increasingly stopped talking about Aborigines as equals in the eyes of God or as Noble Savages and subscribed instead to a race-based view of things.[51] As well as easing conscience, it seemed to explain what was becoming obvious around the world: brought to the test, the coloured races simply could not compete with the white Europeans. A tangle of confusion and conflict, of ideas and emotions, was embedded in white hearts and minds.

When at last the violent frontier seemed to have come to its conclusion, relief from the pangs of conscience was in sight. Yes, there were still some Aborigines left in the distant north,[52] but they would inevitably follow their brethren elsewhere and die out,[53] a plausible proposition given what was thought to have happened in Tasmania and that the Aboriginal population was now less than a tenth of what it had been in 1788. But the story of their disappearance? What would become of that?

Here, interests came into play, along with psychological comfort. Looking forward to a prosperous future as well as back to its obtaining, the landed wanted no challenge to their proprietorship, while the colonists and their leaders wanted no question as to the sovereignty of the nation that would come into being in 1901. Just as there had been no observance of the rules of war and no room for the Aborigines in a physical world that had been theirs, now there would be no room for them in the new constitution, laws, maps or histories of 'Australia'. There would be no treaty, not even compensation. Troubled conscience and material desire conspired to want silence.

In the course of my reading, I found that the phrase 'the great Australian silence' is perhaps the most appealed to and relied upon formulation in the historiography of relations between black and white in this country.[54] But it is in some ways a misnomer. The silence was more than just an end to controversy, and more than a tacit agreement that there was no use in crying over spilt milk. It was an active pursuit, and had been for a long time as part of the everyday work of the frontier. Records of violence were not kept or were destroyed. The files of the Queensland Native Police, for example, were so thoroughly culled and broken up that trying to discover its death toll more than a hundred years after the force was disbanded was little more than guesswork; only extraordinarily dogged forensics recovered and pieced together enough evidence to turn guesses into informed estimates. Cover-ups and white-washes were similarly thorough. When then South Australian premier John Downer was confronted by an outcry over police and vigilante killings in the Gulf country in 1885, he set up a 'private' enquiry that would investigate the activities of the police but not the vigilantes, which would select its own interviewees, give no notice of its (secret) hearings and decline to call the whistle-blower whose evidence had sparked the outcry.[55] Downer's enquiry was chaired by a man who had been one of the vigilantes, and included among its members a former manager of a station notorious for its killings, who was also a son-in-law of the Northern Territory police chief.

Euphemisms and tacit understandings were the lingua franca of the frontiers. The Adelaide *Advertiser* hoped that Constable Gason would 'not be hampered by too many instructions' in the task of teaching the Barrow Creek natives a lesson.[56] When the chief of the Northern Territory police force ordered a punitive expedition into the Gulf country, he told them that 'a too close adherence to legal forms should not be insisted upon'. Such deaths as were reported were routinely put down to 'shot while attempting to escape' or 'resisting arrest'. Police 'went on a picnic with the Natives' or 'dispersed' them or made a locality 'unhealthy' or engaged in 'pacification'. What 'the Natives' were doing, by contrast, was 'treacherous' or an 'outrage' and was often closely detailed, while the consequences inflicted were not.

The 'silence' was more a low murmur than a dead silence, a sup-pression as well as a consensus.[57] It lived in institutions including the law, scholarship, schooling and sites of commemoration and memory, as well as in hearts and minds. Some forms of the silence, I now realise, were used daily by my family when we were in Tennant Creek in the early 1950s. We understood that the Aborigines – like sex, politics and religion – were not to be mentioned in company or outside the family. That this rule was practised as well as prescribed by my father I learned only decades later when he told me about a conversation with the police sergeant, whose house was just two or three down from ours. The sergeant told him that one of the constables wanted to marry an Aboriginal woman. So what? Dad reported himself as saying. He's mad! said the sergeant. He'll be posted to the back of beyond! His career will be ruined! My father had always taken care before this incident, and took every care again after it, to avoid the 'Aboriginal question'. It was only that once, he said, that it got heated.

At school we were told noisy counter-stories, and not just in Social Studies. I was taught nothing about what the frontier had destroyed, but much about what it had built. I was told about the old telegraph station and its history, but not that it was built right beside Jurnkurakurr, the Warumungu's most sacred site, and took their best water supply.[58] A defining memory of my father's Tennant Creek classroom is of watching *Movietone News* in the dark, the 16mm Bell & Howell projector whirring while converting reels of celluloid, sent up on the DC-3, into flickering images of men on horseback driving flocks of sheep that poured fluid-like down eucalyptus-dotted slopes, of Tasmanian axemen on planks jutting out from notches cut high on the base of a giant of the forest, and of mighty plumes of foam gushing from dams far up in the Snowies. All that was not so different from what I found so many years later on the old road from Adelaide to Darwin.

Romance was another form of a muffled silence. At some point during our time in Tennant Creek, I read Jeannie Gunn's *We of the Never Never*, perhaps because we'd stayed at Elsey's Mataranka homestead on the grand trip to Darwin. The book is a saccharine memoir of Gunn's two years as the missus of Elsey,[59] the first of the fourteen South Australian leases to be stocked, in the early 1880s. Unmentioned in Gunn's account is that once the land was taken, Elsey armed its Aboriginal workers so they could shoot Aboriginal 'trespassers', while Gunn's paragons of manly virtue, the white stockmen, took Aboriginal women. That the romance was Gunn's perspective, rather than fact, is suggested by her decision to excise a chapter titled 'A Nigger Hunt'. Gunn was sympathetic to the Aborigines but, like Windeyer, she was trapped between her conscience and the taken world in which she lived.[60]

Perhaps the most widespread (and least toxic) form of silence was the kind of sentimentalism adopted by my mother when she talked about 'Gins Lookout' or the quiet dignity of the old man on the front veranda of Williams' general store. It was at least an acknowledgement that an entire world had just about vanished, albeit coy about how. That same vicarious nostalgia could be found in much harder heads than my mother's. Norman 'Tinny' Tindale, the cartographer of Aboriginal Australia, an entomologist turned anthropologist and possessor of a distinctly empirical cast of mind, chose to place at the beginning of his *magnum opus* one of his own photographs and then spend a page describing its subject and their setting.[61]

An Aboriginal man, woman and child are in the photograph. The man – husband of the woman and father of the child – is leaning on his left elbow and stretched out in lordly fashion. To his right is his wife, smiling. Her heavy breasts and a just-visible thickening of her stomach (Tindale says) reveal that she is pregnant. Their daughter, five or six years old, is standing in front of her parents. The summer rains had been good and so the mother 'had leisure to decorate her daughter's hair with the seed pods of the river red gums'. The photograph was taken just days after these three people had had contact with white people for the first time.

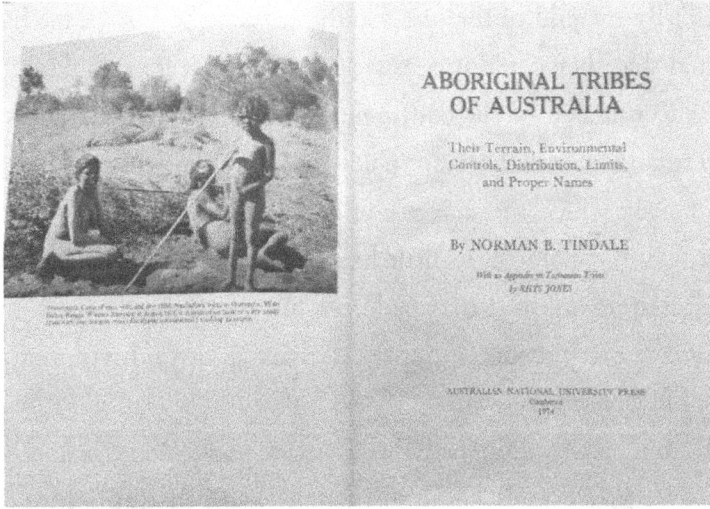

'Tindale chose to place at the beginning of his *magnum opus*'

The sense of loss, not far under the surface of Tindale's lyrical vignette, was my own starting point, first via a slim volume revealingly titled *The Last of the Nomads*, which recounted the search in the far Western Australian deserts for a Romeo and Juliet couple.[62] (They were not, in fact, the last.) I followed that with Blainey's *Triumph of the Nomads*, another of many expressions of our vicarious nostalgia, perhaps even of an undeclared whispering. '[T]he white sails of the English ships were a symbol of a gale which in the following hundred years would slowly cross the continent,' says Blainey in the book's final sentence, 'blowing out the flames of countless camp-fires, covering with drift-sand the grinding stones and fishing nets, silencing the sounds of hundreds of languages, and stripping the ancient aboriginal names from nearly every valley and headland.'[63]

The emotions of that richly evocative passage are a good place to start learning about the Aboriginal experience but, I came to realise, a bad place to stop. Had Blainey continued his story, he would have had to report that the Australian frontier, unlike the American, never 'closed'. By the end of the nineteenth century, the Europeans had all the land that they could use, as well as some that they couldn't. That left up to one half of the continent, a crescent stretching across the north and down into the western deserts and to the southern and western coast, in which the universe of Tindale's map, torn and tattered, was still visible. Some of its little republics had been obliterated, some were still more or less as they had been just over a century before, and others were badly damaged but for all that still there. It was a new triumph of the nomads.

Within this vast crescent, most of a sparse population was Aboriginal. Their lives increasingly became entangled with the Europeans', economically, culturally and sexually. The 'frontier' was now less about who would have the land than about the terms on which both would occupy it. The Europeans kept on finding new things they wanted, so Aboriginal people had to deal with new kinds of white men, missionaries, anthropologists, government officials, road-builders, miners. While often the frontier came to meet the Aboriginal people, they also went to meet it, attracted by kin already there, or relief from hard times and drought, or by the white man's addictives of tobacco, sugar, alcohol. They 'came in', a phenomenon which ended only in the 1980s when small bands of Pintupi people came in from the Western Desert.[64] (They *were* the last of the nomads.) For these Aboriginal peoples, the frontier was now a ceaseless struggle for 'culture'. That included language, health and what we might call 'privacy' and 'agency', as well as living on Country and maintaining ceremonial life. Aboriginal people had to hang on to a sense of who they were as they tried to change it.

Struggles within the frontier were increasingly joined by struggles between it and the post-frontier, its tangled conscience confronted by a relict of its former self. My family travelled from an orderly world of whiteness to a world hinted at in the Social Studies textbook, and then back again. So sharp was the contrast that it was like time travel. I had heard of the Aborigines before I went to Tennant Creek, of course, but I had never met or even seen one. The frontier zone was another country; they did things differently there. The post-frontier tried over and again to get that zone under control and/or averted its gaze.[65] My father was an agent of the post-frontier's civilising effort and an observer of its silence. After one of my trips north I asked him, now in old age, about the Aboriginal mission. No idea, he said. You didn't go there? Or talk to the teacher at the mission school? No, he said irritably, why would I? My family's half-conscious shock prefigured what was in store for Australia when its three defining conflicts – between black and white, between conscience and wants, and between frontier and post-frontier – emerged from behind the silence. The Aborigines were about to be seen and heard once more.

•

Throughout the entire life of the silence that reigned largely unchallenged from the late nineteenth century to the 1960s, there were people who had no impulse to remain silent but no means of doing anything else. How would they speak? Who would listen to them? The Warumungu had a deep, deep sense of loss and a comprehensive understanding of how and by whom it had been inflicted. The *papulanyi* had good reasons not to hear this, and only very exceptionally did they provide a place or an opportunity for the telling. One of the silence's many forms was the silencing of the losers. The camera everywhere rode with the cowboys. Even when newspapers, missionaries and officials reported what was going on, they were whitefella accounts, not accounts by Aboriginal people themselves of what they had seen and experienced.

Something like a hundred and forty years after the clash at Attack Creek, I met Edith Graham Nakamarra, one of those kids who had stolen across in front of the screen at the Pioneer Picture Theatre, one of my contemporaries. Edith's mind's eye saw not a game little Scotsman slogging his way across a hostile continent but an invader. Edith stood with her grandfather, one of those young men at Attack Creek, one of those 'hostile natives'. He turn them back! Edith told me, implacably proud. But that report from the other side of the frontier had been silenced for generations. It is not the least of the ironies of this story that, many years after the events at Attack Creek, Edith's grandfather and his companions were enlisted in the construction of a new way for the whitefellas to hide, even from themselves, what the blackfellas knew all too well.

CHAPTER TWO

1901

O n a mid-winter's day in 1901, a buggy bearing Frank Gillen and Baldwin Spencer bumped along the track through the gap in the McDouall Range and on to the Tennant Creek telegraph station, two or three miles beyond. It was, they later wrote, 'the most forlorn and hopeless-looking place imaginable'.[1] Spencer and Gillen were newly famous as anthropologists of 'primitive man', the Australian Aborigine. They were at Tennant Creek to do the Warumungu.

By now they had it all down pat.[2] They had been on the road since March, basing themselves at a string of telegraph stations and with varying degrees of thoroughness, studying tribes including the Urubunna, the Unmatjera (Anmatyerre), the Aranda (Arrernte) and most recently, the Kaitish (Kaytetye) at Barrow Creek. At Tennant Creek, as elsewhere, they had supplies sent ahead by camel train, for their own use and as currency in their dealings with the Natives. Their support team (a policeman, Constable Chance, and two Arrernte men, Erlikiliakirra and Purunda) soon arrived with the wagon carrying more supplies and equipment, as well as artefacts gathered along the way. They pitched their tent next to the telegraph station and appointed to their staff (as they put it) 'an aged and most remarkable old warrior as "chief witness"', and a 'very intelligent young man "Zulu" as interpreter'.[3] It is possible

Back: Erlikiliakirra, Constable Chance, Purunda.
Front: Gillen, Spencer

that the remarkable old warrior was Edith Graham Nakamarra's grandfather 'Jacob'. Either way, their 'very intelligent' interpreter was Jacob's
nephew and Edith's uncle, Zulu.[4]

Across the creek, the Warumungu were gathering.[5] Why were they
there? They would have known that there was business to be done and
rations and tobacco on offer, but the Warumungu were extraordinarily hospitable and desperately keen to strut their stuff, insistent that
Spencer and Gillen see everything. They performed up to nine ceremonies in a twenty-four-hour period and a total of eighty-eight over a
couple of months, 'the most elaborate and impressive we have seen',[6]
but still only a fraction of the Warumungu repertoire.[7] This elaborate
presentation was certainly an expression of cultural confidence and
pride. It may also have been a form of cultural diplomacy, an effort
to 'strengthen the relationship', as foreign ministers like to say, part of
an ongoing effort by the Warumungu to avoid the fate of their neighbours. Or perhaps it was something more specific? During the early

1890s – a time of drought – the cattle had moved from the northern edge of Warumungu Country almost to its centre, Tennant Creek.[8] Growing pressure on cattlemen there is suggested by the gazetting of an Aboriginal 'reserve' in 1893. The Warumungu knew that Spencer and Gillen were big men; perhaps they saw the visit as a chance to pursue a better arrangement, something of the kind canvassed by Cubadgee?

For Spencer and Gillen, the time with the Warumungu got off to an excellent start, the appallingly windy, dusty and freezing weather notwithstanding, and they never looked back. They admired the Warumungu and liked them, particularly in contrast to the surly Kaytetye.[9] Physically impressive (several of the women, Spencer was startled to find, were taller than him), they were first among equals in a 'nation' that included half a dozen surrounding tribes. Nine weeks raced by in photographing and recording every detail of the ceremonies, in documenting 'traditions' (the anthropologists' word), and in getting their heads around an unusually complex kinship system and a remarkable sign language. During their stay, one of the old men died after days of suffering and failed efforts to sustain him (to which Spencer and Gillen contributed Bovril), providing rich material about medical practices, mourning rituals and burial rites.[10] They also witnessed the ornate courtesy with which a group of Warlpiri visitors was received and entertained.

Perhaps their greatest privilege was a visit to the home of the great *Walunkwa* or 'water snake', several days' ride to the south-east. Along the way, Gillen formed the view that although the country carried plenty of game, it would be no good for cattle. '[U]nless payable gold mines are discovered,' he mused presciently, 'I am inclined to think that here … the Natives will always have a fair extent of country over which they can roam unmolested.'[11] Brought eventually to a craggy, weirdly beautiful waterhole, they were much impressed by 'the reverence shown by the Natives'. Gillen even noticed in himself a fleeting sense of a world crowded with the mystical and the magical.[12] 'I do not wonder that they have attributed [the waterhole's] origin to a mythical monster like the *Walunkwa*,' the Catholic Gillen wrote in his journal. 'I must confess that to a certain extent I shared their feelings.'

When the Warumungu gathered to farewell Spencer and Gillen, after the longest of their stays with a dozen or more tribes, their baggage included a mass of notes, photographic plates, sketches, diagrams and tables and a splendid collection of artefacts, including an item particularly coveted by Gillen: a bone from the body of the man who had died during their stay, dug up then swathed and decorated before being presented to him by one of the dead man's sons.

What were they doing?

Spencer and Gillen saw themselves as bringing a dispassionate science to bear on the long-practised observation of the Australian Aborigine and on the fundamental question of the evolution of *Homo sapiens*. They were confident in the doing that they were defending their many Aboriginal friends against the incomprehension and calumnies of many white men, as well as building upon and bringing theoretical rigor to a small but lively body of Australian 'ethnology', thereby contributing to the emergence overseas of the discipline of anthropology. They believed that their great contribution was the discovery of the 'Alcheringa' or 'Dreamtime' (Gillen's neologism), the revelation that the Aboriginal peoples were the possessors of a vast, intricate and hitherto barely guessed-at spiritual world.[13]

Recent opinion has Spencer and Gillen as archetypal scientific racists. They became such an embarrassment to the National Museum of Victoria – which Spencer did much to establish, including providing a magnificent collection of artefacts – that when I first went there I was startled to find in the lobby two large screens playing a loop of an imagined dialogue in which an old, wise Aboriginal man chides Spencer for his denigrations and Spencer comes to see the error of his ways. At the nearby University of Melbourne, where Spencer was for many years a distinguished professor, the question of renaming the Spencer Building was raised, while on Professors' Walk, where the university's stars are honoured in pavement plaques, Spencer's name is notably absent.

To many present-day anthropologists and other scholars of the Aboriginal world, Spencer and Gillen were marked by the deformities of their times but were nonetheless founding fathers of a discipline grounded in the scientific search for truth that went on to play an honourable role in the long struggle to defeat racism and in the emancipation of the Aboriginal peoples.

My own conclusion: most of the above, and more besides. Their first book, the book that two years earlier had made them famous, had staked anthropology's claim to be *the* authoritative way of seeing the Aboriginal people. The cross-continental expedition of 1901 would put that claim beyond question.

•

Gillen was just eighteen when as a telegraph operator he had relayed messages back and forth between the fatally wounded stationmaster in Barrow Creek and his wife in Adelaide, an experience which, unsurprisingly, he never forgot and often referred to. He was vehement then and long afterwards in his satisfaction that the Kaytetye were given 'such a lesson that they never again attempted an attack'. Aged nineteen, Gillen was on his way north to take up a position as an operator at one of the line's repeater stations and, like thousands before him, he used a diary to jot down observations about the Aborigines.[14]

Our sense of this young man's excitement and deepening fascination is heightened by the way his journey slows as it advances, commencing at speed by train then on stagecoach and buggy, and, finally, on horse-back. Early on he sees layabouts, beggars, half-castes and drunkards. Later there are shepherds and trackers, much valued by pastoralists and policemen. Seven weeks after leaving Adelaide he arrives at Peake, then generally regarded as the point beyond which firearms should always be carried. 'There are dozens of Niggers about here, very few of them possess the luxury of an article of Clothing,' he reports. 'They live principally on Snakes, Lizards and herbage and all look in excellent Condition.' At every stop the nineteen-year-old makes a point of visiting the Natives 'for a yabber' and to build up his word lists. His absence of animosity toward the Aborigines is striking. It might even be that his boisterous, jocular comments about them and their increasingly squalid circumstances betray this young man's moral unease.

Aboriginal people were a familiar part of daily life at Gillen's destination, the Charlotte Waters telegraph station, first as potential attackers, then as mendicants. Gillen used every opportunity to get to know them and their ways. He liked them, and all the indications are that they liked him. He was gregarious, ebullient, open-hearted and generous. His deepening sympathy led him to a second and much less congenial field of study, relations between black and white. His comprehension of the Aborigines and of their experience of the whitefellas took a place in his mind at least as prominent as his earlier outrage at their 'treachery'. This whispering in Gillen's heart sometimes rose to a roar, most spectacularly when in 1891 he recommended that Mounted Constable William Willshire be charged with murder. (Willshire got off, of course, thanks in part to his barrister, Sir John Downer QC, and the public subscriptions that funded him.)

Gillen's extraordinary action against Willshire was taken not long after he had been promoted to the position of post and telegraph master at Alice Springs and hence a special magistrate and sub-protector of

Aborigines. By then he had been in central Australia for fifteen years. He was the most senior public servant for hundreds of miles around, referred to by his mates as the Amir of Alice Springs, the Pontiff, His Catholic Majesty.[15] It was this larger-than-life figure who in 1894 welcomed to his principality the Horn Scientific Expedition, five scientists and a support team assembled by a wealthy South Australian pastoralist.[16] Its brief was to document the geology, botany, zoology, meteorology and anthropology of a stretch of country from Oodnadatta to Alice Springs. After a few days as Gillen's guests, all except the expedition's biologist and photographer, Baldwin Spencer, packed up and set out on the long trek back to the railhead at Oodnadatta.

It was three weeks before Spencer left; by then a friendship with Gillen had turned into a full-blown bromance, not quite an attraction of opposites but close.[17] Gillen was Irish-Australian; almost poetically, he had been conceived on a ship taking his newly married parents from Ireland to Australia, where he was born in 1855. Spencer was English; he had come to Australia not as one of hundreds of thousands of migrants looking for a better life but as a newly appointed professor at the University of Melbourne. Gillen had been earning his own living since the age of twelve, when he got a job as a messenger boy for the postal and telegraph service in the country town where his parents had opened a general store.[18] Spencer, the son of a self-made industrial titan and pillar of the Methodist church in the boom city of Manchester, had left school wanting to be an artist. After a year at Manchester's art school he switched to science at Oxford, where he was so outstanding that at the age of just twenty-six he beat some big names for the plum Melbourne post. Gillen, of working-class, Catholic and Irish provenance, was an ardent Home Ruler with Socialistic tendencies. Spencer was of Dissenter stock, an Empire man, and for Capital. Gillen at thirty-eight was tending to the portly; Spencer, five years younger,

was slight. Both sported big, droopy moustaches. Both were charming
and gregarious; both loved a whisky and a yarn. They followed politics
and world affairs with a nice balance of agreement and dispute. Both
were of a progressive turn of mind, anti-clerical and strong supporters
of development and the push for a white Australian nation. And both
were absolutely fascinated by the Aborigines.

What Spencer knew about the Aborigines came from the academy. While a student at Oxford he had attended the first lectures on
anthropology (or proto-anthropology, really) ever given in England,
and he had helped set up what became one of the world's great anthropological museums, the Pitt Rivers. He had stayed on in Alice to do
field work on local flora and fauna but, late-nineteenth-century biology being a broad church, he also knew that mapping the evolution of
Homo sapiens was one of the hottest fields of enquiry in Europe.[19] He
had read up on Australian ethnology and sought out its two leading
exponents, Alfred Howitt and Lorimer Fison, not long after he arrived
in Australia. Long hours were spent in Gillen's smoky den, crammed
with spears, shields, coolamon and other Aboriginal impedimenta, talking about the Aborigines.

Spencer was scarcely back in Melbourne before the letters began
to flow.[20] 'As I sit here in the old ochre-smelling den, which you know
so well,' says Gillen in his first letter, 'I can imagine you demonstrating the anatomy of a Cockroach to a lot of Callow Youth ... Do you,
I wonder, ever wish that you could transport yourself to the wilds of
the McDonnell's [sic]. I often wish that you could, I missed you very
much indeed.'

Spencer had offered to help Gillen publish at least some of his
immense store of knowledge about the Aborigines; Gillen was hoping
for more but knew that if he was to get it, he would have to find a way
around commitments already made to another scientist fascinated by the

Aborigines. Edward Stirling was not just a big fish in Adelaide and in Australia's compact scientific community; he was the Horn Expedition's official anthropologist. (He was also the surgeon who had operated on Cubadgee's tumour, and presumably arranged for Cubadgee's skeleton to find its way into the museum of which he was director.) Trickier still, Gillen knew Stirling from a previous expedition, had been in frequent contact with him, and had already agreed to help Stirling with his section of the Horn expedition's report – to be edited by none other than Baldwin Spencer. In this awkward triangle, Stirling soon found himself the odd man out. Six months after meeting, Spencer and Gillen agreed to write a book together. As luck and Gillen's high credit with the Arrernte would have it, they were able to base the book on their joint observation of a massive ceremonial cycle conducted on a river flat adjacent to the Alice Springs telegraph station a couple of years after that life-changing first encounter.

For Gillen particularly, the process of writing that followed was simply exhilarating. Spencer kept on firing questions, puzzles, suggestions and requests from Melbourne, while Gillen in Alice Springs chased them down, loving the excitement of the hunt and the stimulus of Spencer's 'seething mind'. His letters ran to many thousands of words (often with no pause for punctuation) and he sent long field reports as well. You work like a steam hammer, he told Spencer,[21] as yet more draft chapters turned up in the post. 'Gillen I never hear from,' wrote one of their mutual Alice Springs friends.[22] '[H]e is working like a Trojan, night and day, at his Ethnological notes. Rumour has it that he recently got up in his Sleep and adjourned to the washhouse from which there presently came a sound of chanting accompanied with vigorous stamping of feet; and on the astonished Night Operator going to see what was the matter, he found the Pontiff, artistically decorated … corroboreeing away like an Aroondah warrior!'

The trouble was that as Gillen's understanding of Aboriginal society deepened so did his understanding of that other field of study, relations between black and white. A few months into the project, one of Gillen's letters to Spencer records his anguish at his own and others' actions in taking Aboriginal 'churinga', inscribed boards and stones of deep spiritual significance. They had been collected in great number by the Horn Expedition and then by one of Gillen's mates, as well as by Gillen himself until he realised what they meant to their owners. He stopped collecting and asked his friend to stop too. He didn't. In the result the Aboriginal man who told Gillen's friend where churinga could be found was put to death for sacrilege. 'This upsets me terribly,' Gillen told Spencer. 'I would not have had it happen for 100 pounds … I bitterly regret having countenanced such a thing and can only say that I did so when in ignorance of what they meant to the Natives.'

There was no cost to such sentiments, of course, coming as they did conveniently after the event. But scarcely a letter of Gillen's fails to remark on the utter demoralisation of the Aborigines, their misery, and the vicious incomprehension of the whites. He reports many incidents of shooting, of unjust punishment, of death from disease. He flares in anger at pastoralists who appropriate the best portion 'for the exclusive use of their stock and relegate the Nigger to the barren wastes which are often destitute alike of game and tradition'. He is scathing about the Europeans' ignorance of Aboriginal religious life, and took or tried to take a step further than asserting its existence, groping toward an understanding of its equivalence. The churinga (he told Spencer) are 'sacred' in the sense that the sacramental wafer is sacred to the Roman Catholic. Aboriginal belief in the magical power of the churinga was like a Lourdes pilgrim's belief in the Virgin Mary. He reckoned that the Dreamtime wanderings were 'startlingly like the wanderings of the Children of Israel'. Missionaries, Gillen said, were intent on wiping out the Aboriginal spiritual universe simply because it was a rival to their own. Gillen was a proto-pluralist.

Sometimes he was even more than that. He was anti-colonialist. 'After I read your last letter I would have given a tenner to be alongside you just to give you ... a bit of my mind in return for your gratuitous attack on my Countrymen,' he stormed at Spencer. 'With that arrogant assumption of superiority so characteristic of your Nigger annihilating race, you sneer at the Irish ... You thank god that you are an Englishman, and I thank God that I am not. I have no ambition to belong to such a race of Hypocrites. The British Lion shows his teeth but everyone, even you who are steeped in prejudice, know [sic] that those teeth are only decayed stumps and the poor old brute cannot bite. The stumps are good enough to crush niggers armed with weapons less dangerous than pea-shooters and that's about all.' Gillen often told Spencer that he was blinded by his imperial allegiance, that he wore 'jingo goggles', that '[your] environment has been too much for you – The hidebound toryism which encircles the walls of all British universities has got you in its grasp.' He foamed at the 'oppressing, restraining, stifling, squelching, and at time annihilating' of the Irish by the English, and at England's 'old policy of crushing the Irishism out of the Irish'. The Irish Gillen was seeing the Aborigines from the white point of view and trying to see the whites from the Aboriginal point of view. Only one of these was of interest to imperial anthropology and therefore to Spencer.

Native Tribes of Central Australia, published only four years on, begins with a long (fifty-page) introduction, a small masterpiece of expository prose, by turns appreciative, deprecatory and exculpatory. Contrary to many assertions, Spencer and Gillen say, Aboriginal society is complex in its social relations and its beliefs. It must not be judged by contemporary European standards; those who would like to do so might care to remember the European treatment of witches. There is

much in Aboriginal lives to admire, even envy (they insisted): a generosity and kindness in their dealings with each other, particularly with
children and the elderly; a lithe gracefulness of movement; remarkable
skills, memory and knowledge of the natural world; and an extraordinary capacity to bear discomfort and pain.

But these capacities and attributes are limited by their stage of
development. There is so much that they *don't* have – 'no idea of permanent abodes, no clothing, no knowledge of any implements save those
fashioned out of wood, bone and stone, no idea whatever of the cultivation of crops … no word for any number beyond three, and no belief
in anything like a supreme being', as they later put it.[23] Their ceremonies are many but each is simple and often crude, performed by 'naked
howling savages' who chant songs, the meaning of which they have no
idea. It is not surprising (Spencer and Gillen write) that on meeting a
much more developed social form, the decay of the Native is as rapid
and complete as it is poignant and, it must be conceded, a matter for a
certain regret. '[T]he black fellow has not perhaps any particular reason
to be grateful to the white man,' they say in a much-quoted passage.[24]

> To come in contact with the white man means that, as a general
> rule, his food supply is restricted, and that he is, in many cases,
> warned off from the water-holes which are the centres of his best
> hunting grounds, and to which he has been accustomed to resort
> during the performance of his sacred ceremonies; while the white
> man kills and hunts his kangaroos and emus he is debarred in turn
> from hunting and killing the white man's cattle. Occasionally the
> native will indulge in a cattle hunt; but the result is usually disas-
> trous to himself, and on the whole he succumbs quietly enough to
> his fate, realising the impossibility of defending what he certainly
> regards as his own property.

That said, it's down to business. Most of the book – two volumes, 200,000 words, nineteen chapters, four technical appendixes, a glossary and an index, with 133 illustrations (mostly Spencer's beautiful photographs) and two maps – is in effect a series of display cases, descriptions of ceremonies (of marriage, initiation, increase), of practices such as 'magic', of kinship relationships, and of 'customs' ('knocking out of teeth; nose boring; growth of breasts; blood; blood-letting; blood-giving; blood-drinking; hair; childbirth; food restrictions' and the like). Although Spencer and Gillen were the first to realise that 'dreaming tracks' crisscrossed a landscape crowded with events and beings, they did not attempt to see them from the inside. Gillen's stumbling efforts to understand the metaphorical content of ceremonies and 'traditions' were abandoned in favour of simple description. No individual is named or thanked; differences in personality, behaviour and outlook are noted, but without specification or examination. The book was first and formidably empirical but its myriad detailed descriptions are linked by an implicit functionalism, an assumption that the many elements of Aboriginal society supported each other to form an exceptionally stable (yet fragile) whole. The only explicit theorising related to feverish speculation about the origins and development of humans then current in European intellectual circles.[25] Spencer and Gillen reported that they found no evidence to support the view, held by some, that the Aborigines were a 'degenerate' form of a once higher race. Nor were Aborigines a missing link. They were human beings at an early stage of evolution – not biological evolution, as was asserted by many, but *social* evolution.

The book's reception exceeded even Gillen's soaring hopes. 'In immortalizing the native tribes of central Australia,' wrote Sir James Frazer, *the* eminent authority of the day, 'Spencer and Gillen have at the same time immortalized themselves.'[26] *Native Tribes* was immediately enshrined in the pantheon of anthropological classics. Spencer went home on a victory lap and returned with his coveted FRS. The book influenced and was relied upon by such giants of European thought as Durkheim and Freud. They were a popular success in Australia as well as an academic success abroad. Spencer in particular was in demand as a journalist and as a lecturer (on one occasion even packing the cavernous Melbourne Town Hall). Gillen was lionised in his hometown and received at Government House. They were celebrities.

Why such acclaim? Why were they installed as founding fathers of an Australian discipline that had already produced a significant body of work?[27] No doubt Spencer's artful cultivation of his European contacts (including Sir James Frazer) had something to do with it.[28] And no doubt their work was exceptionally clear, well documented, well organised and internally consistent. But those are differences of degree, not kind. Their decisive advantage was in their timing. Spencer and his scientific, evolutionary anthropology had provided Gillen with a way out of his agonising, and they then provided white Australia – the bitterness of the frontier at last behind it, a new Commonwealth ahead – with a way to overlook what had been done, and to feel better about what was now theirs. Spencer and Gillen were less forthcoming about the realities of relations between white and black than their disciplinary forebears, Howitt and Fison. They offered a seductive double: an affecting insight into a world now, sadly, almost gone, together with the scientifically established fact that it was no-one's fault, really, just the inevitable and irresistible workings of evolution and progress. Ways were found to send them on a year-long expedition across the continent, to study the northern tribes 'before it is too late'.

•

Spencer and Gillen left Tennant Creek with four months and hundreds of miles still to go, but there was no repeat of their memorable time with the Warumungu. They hastened past the Barkly because (as they'd been told earlier in the trip) the Aborigines there had all been 'shot or driven off on account of their murderous attacks on settlers and their continual depredations amongst the cattle'.[29] Then they left the Line they'd been following all the way from Adelaide and turned right for Borroloola, the Gulf of Carpentaria's only port. Crossing the Gulf country, they encountered some Aboriginal people who were willing to be interrogated and observed, others who did so with ill grace and a few who caused Spencer and Gillen to 'display our stock of firearms so that they might know what to expect if they turned nasty'.[30] They stayed at several homesteads, all but one not much more than bush shelters, and passed others that had been abandoned. Borroloola was like something out of Conrad. Made prosperous in the 1880s by the influx of cattle and miners en route to the Kimberley goldfields, it was now sadly decayed. As the weeks passed in the steamy mosquito-ridden heat of the wet season, with Spencer and Gillen waiting for the coastal steamer to turn up, Borroloola became a purgatory. Eventually they were rescued by a patrol boat sent from Darwin, then just about piped aboard the SS *Duke of Norfolk*. Early in the new year they were back in Melbourne.

In 1904 the second of their two great books of anthropology, *Northern Tribes of Central Australia*, was published. It should be regarded as a sequel to the first, they said, but in fact it was a re-run, with the Warumungu playing the central role given to the Arrernte in the first book. Again there was a long introduction, covering now familiar ground, twenty-five chapters, nearly 800 pages in two volumes, and more than 300 illustrations, including a sketch (Illustration 153) of the item coveted by Gillen, 'Parcel of dead man's bones wrapped in paper bark', as presented to Gillen at his request by one of the dead man's sons.

The great cross-continental expedition of 1901 was the last hurrah for the famous duo. They did make a brief trip back to the Lake Eyre region to check their impressions of the Arrabunna, the now miserable remnants of the people found by the nineteen-year-old Gillen to have been 'in excellent Condition', but that was it. When Spencer had suggested that they really needed two years to do the northern tribes, Gillen had baulked. Even the joys of deeply satisfying work and 'having the little prof all to myself' weren't enough to keep Gillen away from his wife, Amelia, and their growing family. It was for them that he'd given up his eminence as the Amir of Alice Springs and settled for a humdrum existence in South Australia as a country-town postmaster. There came a sad and early end. Still in his fifties, Frank Gillen died of a painful neurological disorder in 1912. Spencer grieved. 'I have missed him more than I can say,' he wrote to Amelia.[31] 'My meeting him at Alice Springs made all the difference to my life, and I like to think that it made, as he told me, all the difference to his.'

While Gillen was living out his life as postmaster and paterfamilias, Spencer was becoming one of Melbourne's most prominent citizens.[32] He was honorary director of the National Museum of Victoria, chairman of the board of the Public Library of Victoria, deputy president of the board of the National Gallery of Victoria and president of the Victorian Football League (VFL), all in addition to his work as a professor of biology. With that came awards, portraits and honours. The FRS that followed the publication of *Native Tribes of Central Australia* was now topped by a knighthood. But over and again his imagination returned to the work with Gillen, to anthropology and to that far-off world of deserts and the vanishing Aborigines. Public life brought prominence but in that other world he had found fame and the intensity of extraordinary experience, and in one way or another he kept returning to it. He made three more trips to the Territory and wrote four more books, all except one loyally naming Gillen as co-author. But there were no more smash hits.

Part of the problem was that Spencer, now working alone, kept on going over the same old ground in the same old way. His mind had been formed thirty or forty years before by the exciting new field of evolutionary biology. Gillen wasn't too far off the mark when he told Spencer that 'the hidebound toryism [of] British universities has got you in its grasp'. Perhaps Gillen would have moved him on, had they still been working together? He was a much more adventurous thinker than Spencer, or at least had been until Spencer's evolutionary doctrine got him in its grasp.[33]

As Spencer approached his sixtieth birthday he ran into a rough patch. He was estranged from his wife and from one of their two daughters. A workaholic before he was a husband or a father, he was badly overcommitted and perhaps facing an existential void. There was nowhere left to climb. The world in which he and his outlook had been formed – 'that arrogant assumption of superiority so characteristic of your Nigger annihilating race', as Gillen had so pungently put it – had disappeared into the maw of the Great War. Spencer had lived his entire life in the safe harbour of England's industrial, financial and intellectual ascendancy in Europe and Europe's in the world, but in just four terrible years much of that was gone. Four of the empires that had entered the war had simply vaporised. The greatest of the survivors, the British Empire, was suddenly broke, and rattled by the stirrings of anti-colonialism and its near-relative, anti-racism. Europe's sense of effortless superiority dissolved in tens of millions of deaths. Who were the savages now?

For whatever reason or combination of reasons, Spencer was an alcoholic. In 1920 he retired to the semi-rural Dandenongs and auctioned off his splendid collection of Australian art. Several years on he found a way out of his personal crisis common among powerful men: a younger woman. He set up discreet house with her in London then sailed in 1929 for Patagonia. Spencer, now in his late sixties, thought that he would find there relatively uncontaminated specimens of primitive humans. It was summer in London but coming into winter in Patagonia. On 14 July, at the ends of the earth, Spencer died and was buried in Punta Arenas.

•

What to make of them? First, a disclosure. I became almost as fascinated by Spencer and Gillen as they were by the Aborigines. On my first trip back to Tennant Creek I followed the old road north, the route taken by the nineteen-year-old Gillen in 1875. In Alice I tramped around the river flat below the old telegraph station, trying to find just where Spencer and Gillen might have set up the humpy from which they watched the last great performance of the Engwura cycle, the experience that formed the heart of their first book. I already knew the old telegraph station from being in Alice for the early part of my secondary schooling. On a couple of occasions I'd been one of the kids from the Hostel for Children of the Inland who rode out and poked about the station, then not long retired from its second career as a notorious 'home' for Aboriginal children, and decades before it was glitzed up as a tourist attraction. Back in Alice after fifty years, I clambered up the rocky hill behind the station and sat where Spencer and Gillen often went for a quiet sunset smoke and a yarn. On the last leg of the trip back to Tennant, I turned off the Stuart Highway to visit the home of the great *Walunkwa* in the Davenport Ranges. There, like Gillen, I did not wonder that 'they have attributed [the waterhole's] origin to a mythical monster like the *Walunkwa*'. On a later trip, I followed the vestigial track off the Stuart Highway, 45 degrees to the right, that had taken them to Borroloola and the end of the great expedition.

I liked them, Gillen especially. He was a large spirit. I felt for him in his hopeless struggle with Spencer's intellectual battalions, in the still-lingering discount applied to his contribution to the partnership, and in his confusions. He was a personification of that essential element of the strange career of great Australian silence, the confused Australian conscience. He veered from satisfaction in the 'lesson' handed to the Kaytetye to raging against the treatment of Aboriginal people by the pastoralists and the cops to finding refuge (and a defeat) in a theory that explained it all away. Spencer was a more resistible character but no brute, or snob. I can see why Gillen loved having him 'all to myself'. So, what follows, severe though it is, may cut them more slack than they deserve.

Spencer and Gillen have often been found guilty as charged. They were what we now call 'racist' at a time when 'race consciousness' and 'race prejudice' were nearly universal in many countries, Australia certainly included. They said some dreadful and very quotable things about Aboriginal people being the human equivalent of the platypus and the like, and that is what is so dismaying on first acquaintance.[34] But once advised to avoid sentimentality (on the one hand) and demonising (on the other), I gradually realised that their thoughts and feelings were not so obvious, simple or quotable, that alongside every chilling phrase or sentence we could set another of warmth or insight, or one of Spencer's respectful, even tender, photographs.[35] They were 'racists' but of a particular kind, and not simply so.

Like Richard Windeyer half a century before, they had come up with a powerful argument without silencing that whispering in their hearts. There was a restless inconsistency in their ideas and emotions.[36] They corrected those who thought that Aboriginal people were at a lower stage of biological evolution, but often forgot the distinction themselves (as in Spencer's notorious remark about the human equivalent of the platypus, for example). At some points they belittled Aboriginal rituals and beliefs that they had documented elsewhere with care and respect.

'One of Spencer's respectful, even tender, photographs':
Utneye Perrurle and child, 1894

They expressed affection and admiration for Aboriginal people and urged their readers to do the same, yet also talked about them as if they were a sub-species. The people Gillen routinely referred to as 'Niggers' were also regarded by him as close friends (preferable, often enough, to the whites). They reminded their audiences, however circumspectly, that the whites took food and water from Aboriginal people then exercised terrible violence if Aboriginal people took the white man's cattle, but they also talked about the destruction of Aboriginal societies as if it were a contagion, something as mysteriously fatal as it was unavoidable. 'All that can be done is to gather the few remnants of the tribe into some mission station where the path to final extinction may be made as pleasant as possible.'[37]

They asked their readers to put themselves in the place of 'Blackfellows', but in practice wrote almost exclusively from the angle of 'Whitefellows'. They were brief and jocular in their references to the old man whom they suspected had been at Attack Creek, but earnest when they remarked (as they often did) on the heroics of the explorers and pioneers (McDouall Stuart particularly) and on the shameful lack of recognition accorded them. They passed through the post-apocalyptic landscape of the Gulf country but Gillen's journal suggests that he was almost miffed that some Aboriginal people were suspicious or hostile. Meeting station-owners on the point of giving up in the face of the 'persistent depredations of the Natives', he took their part and wondered whether we should follow the Americans in 'confining the Natives to definite tracts of country'.[38] Difficult to do, but what is the alternative? Shooting them down? Spencer and Gillen had returned from the site of a human catastrophe bearing stories of what had been there before.

And here is a second reservation about quoting ugly sentences and closing the case: it misses the main point about Spencer and Gillen. Their impact came less from the words they used to describe what they saw than from what they chose to see, from their angle of view. They thought it best to 'draw a veil' over the events that had so troubled the young Gillen, but their anthropology was even more effective than a veil.[39] Don't look *here*, it urged. Look over *there*! It was a way of not seeing and, what's more, it was authorised by science.

In their dealings with Aboriginal people, Spencer and Gillen were often exploitative. The Warumungu got some rations for a couple of months but not much else. Waanyi author Alexis Wright, writing on behalf of the descendants of Jacob and Zulu and the many others who extended their hospitality to Spencer and Gillen, calls them 'rubbish people' for their failure to reciprocate.[40] If it occurred to them that the Warumungu might have been looking for something more from them than tucker, they didn't say so. They certainly did nothing to slow the steady deterioration in the Warumungu's circumstances, and they and their anthropology contributed both directly (via Spencer's reports to government in 1913 and 1924) and indirectly to yet another form of terror, the taking of children of mixed descent from their families. As for the Warumungu's knowledge of what had happened to them and their neighbours, that was theirs to keep for a long time yet.

Perhaps worst of all was a betrayal of trust. They were often asked how had they managed to witness and photograph ceremonies and other events never before seen by white people. The answer, given in emphatic italics I can't recall being used anywhere else in the book: '*both of us are regarded as fully initiated members of the [Arrernte] tribe*', and hence vouched for with tribes up and down the line.[41] In other words, they were not just initiated (Spencer courtesy of being represented by Gillen as his 'brother', by the way) but trusted with secrets which they knew they were going to present to the world. That there was no whispering of hearts on this question represents a number of things, including yet another triumph of wants over conscience and, if I may borrow from the Sermon on the Mount, the power of anthropology to zero in on the mote in the brother's eye yet have not a clue about the beam in its own. On taking leave from the Warumungu, Gillen made a speech in which he urged them to 'discontinue certain cruel tribal rites'. It might have occurred to the proto-pluralist, anti-colonialist Gillen of five or six years earlier that the Warumungu would be entitled to urge the white men to discontinue certain cruel practices of their own, but not the Gillen now fitted out with anthropology's lenses.

What can be entered on the other side of the ledger? The first entry is something not intended by them but nonetheless of incalculable value to the survival and constitution of Aboriginal peoples. In their relentless collection of facts and things, Spencer and Gillen and their anthropology provided a keeping place for knowledge, artefacts, photographs, sound recordings and genealogies.[42] In the case of the Warumungu, some of these have been returned and can be seen in their museum in Tennant Creek, where they say to the *papulanyi*: this is who we are![43]

Second, they were less the founding fathers of a discipline than of its social and historical role. They made anthropology widely known, authoritative and influential. It is true that Spencer and Gillen belittled, infantilised and patronised Aboriginal people, but they also contributed to the long labour of undoing other and worse expressions of 'racism'.[44] They helped make an authoritative way for us to see Aboriginal people as the constructors of a rich, complex and in some respects remarkable civilisation, thus tackling both the armchair theorists in Europe who declared that they were biologically primitive and the local hatred and contempt generated by the violent frontiers.

Third, and most important in the long run, was the method by which they arrived at their correctives. They could say to both the theorists and the haters that their views were not consistent with the known facts. The eponymous sponsor of the Horn Expedition, for example, used much of his introduction to the expedition's report to rant about the base and contemptible character of Aborigines, asserting among other things that they had no traditions and no religion. Spencer and Gillen could demonstrate that that was simply was not the case. They were pursuers of truth (or truthfulness, really) through carefully documented observation, open to test and contest. That there is more to getting at 'the truth' than simple observation is now a commonplace; then, it wasn't. A way of pursuing the truth which began its life in avoiding much of the truth was eventually able to pursue that and other truths about itself.

CHAPTER THREE

1933

I t was many years before another anthropologist turned up in Tennant Creek. This time it was not a famous duo and their support team but a young man at the beginning of his anthropological career. And Tennant Creek was no longer just the telegraph station–cum–ration depot of Spencer and Gillen's day; it was in the early days of a gold rush and about to become a town. Bill Stanner recalled many years later that what he saw was a true 'Never Never' landscape,[1] 'a stretch of bush pock-marked with scattered shafts; a lot of ore at grass; little food, less water, almost no ready money; rough humpies and scores of hard customers with that worst of fevers, gold-fever'.[2] The hard customers wanted to know what he was up to. They thought he was a government agent of some kind, and no wonder. A photograph of the young anthropologist in the field depicts a matinee idol on safari, a darkly handsome chap with a faraway look in his eyes, late twenties, beard (a concession to frontier circumstances) neatly trimmed, hair brushed and parted just so, an open-necked khaki shirt that might have been chosen for him by the wardrobe department. I don't know how he spoke in those days, but recordings of an older Stanner reveal a plummy, Anglophile accent of the kind then mandatory in certain social strata (and for ABC presenters). Given that he'd already been moving in conservative political circles, he probably spoke

'A matinee idol on safari'

then as he did later. To a miner's eye and ear, he must have seemed a government spy from central casting. A small delegation visited his camp and 'offer[ed], in a firm but civil way, to throw me off the field if I tinkered with their affairs'.

Stanner assured the miners that he was 'working on strictly anthropological matters', which was half true. He had been asked to see whether Spencer and Gillen's account of Warumungu social organisation was correct. I'm not sure exactly how Stanner went about this task, but it certainly including seeking out Spencer and Gillen's 'very intelligent young man "Zulu"', now a very intelligent senior man. The other half of the truth is that he *was* an agent of some kind. He was there to find out whether the government should be pressed to constrain the miners and look after the Warumungu. Had the miners known that, and had they also known that in a former life Stanner had been a journalist, he would certainly have been 'thrown off the field'. As it was, he took no chances, kept a gun handy and set himself to finding out what the miners were getting up to and how the Warumungu were faring.

'The Warumungu were in much worse shape'

Stanner found that the Warumungu were in much worse shape than they had been in Spencer and Gillen's time, thirty years before. 'The Warramunga [Warumungu] are not in any real sense living upon their tribal territories,' he wrote. They depended as much as possible upon white food sources, which meant rations handed out at the telegraph station and 'surreptitiously shared by the elder with the younger', plus whatever could be provided by those working on the cattle stations to the north. The old local group system had been abandoned (Stanner said) and with it much of the wider social organisation, but kinship rules were intact and kinship avoidances still 'intensely upheld', conclusions that sit oddly with each other.[3] On the main point of concern there was no ambiguity: there was a tussle between the miners and the Warumungu over the location of their reserve. That was what Stanner had been warned not to tinker with.

In a way it was a phoney war.[4] The reserve had been gazetted back in 1892. No-one, black or white, took much notice of it or even knew where its boundaries were. The whites, including those at the telegraph station, made free use of the land for their stock, but in a concession to the fact of the reserve didn't try to prevent the Warumungu from hunting, camping or performing their ceremonies there. Now, however, it *would* matter. The field was unusual in having gold scattered widely about; the miners wanted the reserve shifted so that there would be no question as to their entitlement to prospect and sink shafts all over the place. For its part, the government wanted what the miners wanted, but it also wanted to protect the Warumungu by keeping them well away from the miners. To these ends, the government geologist and the Territory's sole member of the national parliament had sought and got the agreement of Zulu, 'chief' of the Warumungu. They reported him as saying that his people were willing to have the reserve moved to a perfectly satisfactory alternative stretch of country to the east. Stanner found otherwise. The proposed new reserve was mostly spinifex country, badly watered (inspecting it, he came close to dying of thirst) and a considerable distance from the ration depot and its permanent water supply. Worse, even though the Warumungu weren't to be confined to the new reserve, they and people from surrounding tribes were to be excluded from the old one and hence from a number of sites at which they were obliged to perform certain ceremonies and rituals.

How had this happened, Stanner wanted to know. He asked Zulu and another senior man, 'King' Charlie Jampin. They told him that they had been 'hurried' by the government men and that they now wanted to renegotiate. They didn't want to keep the miners out of the existing reserve, but they did want to make sure that they still had access, and when the mining was done things should go back to the way they were before. Stanner wrote a stiff report on what had happened and added his own concerns about the likely impact of the town and the pub now springing up seven miles to the south of the telegraph station. He made recommendations on matters ranging from water supply to the renegotiation of the agreement and the regulation of movement by both the miners and the Warumungu in the interests of keeping them well apart. His report completed and dispatched, Stanner resumed his solitary journey to his field work in the far north-west.

Stanner later said that what he had seen in Tennant Creek had upset him, 'so the yeast was working'.[5] It was the working of that yeast that made him the guiding spirit of this and many other books. Stanner was the old hand who had warned a new colleague against 'sentimentalising' Aboriginal people, who framed the potent formulation of 'the story of the unacknowledged relations between two racial groups within a single field of life', and who was the first to notice the existence of a 'great Australian silence'. But all that came later, in the 1950s and 1960s, by which time he was deep into the most important intellectual struggle in the history of relations between two racial groups in this field of life.

•

That anthropology was still being done at all in 1934, let alone able to offer a young man the prospect of a career, would have been cause for surprise only two or three years earlier.[6] Spencer and Gillen's spectacular bid to make anthropology the authoritative account of the Aborigines had been followed by a long decline in the discipline's fortunes. Twice it veered toward oblivion.

Anthropology up to and including Spencer and Gillen's time had relied on amateurs – missionaries, public servants, pastoralists, bushmen. Spencer was the only academic among them and he had trained and continued to work as a biologist; Spencer and Gillen were amateurs too. Experts on matters Aboriginal were useful enough to governments as Protectors or to conduct inquiries; indeed, when in 1911 the federal government relieved South Australia of that white elephant the Northern Territory, Spencer himself was sent north to advise on policy for Aborigines and 'half-castes'. But these were gigs; there was no continuing commitment. Academe hadn't come to the party either. Every state capital except Perth had its university (UWA was established in 1911) but all were small, less than affluent and not looking for additional disciplines which offered no vocational prospects. Even Spencer had been knocked back in his bid to get an anthropology program at Melbourne.

Adelaide was the nearest thing anthropology had to an institutional base. Thanks to the overland telegraph and the track and railway that followed, Adelaide provided easy access to relatively 'uncontaminated' Aborigines. Just as Victoria's museum had a wonderful collection of Aboriginal artefacts thanks to Spencer, South Australia's museum had an equally impressive collection courtesy of Edward Stirling. Stirling was the suitor who had been jilted by Gillen in favour of Spencer, the surgeon who had operated on Cubadgee, and honorary director of the South Australian Museum in which Cubadgee's skeleton was displayed. The museum's staff included the exceptionally energetic Norman Tindale. Just down North Terrace was the University of Adelaide, where a professor of medicine and a few colleagues extended a concern for Aboriginal health into anthropology. They set up the Board for Anthropological Research, but there was no anthropology department and therefore no anthropology students or graduates. And anyway, at the university as at the museum, anthropology had emerged from the natural and biological sciences and concentrated on biometrics, demography and the like, rather than social anthropology of the Spencer and Gillen kind. (Among its preoccupations was the relationship between cranial capacity and primitive psychology.) Others of a similar bent worked from the University of Sydney, all in the anatomy department.

Those lobbying for an Australian chair in anthropology – including Spencer, the Adelaide group and senior academics in England – had a stronger hand to play after the Great War than before.[7] They could argue that Australia was now a trustee answerable to the League of Nations for the native peoples of New Guinea. Administrators there would need anthropological insights and should receive anthropological training. Closer to the lobbyists' hearts, the Aborigines had not died out, or not yet anyway; there were still 'full-bloods' living in the traditional way in many of the nooks and crannies of the vast frontier zone. Their way of life should be documented 'before it is too late', of course, but as the most primitive of the world's many races, they had a special role to play in an emerging 'science of Man'. Third, even if 'full-blood' numbers were falling (and no-one really knew), 'half-castes' were on the increase. The political fact was that the Aborigines – if indeed 'half-castes' were actually 'Aborigines', as some thought they were and some thought they weren't – presented a problem, a threat to White Australia and its moral fibre, an embarrassment abroad and a source of rumbling disquiet at home.[8] Expertise was called for.

Much of the lobbyists' effort had been directed at Australian universities and governments, but the South Australians went elsewhere. In 1923 they pitched wealthy US foundations, with immediate effect. Encouraged by strong expressions of US interest, Australian state and federal governments agreed to chip in too. By 1926 a foundation professor had been appointed – not at Spencer's University of Melbourne or, to the intense chagrin of the Adelaide lobby, in Adelaide, but at the University of Sydney. Influenced by Australia's Trusteeship responsibilities and by the US race theorists who had encouraged the foundations to get involved, the new department of anthropology would look more toward the Pacific than inland, and toward physical rather than social anthropology.

The foundation professor had other ideas, however, and proceeded to implement them with dispatch. A.R. Radcliffe-Brown (not long since plain Alf Brown, a lower-middle-class lad from Warwickshire) was an extraordinarily flamboyant figure.[9] 'A tall man with a distinguished air and presence, strikingly handsome in his prime, he often captivated people as much by his charm, wit and cultivation as by the appeal of his ideas,' reported one of the captivated – Bill Stanner – many years later. 'He was a particularly brilliant teacher who was so much the master of his subject, and of the arts of the rostrum and seminar, that he would expound the most difficult topics without notes or any outward sign of preparation. His writings gave the same impression.' Radcliffe-Brown was as headstrong as he was flamboyant. More engaged with the Aborigines than with the Pacific islanders, he was also more than happy to leave physical anthropology to others. He wasn't interested in divining the position of Aborigines on the evolutionary ladder either. What he *did* want to do was analyse how societies construct and maintain themselves. His was a new kind of anthropology, a rigorous theorisation of the way many parts of complex social orders comprise a structured whole, an approach which he expounded with charismatic flair. Radcliffe-Brown soon had half a dozen workers in the field gathering evidence which, he said, would be 'of the very greatest importance for a comparative science of culture'.[10] He was confident that this science would have its uses but that wasn't the point of doing it, or not yet anyway.

His eyes fixed on far theoretical horizons, Radcliffe-Brown took insufficient notice of events closer to home. The funds for his chair came from the US via the Australian National Research Council, the members of which he failed to keep on side, while at the university 'an air of academic superiority and a somewhat exotic and social pose raised [as one acid pen put it] a slight barrier between himself and some of his colleagues'. Five years after taking Sydney by storm Radcliffe-Brown was on his way to a chair at Chicago, his field workers dispersed and their expeditionary gear consigned to storage. Social anthropology in Australia was in serious and perhaps fatal trouble, again.[11] An acting professor was followed by an acting lecturer, one of Radcliffe-Brown's field workers, Adolphus Peter Elkin. Elkin later said that he was 'given the helm of a sinking ship'. In fact, the ship was being scuttled. Students were warned that teaching in anthropology would cease at the end of 1933; it was Elkin's job to wind things up. But Elkin, like Radcliffe-Brown before him, declined to accept his brief. He was to stay at Sydney for the rest of his long life, making it the capital of a growing empire of anthropology and retrieving Spencer and Gillen's efforts to make anthropology the definitive and most influential of Australia's stories about the Aborigines.[12]

·

Elkin shared Radcliffe-Brown's enthusiasm for field work and for a social anthropology of the Aborigines, but in every other respect he was Radcliffe-Brown's antithesis. Elkin said of his predecessor (in an obituary that was the source of the acidic remarks quoted above) that Radcliffe-Brown was a 'starter', not a builder – fair comment given that Radcliffe-Brown was three times a foundation professor of anthropology (in Cape Town, Sydney and Oxford) and once a foundation professor of sociology (in Egypt).[13] Radcliffe-Brown laid the foundations, Elkin acknowledged in a characteristically arch manoeuvre, but 'foundations without superstructure are of no use ... building superstructures requires persistence, patience, willingness to modify plans, and an appreciation of the context in which a university ... exists'. Where Radcliffe-Brown offended, Elkin cultivated. Where Radcliffe-Brown was in ceaseless motion, Elkin established himself at Sydney and never budged. Elkin was a powerful presence but through 'persistence, patience, willingness to modify plans, and an appreciation of the context in which a university ... exists', not charisma. Beaky, thin-lipped, grey-suited, Elkin contained not a jot of flamboyance. He had a clear, sharp mind, theoretically alert but impatient with theoretical castles in the air. He was an eclectic thinker but an orderly one, fond of mental pigeonholes – the four phases of contact between white and black, the four stages in the development of the discipline of anthropology, the nine areas on which future research should concentrate, and so on. In important part he conducted what amounted to an intellectual counter-revolution, reaching back over Radcliffe-Brown's structuralist theorising to the grounded empiricism of Spencer and Gillen. And far from being indifferent to the uses of anthropology, Elkin gave good works parity with science.

From our vantage point this radical rethinking of anthropology and its purposes is hardly surprising. At the time of his appointment to a temporary lectureship and, soon after, to the chair, Professor Elkin was also the Reverend Elkin. From Monday to Thursday, he could be found at the university; from Friday to Sunday, he was in his parish at Morpeth in the Hunter Valley, north of Sydney. Elkin was a missionary, but not of the old kind. Eschewing life among the Natives, he sought influence over public opinion and official policy, and power within the machinery of the state and the organisations of civil society. But by Elkin's own account, the one thing did not automatically flow from the other.[14] He had commenced as one of Radcliffe-Brown's field workers in 1927 'with no humanitarian motive at all', he said, and with no interest in 'the contact situation' either. 'My task was to record and analyse aboriginal social organisation, ritual and mythology,' he said, 'and to that task I stuck.' He began as a salvage anthropologist, pure and simple, but he found it impossible to be 'in the field' and *not* notice 'the contact situation'.

Almost unconsciously at first (he later recalled) but with steadily increasing force, the realities of the present social order pushed against those of the past. He got to know Aboriginal people, some 'civilised', others making contact with a white man almost for the first time. 'They looked after me ... and they did their best to explain their language and culture to me,' he said. Like many before and after, Elkin was falling for the Aboriginal people, the very people he soon saw walking along 'each fastened by a light chain extending from a neck-band on one to a neck-band on the next'. He found gaps in genealogies left by individuals who not long before 'had been shot and whose bodies had been burnt by a punitive expedition led by two policemen'. Working in South Australia later, Elkin, like Stanner, was an object of frontier suspicion. It fell to the publican at Horseshoe Bend (south of Alice Springs) to reassure the local cop that he could speak freely in Elkin's presence because Elkin was 'alright' – meaning, as Elkin later said, '[that] I was just a scientist and not a busybody'. Elkin also recalled meeting a missionary who thought that the pastoralists had cause for grievance because the Aborigines came to the waterholes and frightened the cattle. The code of silence was being policed in the frontier zone against signs of its weakening in the post-frontier.

Interest in the Aborigines had flagged after Spencer and Gillen, but was now rising again; 'sympathy' was increasing. The murmur was becoming a low rumble.[15] Writers and journalists, artists, churches, women's groups, trade unions and a prospering Communist Party, as well as organisations like the Association for the Protection of Native Races (APNR), drew attention to the 'plight' of the Aborigines. Increasingly, Aboriginal people spoke for themselves. Political resistance – organised efforts to change white Australia's attitudes and policies – came from Aboriginal people in the post-frontier south, survivors of a defeat now several generations away, as well as from the 'sympathetic' whites. During the 1920s, associations of Aboriginal activists appeared in several states and at the national level; by 1938, the Australian Aborigines League was able to organise a National Sorry Day to mark the one hundred and fiftieth anniversary of the arrival of the First Fleet. Aboriginal people were using the Europeans' ways to struggle against them.

On the receiving end of this gathering unease were the state and federal governments. They were attacked for what they were doing and for what they weren't. From the middle of the nineteenth century they had turned to legislation and regulation to 'protect' the Aborigines, two-thirds of whom lived in the frontier north. By the end of the 1930s New South Wales had passed fourteen pieces of legislation bearing on Aborigines, Victoria had passed eighteen, Western Australia twenty-four, South Australia twenty-five and Queensland twenty-nine, while the Commonwealth, responsible for the Northern Territory, had promulgated thirty-eight ordinances.[16] If you were classified as 'Aboriginal' and were within administrative reach, one historian records, you could be told where to live, whether your children would be raised in an institution, how much money you could be paid as an employee and how you could spend it, whom you could associate with, even whether you could marry the person of your choice. (Permission was given for the celebration of the marriage of twelve female 'half-castes', noted the Northern Territory's annual report for 1933–34, seven with Europeans and five with male 'half-castes'.)

These measures of 'protection' did little to quiet whispering hearts. They didn't protect, and often gave offence as well. But what really turned disquiet into a movement was a steady flow of 'incidents', including 'reprisals' that post-frontier Australia thought belonged in a half-remembered past. In 1926 came reports of killings in the Kimberley – the killings that produced the gaps in Elkin's genealogies. That was followed by the infamous Coniston massacres in 1928, police-led vigilante raids in reprisal for the spearing of a white trapper on Coniston Station, north-west of Alice Springs, and for an attack soon after on the owner of a nearby station. Dozens of Warlpiri men, women and children were hunted down, Queensland-style. Not long after a government whitewash of those events came official talk – a proposal by the administrator of the Northern Territory, in fact – of mounting another reprisal, this time in Arnhem Land. A policeman sent to investigate a number of killings by the Yolngu had been fatally speared.

This time, however, the reprisal didn't happen. An outcry in southern cities precipitated a complicated series of events in which the move for a reprisal was halted, but a number of Aboriginal people were brought to trial and found guilty.[17] Prominent in the outcry was Professor A.P. Elkin. In mid-1934 Elkin spoke at a packed protest organised by the APNR, missionary societies and trade unions. Rather than follow other speakers in 'fireworks and emotional appeals', Elkin offered what he called a careful analysis of policy and court procedures. A couple of days later he took a phone call from the prime minister. Press reports in London caused the dominions office to contact the high commissioner, who contacted the prime minister, who called Elkin. The prime minister told Elkin that 'the Government, acknowledging the pressure of public opinion in Australia and the interest in England, was prepared to take a broader, juster, more humane and forward-looking view'. Elkin had just what the prime minister was looking for.

Elkin's rising humanitarian instincts made him active in the cause; by 1933, newly elected as president of the APNR, he was close to leading it. Along the way he had become impatient with protests and reviews and commissions of enquiry that went nowhere, and with protection policies 'implemented by sincere Protectors and other officials' which 'did nothing to stem injustice, cruelty, atrocity and aboriginal depopulation'.[18] He knew from his own experience that the centre and the north 'was a world of its own, insulated from the south, and beyond the rangs [sic] of the benign intentions of governments'. To counter it, governments and critics alike must 'adopt the view that the aborigines need not die out [and] implement positive policies of health services, education and employment to fit themselves for a place in our Australian world'. Elkin wanted the state to bring the vast frontier zone to heel. The way to do it was *strategy*.

That is what Elkin offered the prime minister, and that is what a prime minister adrift gratefully accepted. There followed, Elkin reports with satisfaction – he was a relentless chronicler of the rise and rise of anthropology, and liberal in his use of the vertical pronoun – change in the form and/or substance of the policy and methods of every government except the Victorian. A couple of years on, Elkin suggested 'assimilation' as the goal of these new policies, and in short order 'the term assimilation became official'. Pursued with proper regard for the psychology and 'group life' of the Aborigines, it was the best and only option: contact was fatal, protection a failure, and complete segregation impossible. In 1938 the minister for the interior announced 'a new deal for Aborigines' with the goal of 'assimilation' at its centre.

In a fever of activity, Elkin was building anthropology's science as rapidly and successfully as its good works. He was not a system-constructor like Radcliffe-Brown. In fact, he saw integrated theories in general and functionalism in particular as obstacles to thought and to policy, overemphasising as they did the rigidity of Aboriginal culture and underestimating real-world complexity. Science was the only proper basis for policy and administration, but it had to be eclectic, not 'pure', a humane science,[19] alive to the humanness of the Aboriginal people – including, notably, of Aboriginal women.[20] He was head of the only university anthropology department in the country (a distinction retained until 1950), editor of *Oceania*, the leading scholarly journal, producer of hundreds of reviews, comments, digests, notes, articles, recollections and surveys, chair of the national allocator of funding for field work, the Australian National Research Council (ANRC), a relentless

networker, author of a popular digest of a growing academic literature
(*Australian Aborigines: How to Understand Them*), and wielder of the title
'professor' at a time when it was accorded a respect bordering on awe.[21]
By 1938 Elkin could boast of his department's twenty-four extended
anthropological expeditions and many shorter ones, most during his
tenure. Elkin was becoming a household name and the most powerful man in Aboriginal affairs, a triumph for him and for his concept of
anthropology. He was cock-a-hoop. Stanner was not.

•

Stanner's 1930s were very different from Elkin's. He returned from field
work in the Daly River region to find that his report from Tennant
Creek had spurred Elkin and the ANRC to vigorous protest about the
immanent dispossession of the Warumungu – to no effect.[22] Only two
weeks after Stanner had left Tennant, the old reserve was revoked and
the new one gazetted. The new reserve, said the minister in announcing
it, was 'a large area well-watered, and apparently in every way suitable
for the natives', none of which was true.[23] Later that same year, popular novelist-cum-journalist Ion Idriess was in Tennant on the lookout
for material, and joined the local butcher in his daily round.[24] 'With
Jock I roamed the entire circumference of the field, visited every camp,
every claim, in his meat truck. Fifty miles each daily trip all round the
compass, the "hub" being the pub and a dozen shacks round which the
future prosperous town would be built, bumping out into the sunlight,
dodging the spinifex tufts out into a dreamy vastness which westward
knew no township even for a thousand miles.' Less than a year later
700 leases were scattered across a thousand square miles.[25]

In 1935 the minister honoured the booming field with a visit and
was treated to a corroboree,[26] 'a spectacle which as civilisation advances
is becoming increasingly rare', the Adelaide *Advertiser* pointed out.[27]

'Completely naked ... bucks and lubras' were reported to have performed their dances 'under the direction of Zulu'. Soon a bigger town was planning a bigger spectacle to celebrate the taking of 100,000 pounds' worth of gold from the field. Warumungu 'scouts' were sent out to bring members of the neighbouring Warramulla tribe to an 'Inter-tribal' corroboree. Back in Sydney, Stanner got wind of this plan and penned an angry protest. The Warramulla, he wrote in a letter to *The Sydney Morning Herald,* unlike the Warumungu and many others, were 'still in a very primitive state'.[28] Under no circumstances should they be permitted to proceed to Tennant Creek. If not prevented from so doing, 'the tribe will keep on returning until it is a parasitic rump' and its 'extinction [will be] a matter of a few years'. Days later came the report that 'King Billy, majestic in loincloth and towering headdress', supported by his 'first man' Zulu, had led the Warumungu on the dance ground, followed by the Warramulla, 'primitives who wander uninfluenced by white control over the barren desert north of Tennant Creek'. Screaming their chants and leaping wildly, the dancers brandished their spears. Exhibitions of spear- and boomerang-throwing followed.

The miners won, Stanner said bitterly many years later, and the Warumungu lost. The miners and the town brought the grog and the venereal disease, as Stanner had foreseen. Perhaps because he'd been asked to focus on the land question, Stanner seems to have overlooked the impact of other events on the Warumungu. Coniston was almost as close to Tennant Creek as to Alice Springs; the riverbeds along which the Warlpiri had fled and were hunted down were closer still. The Warumungu must have been reminded that the bad old days of white terrorism weren't over after all. Whether or not that was the case, the massacres brought an influx of Warlpiri and other refugees to the rations, water and presumed safety of the telegraph station. Then, as the population of the nearby town swelled from the hundred or so at the time of Stanner's visit to six times that number, the policemen arrived, three of them. The protection they were charged with extending to the Warumungu included taking 'half-caste' children, a policy advocated by Spencer among many others.

Geography was fortune, good and bad. By virtue of living more than a thousand miles from the eastern and southern coasts, the Warumungu had been out of harm's way for a hundred years longer than the Cadigal on the southern shore of Sydney Harbour. On the other hand, the accident of being on a line drawn between a southern settlement and a northern one brought the Warumungu their first frontier decades sooner than it reached people in the western deserts and in the north-west, in Arnhem Land and on Cape York. Then came the cattle, taking their good country to the north but leaving the rest. Next came the police, who took their children, and the miners, who took much of what the cattle hadn't wanted but at least left the ration depot at the telegraph station, and with that their access to the creek and the most sacred of their sites, Jurnkurakurr. Then, even that went: the Warumungu were in the way of the soldiers.

By 1940 the old track along the line was being turned into a sealed highway, along which came tens of thousands of soldiers and their support crews. The Territory's director of native affairs, evidently feeling himself to be on the high moral ground, was able to assure the National Council of Women of Australia, anxious about the welfare of Aboriginal women, that 'all places within a radius of 5 miles from the new road and the camps of the workers' had been declared prohibited areas for Aboriginals, and that 'a large number of Aboriginals' had been transferred from the telegraph station at Tennant Creek to 'a watering place 20 miles distant … and there rationed'.[29]

That left the Warumungu with a grim consolation: through four successive waves of invasion they had managed to avoid the deadly violence visited upon neighbours to the south (the Kaytetye in 1874), to the north (the peoples of the Barkly in the 1880s), to the south-east (the Alyawarre in the early 1920s) and to the south-west (the Warlpiri in 1929). They had survived.[30]

•

In 1936 Stanner took himself off to England to do a doctorate with Radcliffe-Brown, who had moved on from Chicago to take the new chair at Oxford. It was Radcliffe-Brown's riveting lectures that had caused Stanner to abandon journalism for anthropology in the first place, and he wanted more. He found that he couldn't earn his keep in Oxford and so went instead to London and the LSE to work with the other great exponent of structuralist anthropology, Bronisław Malinowski. In the course of that work there were more angry letters to the editor to be written, one of them in *The Times* (where, perhaps not coincidentally, he was working as a subeditor and leader-writer) causing a stir, to no avail as usual. As Stanner argued the case over and again, he was coming to think that the problem lay less in the volume of protest than in its content, in his own outlook and discipline.

Stanner's sponsor and research supervisor, Elkin, seemed to think that anthropology – *his* anthropology – was not just useful to policy but its golden key. As one sympathetic critic put it, Elkin set himself up as the expert.[31] 'He, the professor of anthropology, knew best.' In fact, there was as much conflict and confusion among anthropologists as in official circles and public debate. At one end of the spectrum was Sydney-trained but Melbourne-based Donald Thomson, who, to Elkin's intense irritation, was using work with the Yolngu in Arnhem Land to argue against assimilation and in favour of complete segregation of the remaining tribes of 'true' Aborigines. At the other end was Tindale in Adelaide, also irritatingly out of Elkin's direct control, trying to deduce capacity for assimilation from biology ('half-castes' versus 'quarter-castes' versus 'octoroons').[32] Anthropologically informed protectors disagreed over whether 'miscegenation' was the problem (because it increased numbers of coloureds) or the solution (because the colour would breed out). Elkin wanted to assimilate the Aborigines while respecting 'Aboriginal psychology' and 'Aboriginal group life', but how exactly would that be done? Who would manage the many paths to equality and citizenship from starting points ranging from Thomson's Yolngu to urban intellectuals like tenor Harold Blair, inventor and author David Unaipon or activist William Cooper? And how, on the other hand, could segregation work? Where would it lead? Stanner's own plea for the segregation and protection of the Warramulla trailed off into implicit despair. Anthropology's thinking was as muddled as anyone else's.[33] It couldn't even decide who was 'Aboriginal' or whether 'extinction' was being avoided or if it could be.

Anthropology might have become the most influential of Australia's stories about the Aborigines, but Stanner had seen that in the places that really needed influencing it was practically inaudible, drowned out by other stories Australians were telling themselves: the Development of the North story, the Nation for a Continent story, and the Hardy Pioneers story. In Tennant Creek, Stanner had watched the frontier zone enlist the government in thumbing its nose at the whispering hearts of the post-frontier. It wasn't that governments were unaware. As Stanner later pointed out, they had any number of reports at their disposal, including Stanner's own about the miners and the Warumungu.[34] Symbolically enough, that report had disappeared somewhere in Canberra, only to reappear quite by chance in 1979. It was a question of interests, and priorities. A government in the midst of a great depression, stuck with a white elephant that had cost many millions since taken over from South Australia in 1911, saw the Aborigines as a trifling obstacle between it and what might well be another Bathurst or Ballarat or Bendigo or

Kalgoorlie.[35] Yet it was in government that Elkin rested most of his hopes. Looking back on all this, Stanner saw a younger self who was 'steeped in Spencer and Gillen' (hence all the talk in his Warramulla letter about primitives, the drift to extinction, the doomed tribe and so on), who knew that he didn't like it, but who couldn't work out why. Elkin doubted nothing; Stanner doubted everything.

PhD done and accolades earned (Malinowski is reported to have declared him the 'most original' thinker in his seventy-strong seminar), Stanner got his first real job as an anthropologist, in Kenya. In London and then in Africa Stanner met people, read books and saw things that confirmed him as bear to Elkin's bull.[36] In 1937 the state and federal ministers for Aboriginal affairs met for the first time to endorse what became the Commonwealth's 1938 new deal for Aborigines, for which Elkin took much credit. Stanner, now possessing the voice that was to become so familiar, was not persuaded.[37] 'Here are high official aspirations, unimpeachable liberal social principles, an ambitious paper plan, an objective dimly conceived and pleasantly worded,' he wrote. 'Here, apparently, is belief that prejudiced men, case-hardened viewpoints, vested interests, a bureaucracy with a long tenure of office yet to run, and a proven difficult environment will belie their history and become conveniently malleable ... Policy is put into operation with its head in a whirl, accompanied by the hope that things will sort themselves out ... This is where defensive official myths start, and this is also why it is so hard for both officials and public to see where truth lies.'

What Stanner saw in and knew about Tennant Creek richly illustrated the confusions and impotence of both anthropology and policy, but my guess is that that was not the town's main contribution to his ferment. That lay, I think, in his conversations with Zulu and Charlie Jampin, the telling and hearing of the story of what had happened. No doubt their account was, as Aboriginal accounts given to whitefellas usually are, undemonstrative and terse to the point of being cryptic. But Stanner was a good listener. Unlike the miners and the government men and the minister and the reporters (indeed, unlike Spencer and Gillen in their conversations with the selfsame Zulu), Stanner wanted to hear. My surmise is that in listening to Zulu and Charlie Jampin, Stanner heard all that they weren't saying, and heard also the thousands of other stories each different, all the same about what happened when the whitefellas turned up. Where did those stories fit in anthropology? Anthropology did take in 'cultural change' (number seven on Elkin's list of nine areas requiring further research), but Zulu and Charlie weren't talking about 'readjusting themselves to conditions arising from a clash of peoples and culture', as the cultural change perspective would have it.[38] They were describing the exercise of power, unrestrained and backed by violence. Elkin's anthropology was a big improvement on Spencer and Gillen's because it attended to the here and now as well as to the world before. But what had happened in between? Elkin was well aware of frontier realities. He had seen them. But they were not his or anthropology's subject matter. In London and then in Africa, Stanner came to understand what he'd first sensed in Tennant Creek.[39] His science wasn't telling the truth, or not the one that mattered anyway.

CHAPTER FOUR

1958

Being 'transferred' from the telegraph station to 'a watering place 20 miles distant ... and there rationed' turned out to be the nadir of the Warumungu's fortunes. They might have been shoved out of the whitefellas' way, yet again, and banned from 'all places within a radius of 5 miles from the new road and the camps of the workers', but that turned out not to matter so much. Losing access to Jurnkurakurr was a blow, but the rations were still being provided for those who couldn't do without, and those who had been living and working on the stations continued to do so. For a lucky few there was now another option: army work, which offered a decent wage and decent living conditions, a shock for the station-owners and an eye-opener for Aboriginal people. The 'watering place 20 miles distant' from the telegraph station referred to by the Territory's director of native affairs soon replaced by another, at Phillip Creek, where something more and better than a 'ration depot' emerged, a 'mission', a home base and general service centre for an increasingly mobile people. The white *quid* was still very much larger than the Aboriginal *quo,* to say the least, but it worked. In the cattle and at the mission and in the relationship between them was an arrangement, negotiated by the *wumparrani* and the *papulanyi,* with something in it for both.[1] In not much more than a decade it would all be gone, brought down by friendly fire.

•

Abandoned in 1956, there is little left of the mission now apart from a few stubby bits of mudbrick walls left standing on concrete slabs, once the superintendent's house, the kitchen, a hall, the laundry, the ablutions block, the dormitories – a dozen or more buildings in all. Set among spindly trees, most grown since the mission's short life came to an end, and with a sweet waterhole less than a hundred metres away, it didn't look like the concentration camp of my imagining.[2]

Phillip Creek, as the mission was known, was a very late addition to the long list of missions established in every colony and state from the 1820s.[3] Unusual in some respects, it was like its many predecessors in one crucial respect: it set out to bring up Aboriginal children, and particularly children of mixed descent, in the European way. Hence the dormitories and the hall that served as dining room, church and schoolroom. Why did the parents go along with it? Because there was no real alternative. The capacity to enforce came with the control of

Missions were established in every colony and state from the 1820s

rations. It was 'mission policy' that children of school age live in the
dormitories, go to school and go to church. That might have its advan-
tages – teaching the children whitefella ways for life in a white world,
offering a better diet than the families themselves could as well as a safe
place for the children to stay while the parents went looking for work –
but these were consolations rather than reasons.

When decades on I asked my age-mates about life at the mission,
they gave straightforward accounts of a complicated experience.[4] School
was mostly tedious, sometimes worse. They remembered bitterly being
hit by teachers; Aboriginal children were never hit by their own people.
They smarted at the humiliation of being told by white teachers that
their Aboriginal ways were no good. They resented being told by one
of their teachers that they were children of God and as good as anyone
when that wasn't how they were treated. I found in government files
about the mission a text that the older children were required to copy
out ('in your best writing') and then, one by one, read aloud.[5] 'I must
be polite because I live with other people,' the text began. 'If I am rude
everybody knows that I am selfish and disgusting, and they feel sick
when they look at me ... When I am *always* swearing without caring
who is listening to me I am *not* being funny or smart ... I am really telling everyone that I have a filthy mouth and am not fit to live with pigs.
I must have good manners because I do not want my friends to live like
a pack of howling dogs. I must have good manners because I do not
want to be a slimy, obscene animal.' That wasn't the worst of it either.
The superintendent would take the girls swimming, Edith Graham
Nakamarra recalled, 'and we was thinking "Ah what's this boys don't
come" ... his wife went away for holiday to England and he stop by his
self'. Worst of all was the day when the kids from the dorm reserved for
the 'half-castes' were taken away, to Darwin.[6] The mission did introduce
the children to white ways, but it couldn't stop them being Aboriginal

and it couldn't turn them into white kids. Contrary to its intentions, it gave them daily instruction in the fact that they were not white, and that they belonged to each other.

There were modest offsets. Some of the kids saw their mothers every day because it was their mothers who did the daily work of cooking, cleaning, washing and supervising the dormitories. Most had family who visited and who sometimes took the kids back to their own world, over the Christmas break particularly. The older girls found ways to evade white authority, sneaking out of the locked dorms at night for assignations. There were things to look forward to, singing hymns on Sundays, Saturday nights at the pictures. Some of the whitefellas were kind, and kindly remembered. I was put in touch with one of them, now an old man living in Darwin. On a trip there to see what was left of the shot-up town I'd seen as a kid – hardly anything – I visited the old missionary in his cottage, set among greenery on his son's hobby farm.[7] 'It wasn't like you hear these days,' he insisted several times. His own memories were mostly happy ones, of the kids particularly. 'Oh, they were lovely kids,' he said, as I listed the names of the people I had by then met in Tennant Creek. His wife got out their photo albums, and there they were: little Bunny, Judy, Teresa and the others. The old missionary's Phillip Creek was a pastorale of expeditions with the men to shoot goanna and roo, and regular calls on the camps to make sure that everything was okay. 'It wasn't like you hear nowadays!' It sounded like the calm, gentle place I had seen on a blue day, a lagoon bordered by spindly but graceful gums and the remains of a place of refuge.

For the adults, the mission was indeed more their world than it was the whitefellas'. There was only a handful of whites there at any one time, mostly just the superintendent and a teacher and their spouses. Aboriginal people provided most of the labour to establish and run the place, which they did for not much more than rations, but that was true of the Europeans too. 'The Lord will provide!' the old missionary declared several times as we talked. Demobbed in Melbourne after the war, he had been at a loose end, with no sense at all as to where his future might lie. Then, as he crossed his usual bridge over the Yarra one day, he looked up at something he had often seen but not *understood:* a giant billboard depicting a broadly grinning Aboriginal man in a crisp white Pelaco shirt. There it was! He must work for the welfare and salvation of the Aboriginal people, which at Phillip Creek he did.

For most of the Aboriginal population of 200 or more, the little mission compound was a place to visit once a week or so to get rations, or to see the children. Living in squalid camps scattered up to 20 kilometres 'outside the fence', they came and went. They weren't so much kept in as kept out – out of the town, 50-odd kilometres down the road, and out of a mining field five times the size of the two old native reserves combined.

The Warumungu were heavily outnumbered at the mission by Warlpiri people, most of them refugees from the Coniston events of twenty years before. Through two senior men, Nat Williams Warano and Engineer Jack Japaljarri – Warumungu and Warlpiri respectively – an accommodation was worked out.[8] The Warlpiri, accepting that they were on Warumungu Country, deferred to Warumungu authority. In a deal that says much about who had power over whom in 'traditional' Aboriginal society, as well as its diplomatic capacities, Warumungu men could marry Warlpiri women and the children of those unions would be Warumungu. The two groups also agreed to share a ceremonial ground and to participate in each other's ceremonies. Edith Graham remembered the excitement of being taken there to watch the men's payback fighting.

Nat Williams Warano (on left) and Engineer Jack Japaljarri (on right),
with a man identified only as 'Banjo'

Nat Williams and Engineer Jack also managed the relationship
with the mission. Both had worked in the cattle and then with the army
during the war, acquiring skills later put to the service of the mission.
Williams was a man of many parts. Known for his skill as a tracker and
as an artist (he painted artefacts and sold them to tourists), Williams
was also a capable builder, responsible for the mudbrick construction
so vastly superior in the baking heat to the usual galv. Engineer Jack, as
the name suggests, maintained and repaired engines and motor vehicles. As important as practical skills in the white world was an ability
to deal with the whitefellas. Williams inherited a long experience of
that relationship – his father, Jacob, was among those who 'turn them
back' at Attack Creek, and his uncles included Cubadgee, who had
dreamt of sharing the land with the *papulanyi,* and Zulu, chief liaison
officer with Spencer and Gillen and subsequently a key contact for Bill
Stanner. Engineer Jack, by contrast, had had only intermittent contact
with whitefellas for the first eighteen years or so of his life, just enough

to be tempted by their addictives. With a couple of companions the young man had set out on what turned out to be a long walk north of Warlpiri Country in search of tobacco, eventually found hundreds of kilometres away at Wave Hill Station. His timing was fortunate; during his absence many of his people died in the Coniston massacres. Engineer Jack stayed in the north, working in the cattle and then at an army staging camp not far from Tennant Creek, before joining Coniston survivors at the Phillip Creek mission.

An advantage of the mission was its location on the northern fringes of Warumungu Country and therefore the southern fringes of the Barkly, close to the people on the stations, Rockhampton Downs, Brunette Downs, Brunchilly, and close to casual work, droving particularly, for which the mission served as an employment broker. Constant movement was the lifeblood of the northern Aboriginal social order, essential to the maintenance of relationships and of ceremonial life. The more they were dispersed and mixed up by disrupted territorial arrangements, the more the movement was needed and the more useful the mission as a home base.[9]

Aboriginal people on the stations weren't imprisoned but they were tethered, as the station-owners and managers well knew.[10] The stockmen and the women working around the homestead were there for various combinations of reasons.[11] They might have liked the work (the men particularly) or the missus (the women); they needed the handouts of clothing, blankets, meat sometimes, flour, sugar, tea, tobacco, as well as a little money to support themselves and those with whom they were obliged to share, many of them back at the mission; they could come and go; and they were on or close to Country. And besides, where else was there?

On the stations, much depended on the owners and on the man (and missus) on the spot. The big absentee landlords like Vesteys and

Bovril were typically harsh at best, cruel at worst.[12] The smaller family-owned properties were generally not as bad. Among the most exceptional of the relationships between black and white in the cattle, and certainly the most remarkable in the experience of the Warumungu, was with the Wards, and especially Mrs Mary Ward. The Wards' Banka Banka has a special place in the memories of both black and white in Tennant Creek and in the history of relations between them. It has a small but vivid place in my memory too, for that lunch served by Aboriginal women padding softly across the cool concrete floor of a homestead set (in my memory anyway) among lawns and peppercorns. It was high on my memory-lane checklist.

Banka Banka had been established not far north of the telegraph station in the wake of the great 1880s cattle invasion by Tom Nugent, a Territory 'identity'. The homestead was close to the road and it was there that Spencer and Gillen stayed on their third night after leaving the Warumungu. 'The Station buildings are of a most primitive type,' Gillen's diary records.[13] 'Nugents [sic] room is decorated with framed coloured prints of fighting men, pugilists, and I am shocked to find that so many of them bear unmistakably Irish names.' There were pictures of Gladstone, Kruger and Banjo Paterson too (although Gladstone didn't warrant a frame).[14]

Forty years later Banka Banka was bought by Ted and Mary Ward, and it was they who gave the station its modest fame.[15] Mary had trained and worked as a teacher in Perth before she was posted to the far northern port town of Wyndham, where she met and married Ted Ward, head stockman on one of the region's many cattle stations. In 1935 the Wards got that 'worst of fevers, gold-fever'. They upped stakes for the rumoured boom hundreds of miles away in Tennant Creek, and there struck it rich. Their Blue Moon mine was among the most lucrative of the pre-war sites, renowned for yielding around 80,000 pounds worth of gold in very short order. The Wards bought Banka Banka with the proceeds and made it a showplace for its gardens – a matter of historical record, I was glad to learn – for its hospitality to the many passers-by, and for the relationship there between black and white.

Banka Banka was a Warumungu stronghold and several of my Aboriginal contemporaries turned out to have been Banka Banka people, among them Kathleen Fitz Napanangka.[16] Mrs Fitz was a decade or more older than me, and it is very likely that she was among the Aboriginal women who had padded quietly across the cool concrete floor to serve our lunch. But the garden isn't *there* anymore, I said when we first met. It's gone! Mrs Fitz said, Ah, that was terrible. They knock it down! I nearly cry for that! Banka Banka belonged to Mrs Fitz in a way that it did not and could not belong to the Wards. In another of those moments when time shrinks and history practically vibrates in the air, I learned that Mrs Fitz's family had been on Banka Banka since Tom Nugent's day, or, perhaps it would be more accurate to say, since the days of the invading cattle and cattlemen and their mayhem. Mrs Fitz's grandmother Alice Nampin was a Garrwa woman; it was she who had been brought from the Gulf country to Banka Banka and 'given' to Nugent by a fellow cattleman.[17] One of Alice Nampin's daughters was Mysie, and one of Mysie's daughters was Kathleen. Kathleen married Fitz, Banka Banka's head stockmen, and like her mother and grandmother before her Mrs Fitz 'grew up' her children there, Priscilla, David, Billy, Louie, Betty and Ray.

Mrs Fitz worked daily with Mrs Ward and spoke well of Mrs Ward's regime, as did the government inspectors.[18] On Banka Banka everyone got three meals a day ('good tucker alright'). White employees who mistreated Aboriginal people were sacked. The Wards believed in sharing the work around so that as many Aboriginal people as possible got at least some money in the pocket. The money didn't go on grog, as was often the case elsewhere; grog was banned. So were dogs. Mrs Ward was tireless in matters of clothing, hygiene and welfare. She sent children to Alice for schooling at her own expense, and in later years set up a school on Banka Banka. She refused to allow the government's patrol officers to take 'half-caste' children from their families, still common practice elsewhere. Before Mrs Ward's time on Banka Banka four of Kathleen's older siblings had been 'taken', and Kathleen herself had a terrifyingly close shave.[19]

It is not difficult to spot the tarnish on Mrs Ward's halo. 'Very hard lady,' Mrs Fitz said. The federal government's child endowment payments, made via the station-owners, were kept by Mrs Ward to set against the costs of feeding, clothing and educating the children. For the discovery of gold on the Blue Moon lease and hence for Banka Banka itself, the Wards had Warumungu man Frank Juppurla to thank, and of course the gold came from Warumungu land. Banka Banka itself was just another slice of Warumungu Country taken by the whitefellas for their own use and exchanged among them as if it had nothing to do with the Warumungu. When Mrs Ward eventually sold up for the then-colossal sum of a million dollars, the money went to her and not to Frank Juppurla or the many other Warumungu people whose unremitting work had made the Blue Moon fortune and Banka Banka a showplace.[20] But it is also true that Mrs Ward understood and wholeheartedly accepted what many others ducked or fudged: she had entered into a relationship with the Aboriginal people, and with that came responsibilities. She kept her side of the bargain, in her way. Widowed and with her life drawing to a close, she bought five houses in Tennant Creek for Banka Banka people and built a substantial hostel for them as well. She faced down those in the town who objected.[21] On Banka Banka she worked with the Aboriginal people to find a place for them in a white world, and she tried to find a future for them and for their children.

There was a third party to the relationships between black and white at both the mission and in the cattle: the government in far-off Canberra. Its first substantial interventions came through the army, and then through access to the welfare system. Beginning with child endowment in the early 1940s, Canberra extended one social welfare benefit after another to Aboriginal people until by the late 1950s they had on paper the same access to the system as everyone else.[22] Of greater impact, in the short term, was the army.[23] Its massive construction program in the north required a lot of labour, on the spot, immediately. It set up camps and its decent wages, housing and nutrition gave many Aboriginal people (men mostly) whitefella skills as well as the confidence to use them.

Those shocks to the feudal regime of the cattle stations during the war were followed after it by stronger regulation of wages, of rations and of living conditions, bearing down on the worst of the neglect, exploitation and mistreatment. Things that would have passed unremarked before the war now didn't. In 1955 the owners of one of the stations on the Barkly were sentenced to six months' hard labour (and substantial fines) for horsewhipping three of their Aboriginal employees.[24] The mission had earlier felt these same winds of change. The teacher who had set the 'not fit to live with pigs' exercise was moved on, and the superintendent who took the girls swimming but not the boys was arrested one day and on his way to jail in Alice Springs the next.[25] The government followed up by getting rid of the dormitories that had separated children from their families, appointing a trained teacher, taking over the admin and improving facilities and provisioning.

•

In 1951 the Territory got a new minister in Canberra. The minister entertained little doubt about what needed to be done in the Territory, or his own capacity to do it.

Paul Hasluck was an ardent proponent of assimilation, but, as was typical of the man, he had arrived at that position in his own way. His thinking owed relatively little to anthropology or Elkin or the federal government's 1938 'new deal' for Aborigines. As a young journalist in the West, that vast third of the continent in which the line between frontier and post-frontier society was still blurred, he had taken an interest in the very visible Aborigines in and around Perth. His exposés of their condition brought a passage north, 'embedded', as we would now say, with a royal commission on the Aboriginal question. That led in turn to part-time postgraduate study at UWA. Perhaps if he'd been in Sydney he would have opted for anthropology, as Stanner had done not long before, but Sydney was two thousand miles away, and UWA had no anthropology. But it did have a history department. Hasluck's master's thesis became *Black Australians*, that rarest of birds in the great Australian silence, a history of relations between them and us, taking the particular case of Western Australia from the arrival of the British governor in 1829 to self-government sixty-odd years later.

Black Australians told a story and reached conclusions which Hasluck was still defending in the last of his many books more than forty years later.[26] When a Western people occupies the land of a primitive people, he argued, it is the invader alone who, by virtue of superior power, can manage the inevitable process of change. In Western Australia the invading power began with honourable and achievable objectives but quickly lost its grip. The Colonial Office in London instructed its proconsul to treat the natives as British subjects, to civilise them and to guarantee their physical well-being. Had these instructions been acted upon, the 'eventual absorption' of the black population by the white would have been assured. But they were *not* acted upon. In Western Australia, as elsewhere, 'settlers in successive new districts were almost continually facing the urgent problems and dangers of first contact' and in no position to control a dynamic process or to take responsibility for the necessarily 'slow adaptation' by the Aborigines to white society. Those who should have taken that responsibility and who said that they would take that responsibility did not. 'The Home Government was not prepared to pay for the ideal it had declared,' Hasluck found, and it had failed to keep its ideal 'steadily in view'. When eventually the Imperial government ended its rule of 'uncertainty, inconsistency and neglect', it handed to the people of Western Australia 'the sacred charge of several thousands of human beings', now 'ill-kept, contaminated, hopeless and despised'.

Hasluck's account ended with the transfer of responsibility for Aboriginal people to the new state government in 1897, but an epilogue drew the contemporary moral. On those who took the land and disturbed an ancient way of life was laid a solemn Christian duty 'to lead the native into the benefits of their civilization and the brotherhood of their faith'. Governments both Imperial and Australian had failed in that duty; the task must now be taken up again. They should 'return from the present limited concern with native welfare to the old conception of the native as a British subject, and as a fit candidate for civilization'.

The book earned for Hasluck a glowing notice from the only reviewer who mattered, Professor A.P. Elkin, head of Australia's only university anthropology department.[27] 'Mr Hasluck's book is an outstanding contribution to historical research,' Elkin declared. 'He has ... provided an essential historical manual for all engaged in administrative work amongst the Australian Aborigines.' By the time the review appeared in 1943 Hasluck had no need of Elkin's imprimatur or an academic career; he was in Canberra, and on his way up.[28] Hasluck had landed a job in the infant Department of External Affairs. Starting out in postwar planning, his career prospered along with the Allies' fortunes and Australia's emergence as the champion of the 'smaller powers'. He hit the big time at the San Francisco conference to establish the United Nations, where he was among other things a member of the committee that drafted the UN Charter. Success in San Francisco took him to New York, representing Australia on the Security Council, the new epicentre of international politics and the focus of hopes for a new world order made hostile to 'racism' (a new term) by revelations of Nazi atrocities, and by a new understanding of race as a cultural construction built upon biological difference rather than arising from it. Impelled by the ideal of a common and equal humanity, an aversion to racial segregation and a fear of racial strife of the kind that so disfigured American life, Hasluck was convinced that assimilation based on equality was the only way out as well as the only humanly decent one. It was a common-sense of the age, and he took it with him when he left the bureaucracy for politics, where history's improbable turn gave him powers and responsibilities in the Territory not unlike those of the first British governor of Western Australia.

Hasluck's elevation gave Elkin hope that he and his discipline might make a comeback. Anthropology hadn't had another near-death experience of the kind that came after Spencer and Gillen and then again when Radcliffe-Brown left Sydney; indeed, it remained the most authoritative voice on matters Aboriginal, and its pioneering appreciation of Aboriginal culture now suffused the work of poets, novelists, filmmakers and artists. But the run that so exhilarated Elkin through the 1930s had come to an end with the war and would not return. Elkin's clout was much diminished. His department lost half its business soon after the war when the government established its own institution to train administrators for service in Papua New Guinea, and the 'positive policy' for Aborigines built up in the 1930s was now running a distant second to PNG. Surely the new minister, as convinced in his

assimilationism as Elkin himself, and in Elkin's debt thanks to that glowing review of *Black Australians*, would turn things around? Words of
mutual admiration were exchanged. 'We have rested heavily on foundations which you laid,' the new minister told Elkin.[29] Elkin perked
up, reciprocated, and looked forward to rejoining the charmed circle.
But nothing came. Months passed and eventually Elkin lost hope. 'I do
not think anybody outside Canberra ... has any influence whatever,' he
concluded sniffily. 'This seems to satisfy the present Minister.' In the
1930s the national government had depended on Elkin; now it didn't
even consult him. Hasluck would be his own Elkin.

Much of Hasluck's ministerial energy was spent on Papua New
Guinea, his other responsibility as minister for territories, and he was
additionally cramped by the states' control of 'their' Aborigines, but in
the Northern Territory he could do almost as he pleased. With extensive
control over a Commonwealth territory and its Aboriginal inhabitants,
equipped with a lucid mind and a tremendous capacity for work, the
tides running his way and the author of one of a handful of thoughtful, well-informed books about policy on relations between black and
white, this personification of the post-frontier whispering heart set out
to bring the frontier zone and its Aborigines into the mainstream of
Australian life. Those shards of a broken social order would (as he put
it in his most relied-upon formulation) 'attain the same manner of living ... enjoying the same rights and privileges ... as other Australians'.[30]

The problem was: how? It was easy enough to grant full legal equality to those who were 'ready' for it, but what about those who weren't?
And who would decide who was 'ready' and who wasn't? Unlike the
relationship between the Aborigines and the stations, assimilation wasn't
a deal. It wasn't even an offer. The government that installed a trained
teacher on the mission also told the teacher that 'the policy of assimilation demands a lingua franca ... [and] that lingua franca must be

English'.[31] Aboriginal languages were not to be used, even in the playground. 'Weren't allowed to speak language,' Edith Graham Nakamarra recalled, 'not allowed, only had to speak English. We used to talk in the bush alright, only bush.' The government that got rid of the dormitories and arrested the molesting superintendent also provided the truck and trainee patrol officer who turned up at the mission one day, loaded up sixteen half-caste kids and took them off to Darwin, where they would be readied for life on the lower rungs of white society. The government that extended 'real and unconditional legal equality' to many mixed-race people told the rest that they weren't ready for real and unconditional equality and would be wards of the state until they were.[32] But on what basis would readiness be determined? Worried officers in the field were told to draw up a Register of Wards, and that for that purpose 'race' – in the supposedly jettisoned biological sense – would do.[33] 'Full-bloods' were in this infamous 'stud book', the rest weren't, drawing a line right through the unmanageable complications of reality, including the reality of many mixed-descent Aboriginal families.

Compulsion combined with ignorance to generate unforeseen consequences. In 1956 the trucks were at the mission again,[34] this time to ferry the entire population 250-odd kilometres south to a 'model settlement', purpose-built complete with airstrip, power station, government offices, a police station, school and hospital plus a bakery and workshops, supposedly serving as a way-station for Aborigines on the high road to becoming Australians different only in the colour of their skin – Black Australians, as Hasluck had put it in the title of his book. 'There's a place in the Centre/And we call it Warrabri/Where we all live together as one', went the official Warrabri anthem. In fact, Warrabri – the name an Orwellian compound of 'Warramunga' (Warumungu) and 'Warlpiri' – was a disaster.[35] The Warumungu were no longer just kept out of the town and the mining field; now they had been taken from Country. Warrabri was in Kaytetye country. The Warumungu were effectively deported. The easy movement between the mission and the stations to the north – Banka Banka, Rocky and the rest – was gone. Worse, there were four language groups at Warrabri, not two: the Kaytetye, of course, and the Alyawarre as well as the Warumungu and the Warlpiri. The careful arrangement worked out through Nat Williams and Engineer Jack lost its foundation. The idea was that the 'model settlement' would train people up for jobs in the mainstream economy. But where were the jobs for 'those Black Australians'?

In 1958 an anthropologist little known outside the academy but well-respected within it addressed his colleagues at the annual Australian and New Zealand Association for the Advancement of Science (ANZAAS) conference. He took as his text a publication prepared by Hasluck's department to explain how the government's policies would help Aborigines 'attain the same manner of living … as other Australians'. Who do we find in this publication, the anthropologist asked rhetorically. We find the Noble Friend of the Aborigines.[36]

> He is every good Australian. He is a man of sympathy, readily moved by Aboriginal sufferings. He seeks to keep a steadfast alliance between a warm heart, a cool head and steady hands. He is a man who always asks: "What are the facts?" When the facts inevitably prove complex, he always says: "Let us understand this question, wisely, clearly, exactly." Then, having strained understanding, he settles down to do what is needed … The image is one of modern Everyman. Idealist, yet practical; rational, but warm-hearted; with an ear to the ground but with an inner vision to see three generations ahead. And what is the vision? The former Aborigines distinguishable from us only by skin colour, if that.

The anthropologist was, of course, Bill Stanner. He might just as well have burned Hasluck in effigy.

•

In Kenya with his recently minted PhD when the Second World War broke out, Stanner had returned to Australia to take odd jobs in journalism, in imperial administration and as a staffer to successive ministers for the army. From the last of these positions he devised and then commanded the near-legendary Nackeroos, a surveillance unit operating on the northern coastline in the wake of Japanese raids on Darwin in close cooperation with the Aborigines.[37] Success there brought promotion (from major to lieutenant colonel) and a posting to GHQ in Melbourne, where he worked on planning for the postwar world. Demobbed, he was back in the gig economy again, shuttling between Australia, London and various outposts of Empire, writing decolonisation policy as well as doing a short stint as principal of a tertiary college in Uganda. It was not until late 1949 that – at last! – he got a proper academic job, at the new Australian National University in Canberra.

At the ANU Stanner was supposed to concentrate on problems of 'transition' in the Pacific territories for which Australia was now responsible (he was Australia's rep on the South Pacific Commission), but he kept going back to that nagging problem of how to see the Aborigines in a way that was, as he later put it, informed, detached and respectful.[38] In work punctuated by several trips to the far north-west and the Murinbata people, Stanner crisscrossed a broad intellectual landscape, starting over and again from different points, each time heading in a different direction, 'trying out on old and new facts new ideas', as he later recalled.[39] A study of 'Aboriginal territorial organisation' grappled with constantly changing relationships between individuals, group and place. In work of 'intuitive genius' (as one of a later generation of anthropologists put it), he plunged into the *meanings* embedded in Aboriginal religious practice.[40] In these two fundamental investigations (which some argue anticipated Lévi-Strauss),[41] Stanner was trying to shift his discipline from its preoccupation with observable behaviours and structures and toward understanding experience and action, and from what was inferred to have been there before to the real circumstances of present lives.

In the middle of all that was the question of how to understand relations between black and white, a matter which Stanner was uniquely well equipped to tackle. The years in London and Kenya combined with the apparently lost war and postwar years to make him the only Australian anthropologist of the Aborigines to have spent extended periods of time outside Australia, the only one to have seen other tribal societies 'in transition', the only one to have been deeply involved in the tumultuous business of decolonisation, the only one to have spent much of his working life in one kind or another in public life, trying to work out what to do as well as trying to understand what is, and the only one trying to pin down just what it was in his discipline that made Australia's racial order seem 'natural and unalterable'.[42] It was not until 1958 that he was ready to lay his conclusions before his peers, and to burn in effigy the Noble Friend of the Aborigines.[43]

Conclusions laid out at length and in compelling detail can be simply stated: the story we have been telling ourselves about the Aborigines and our relations with them was, for all intents and purposes, a fiction. Anthropology had inherited from its founders a view of Aboriginal society as an intricate, unchanging structure, fragile to the touch, a view from which anthropology had not yet escaped. The discipline had to address the puzzle of continuity *and* change. Yes, the Aborigines had indeed been the victims of European power, but not only or not simply so. No, their culture is not in decay or collapsing; it is undergoing a profound change in which the Aborigines themselves are playing an active part and through which they are changing themselves as fast as they can. And no, they are not being Europeanised. 'Various European things – our authority, our customs, our ideas and goods – are data, facts of life, which the Aborigines take into account in working out their altered system' – but it is 'plain as daylight that this system is still fundamentally Aboriginal in type'. Not only are the Aborigines not being turned into Europeans, they do not *want* to be – and even if they did, they couldn't.[44] They do not know how. The Aboriginal and the European ways of being in the world are fundamentally different. Indeed, if one tried to invent two styles of life as unlike each other as could be (he said) 'one might well end up with something like the Aboriginal and the European traditions'.

We struggle to comprehend the Aborigines just as they struggle to comprehend us. 'Have we [and here Stanner addresses his colleagues directly] truly understood the process by which the modern Aborigines are, to some extent at least, transforming themselves as well as being transformed by things beyond their control?' It is not only that we have failed to comprehend them. We have been oblivious to ourselves. Here, Stanner turned to the publication in which the Noble Friend of the Aborigines appeared, that man of sympathy, readily moved by Aboriginal sufferings who, with an ear to the ground and an inner vision to see three generations ahead, the vision of 'former Aborigines distinguishable from us only by skin colour, if that'. Stanner didn't want to just see 'the blackfellows' point of view', as Spencer and Gillen had once urged; he wanted us to see what they had been seeing.

There was a whiff of patricide as well as heresy in this denunciation of Hasluck and of assimilation. It was Elkin who had inducted Stanner into the discipline, supervising his research and funding his field work (including getting him to stop off in Tennant Creek to see what the miners were up to). It was at least in part to Elkin that Stanner owed his preoccupation with making a truly useful, morally informed science. Now the apprentice had gone far past the master and, while carefully distinguishing Elkin's version of assimilation from Hasluck's, had effectively declared both to be based on a misconception of the Aborigines as well as of their relations with the Europeans.

My good acquaintance Fay Gale was there, and forty years later she bubbled with excitement at the memory. It was tremendously influential, she said. Perhaps so, but not then it wasn't; it was noticed only to be dismissed. At the following year's ANZAAS conference the minister himself addressed the same group of anthropologists.[45] Hasluck, now eight years into his reign, was established as the great champion of assimilation, and assimilation was established as the way of the future. Even organisations run by and for Aboriginal people generally supported assimilation, albeit with reservations.[46] Its promise of 'equality' seemed to offer a way out of treatment reserved for Aboriginal people and for them alone. Hasluck was politically unassailable, and in no doubt as to the rightness of his cause. Accusing the critics of selfishness and a lack of genuine concern for the Aborigines, he launched into a presumably unconscious parody of Stanner's Noble Friend of the Aborigines: 'How many poor wretches have been dragged into the arena of social controversy and butchered to make a reformer's triumph or a prize-winning newspaper story?' Hasluck asked the anthropologists. How different was such moral vanity from the humility of government, that 'sheltering, protecting, guiding, teaching and helping and eventually, as the final … act of welfare, quietly withdrawing without any proud fuss when the aboriginal enters the community'? In a long address, Hasluck avoided direct reference to Stanner's remarks of the previous year; the critics guilty of selfishness and a lack of genuine concern for the Aborigines went unnamed.

•

Among the puzzles of the story of race relations in Australia is how two of its most prominent protagonists, men so alike in so many respects as to be near doppelgangers, could reach such radically opposed conclusions about it.

Bill Stanner and Paul Hasluck were both born in 1905 into modest circumstances. Both bore a slightly toffy three given names rather than the usual one or two: William Edward Hanley Stanner and Paul Meerna Caedwalla Hasluck. Both rose in the world via very similar routes; both became journalists and studied part-time at university. Both inclined to and got involved in politics, both on the conservative side. Both spent time as public servants working on planning for a postwar world. One flirted with politics and ended up in academe, the other flirted with academe but ended up in politics. Both were intellectuals who saw scholarly insight and public policy as two sides of a single coin. Both found much in politics distasteful, even repellent. Both were correct to the point of puritanism in their public and personal lives. Both were solitary souls with a strong sense of apartness; each was determined to be his own man. For both, writing and writing well was a lifelong preoccupation; both were stylists with an eye for just the right word and the pungent formulation, and both dabbled in poetry. Both were close observers of their colleagues, in meetings particularly, drawing passable caricatures and writing nicely turned profiles. In their mature years they even looked somewhat alike: of middle height, a little overweight, round-faced, clipped moustaches, thinning hair brushed neatly back. They bore themselves in much the same way too, inconspicuous in dress and reserved in manner, although Hasluck's persona and accent were more recognisably Australian than Stanner's. Among friends both were excellent company, witty, and splendid raconteurs. Perhaps most strikingly, both possessed urgently whispering hearts. Both were appalled by what they saw in the frontier north and both spent much of their careers in Canberra just a mile or two away from each other, on opposite sides of the lake, trying to work out what should be done about it.

What differences might explain such different conclusions? They grew up in very different cities. In Stanner's Sydney the frontier was four or five generations away; in Hasluck's Perth it wasn't far away at all, in time or in distance. They encountered Aboriginal people in very different ways. Stanner was drawn to anthropology as a kind of time machine that might transport him to that other universe; Hasluck observed what was becoming of that universe from a distance.[47] Their wartime and postwar experiences were different too. Stanner spent those years, as well as the years before, much closer to the ground than Hasluck. While Stanner was trying to understand the profoundly different Aboriginal world and the bewildering impact on it of the Europeans, Hasluck was drafting the rules of a new international order. A difference in temperament was marked and perhaps fundamental. Hasluck yielded nothing to Stanner in his sense of decency and obligation, but he was a difficult man, often 'brusque, demanding and aloof', and the older and more senior he became the more difficult he became, a trait given ample scope in his years of something close to despotism as minister responsible for both the Northern Territory and Papua New Guinea.[48] And Stanner? There was something almost saintly about Stanner, said his old friend and colleague John Mulvaney. To Fay Gale, a member of the next generation of scholars, he was simply 'wonderful'. Among squabbling, territorial, petty-minded anthropologists particularly, Stanner was often the only grown-up in the room. In his devotion to the Aboriginal cause, he was almost heroic as well as almost saintly. Hasluck's impulse was to correct, to bring order, to demand and, if necessary, to control; Stanner's was to comprehend, to support, and to defend those in no position to defend themselves. Under the differences in understanding and policy were different ways of facing the world.[49]

Stanner's address to the anthropologists in 1958 and Hasluck's response in the following year marked the beginning of one of the most bitter and consequential disputes in Australia's intellectual history. It set the terms of a controversy which has flared off and on ever since, helped to turn what had been a more or less bipartisan area of policy into an ideological and party-political battlefield, and made Hasluck and Stanner standard-bearers for forces ranged against each other. Hasluck's assimilationism is to this day a litmus. To some it was a golden age of policy, the fatally lost direction, to others the purest expression of the arrogance of power.[50] Both views are tributes to the clarity and vigour of Hasluck's argument, as well as the zeal with which he turned it into policy. His gaze was still that of the governor of Western Australia and the settlers, figures now seen by Stanner as the Aboriginal people had been seeing them ever since 1788, 'very clever people, very hard people, plenty humbug', as one of his Aboriginal friends put it.[51] From there, assimilation didn't look like the way out at all. It was, to invert Clausewitz, the continuation of warfare by other means, a racist kind of anti-racism, its equality of individuals blind and implicitly hostile to the parity of peoples. If we keep going in that direction, Stanner told his colleagues in 1958, there's going to be real racial strife.[52]

CHAPTER FIVE

1967

E arly in 1965 the North Australian Workers Union lodged an application to the Commonwealth Conciliation and Arbitration Commission to have all pastoral workers in the Territory, black and white alike, paid on the same scale.[1] The NAWU declined to lead any evidence or call any witnesses on the grounds that wage equality was a matter of self-evident and overriding principle. The task of arguing that it wasn't so simple fell to the employers and their team, the later-infamous John Kerr QC and his junior, Hal Wootten.

In his later years Wootten recalled the depth of his own and his colleagues' ignorance about all matters Aboriginal, including their conditions of life and work on the Northern Territory's cattle stations.[2] Wootten's crash course of instruction took the form of a week-long tour of Territory stations (including several on the Barkly) by light aircraft.[3] He was surprised to find that the employers' case would not be as self-serving as might at first be thought. The employers, unlike southern lawyers, were not completely ignorant about Aboriginal lives. None saw Aboriginal people as equals (Wootten found), but many did want to avoid unfair discrimination and on the whole they supported the goal of assimilation. Some Aboriginal stockmen worked in much the same way as the whites (the employers said) and should be paid in the same way, but most – for reasons tribal and cultural – did not, could not, and did not want to work like that. Wootten found the employers to be 'keenly aware how painful it would be for them [Aboriginal people] to be separated from their traditional lands', and they didn't want it to happen, as it certainly would if all were to be paid full award rates. Insisting that equal wages would price Aboriginal labour out of the market, the employers were in effect arguing that any new award should build upon the kind of arrangements that had obtained at Banka Banka, with the stations supporting the whole group and paying full wages to individuals as the exception rather than the rule.

Eighteen months after the NAWU's application, the commission handed down its decision. Wages would be equal. For all its agonising, and there was much agonising, the commission had been unable to think its way out of the box of assimilationism. There were two alternatives and two only: equality or inequality. 'We do not flinch from the results of this decision,' said the commission, 'which we consider is the only proper one to be made at this point in Australia's history. There must be one industrial law, similarly applied, to all Australians, Aboriginal or not.'[4]

Of course, the commissioners were not the ones who had to do the flinching. The demand for Aboriginal workers varied from one time and place to another.[5] They had already been losing ground to technology: motorbikes instead of horses, new kinds of fencing displacing boundary riders, electric appliances displacing women in the homesteads, roads and trucks displacing drovers. (My father took us out bush one day in 1953 or thereabouts to see the last of the cattle droves, run by the young female drover Edna Zigenbine.) The compact between black and white was under other pressures too. A parliamentary inquiry reported in sombre tones on the impact of money, cars, grog and a new spirit of defiance.[6]

These developments turned the commission's decision into a rout. On some stations and for some people, the impact was immediate and dramatic; for others, employment gradually dried up and numbers shrank until there was no-one left.[7] The deal between black and white was dead. In one way or another, sooner or later, across the Territory and then, when the Commonwealth's decision flowed on to the states, across the entire frontier zone, Aboriginal people moved off the stations and into settlements and towns, out of the economy and onto welfare.[8]

•

In 1955 Tennant's prospects brightened.[9] The good thing my father had got onto per kind favour of the postmaster turned out to be a very good thing indeed. In what were already being remembered as the good old days – that is, before the war – miners were mostly gougers, hardy scrabblers who roamed around the spreading field prospecting, and when their luck was in they scratched and blasted out a shaft sufficient to get at the gold. After the war the miners were mostly companies, not gougers; they had capital, expertise and equipment for scientific prospecting and for big, deep mines. Peko, the sure thing, led the way, finding copper as well as gold, and others followed. Tennant had a population of around 600 before the war and for a decade afterwards. Then it started to climb.[10] By the end of the 1960s it had just about tripled to 1800 in the town with another 750 in five company townships scattered around the field (Peko, with 390 residents, the biggest of them). The old shanties began to disappear in favour of houses that might have been transplanted from any Australian suburb. Some even had a garden. Water, which had been carted at considerable expense from a bore at Seven Mile, was now on tap. The vastnesses of Paterson Street, aka the Alice–Darwin highway, turned into a dual carriageway with a wide (and green!) median strip down the middle. Tennant's slender social infrastructure filled out with the addition of a golf club (1957), Uniting and Lutheran churches (1960 and 1965), a Limelights club (it took out the Mt Isa drama festival prize for best production in 1965, its very first year), a bridge club, a Lions Club (1967), a youth club and a senior citizens club (both early 1970s), an Apex club (1978), even a Toastmistresses club (1978), which had as its 'ultimate objective' the 'development of the individual person so she or he will be better prepared to meet the challenge of the times'.[11] The redoubtable Country Women's Association, which claimed to be Tennant's oldest continuously operating association, mounted 'functions' that included an art prize, a cookery show and a disco. The highlight was the 1963 royal visit; it precipitated the formation of a St John's brigade to meet the needs of the anticipated crowds. The two general stores morphed into supermarkets, the two pubs were joined by three motels, three restaurants, a pharmacy, a taxi service, a travel agency and a swimming pool. There were growing pains. Peko's management complained that here they were in the middle of a mining boom, saddled with inadequate transport and communication services, while the residents complained about poor drainage, scarce housing, and overcrowding and understaffing at the school. But Tennant was *going ahead*. And then, just as it was starting to look like a normal Australian town, the Aborigines turned up.

In our time in Tennant, Mrs Hare and her three sons were the only Aboriginal people living in the town. When Mr Hare wanted to employ an Aboriginal man to help with his nightsoil rounds, he had to satisfy officialdom that he'd been unable to find a white man who would do the job, then enter into guarantees as to the accommodation, keep and conditions of employment for Tennant's fifth Aboriginal resident.[12] A decade on, five had swelled to eighty-four and over the next ten years that number tripled, from which point growth slowed but continued. The Department of Aboriginal Affairs (DAA) was unhappy. A few mixed-descent people employed and living in the town were welcomed as evidence of assimilation at work, but most of Tennant's Aboriginal population had settled in camps on the fringes of the town, a different matter entirely. In the late 1960s the department's point man had succeeded in moving most of the camp-dwellers back to Warrabri or to the stations whence they'd come, and had issued instructions to his subordinate to 'dismantle and remove all the makeshift dwellings … to the rubbish dump'.[13] A few camp-dwellers, however, had refused to shift, and many of those who left soon returned. Repelled by Warrabri, pushed off the stations, attracted by the town and the possibility of boom-time jobs, licensed by assimilation's rhetoric, no longer afraid of the whitefellas, they declined to go on doing what they were told. Aboriginal people were coming into history, in both senses of the word.

Soon Tennant was ringed by camps ordered by language and country – Jingili, Mudburra, Warlmanpa, Wambaya and Warumungu to the north, Wakaja to the east, Alyawarre to the south-east, Kaytetye and Anmatyerre to the south, Warlpiri to the west.[14] Tennant was more like a laager than the normal Australian town it aspired to be. Mrs Ward's provision for Banka Banka people – first the five houses dotted about the town and then the hostel on the town's fringes – provoked an uproar.[15] The townspeople didn't want to do the government's assimilating, and while the people in the camps did want clean water, power, sanitation and health care, they didn't want to be assimilated either. In this, they were not alone.

•

Hundreds of kilometres north were the Yolngu, a powerful Arnhem Land tribe who, like the Warumungu, had found themselves dispossessed by the government at the behest of miners. The Commonwealth had given the Swiss giant Nabalco a lease right in the middle of land 'reserved' for the Yolngu, and in came Nabalco with heavy machinery, roads, hundreds of whitefellas, shops, houses, the lot. However, the

Yolngu in the early 1960s were better placed than the Warumungu in the early 1930s to put up a fight.[16] Their Country was well off the white-fellas' beaten track and of no use to the pastoralists, so they were very much a going concern. They had correspondingly little experience in resisting white incursion, but impressive form nonetheless. In the early 1930s they had killed several traders, variously recorded as Japanese or Macassan, thought to have interfered with Yolngu women. When the administration sent out a police officer to investigate, they killed him too. (It was these events and talk of a reprisal expedition that provoked an outcry in the south, marshalled by the newly appointed professor of anthropology at the University of Sydney, A.P. Elkin.)

The Yolngu's social and political organisation remained in good working order, and they were able to use assimilation's recently granted rights to further their cause. In 1963, with the help of white allies, they sent the now-revered Bark Petitions to Canberra, one in Yolngu Matha, the other in English.[17] The petitions used language undreamt of by Zulu Jappangarti and 'King' Charlie Jampin when they told Stanner what the government and the miners had done to them. The Yolngu declared that they spoke for 'the Indigenous owners and occupiers of Australia', and demanded 'permanent control and enjoyment of our ancestral lands'. Then they went much further: they wanted a *treaty*, a treaty 'recognising our *prior ownership*, continued occupation and *sovereignty* and affirming our *human rights* and *freedom* [emphases added]'.

The Bark Petitions created a small media sensation and a flurry of parliamentary talk, but even so it was not long before they were upstaged by the Warumungu's near-neighbours, the Gurindji. The Gurindji's charismatic leader Vincent Lingiari had agitated for equal wages on the stations, and when the arbitration commission decided to delay implementation of the new award for a couple of years, Lingiari was incensed, and led the Gurindji out on strike against their employer, the British giant Vesteys.[18] To strike over wages seemed to suggest think-ing much less advanced than that of the Yolngu. Was it just the money they were after, or the 'industrial justice' for 'all Australians' of the kind that so animated the unions and the commission? Stanner stared at the question, as at many others, with the cold eye of a fish, and con-cluded that yes, they were after the money and so they should be.[19] His extended analysis of the case reported a growing 'money-hunger' and a 'steady build-up of demand for European goods' among Aboriginal people in the Territory, a result of the rapid expansion of the cash economy and price inflation. Against Stanner, and with the advantage of hindsight, Wootten argued that for many Aboriginal people in the north the struggle wasn't only or even mainly about wages or equality but something larger than either.[20] It was about dignity. The Aboriginal campaign for equal wages expressed a growing anger at a long experi-ence of injustice, disrespect, insult and shoddy treatment, and it gave way to a bigger goal. The Gurindji were not simply 'Australians' of the commission's imagination, and they soon moved on from wages: they wanted their Country back. They, like the Yolngu, did not wish to un-be who they now were.

Resistance in the frontier zone, led by the Gurindji and the Yolngu, inspired and was inspired by Aboriginal people mobilising in the south. Those now referred to as First Peoples around the world were up in arms, and rapidly increasing numbers of their former colonisers gave loud sup-port. Australia's racial regime – which still included the White Australia policy – incurred growing international odium and was rapidly losing support at home. A referendum held in 1967 saw an astonishing nine in every ten voters supporting equality for Aborigines as they seem to have understood it.[21] Hasluck was entitled to see the vote as vindica-tion of his long campaign to give Aboriginal people 'the same rights and privileges … as other Australians'. But equality of rights hadn't brought equality in employment, housing, health or education, and far from being or agreeing to be 'assimilated' as Australians differing from others only in the colour of their skin, these Australians increasingly saw themselves and demanded to be seen as Aboriginal Australians. Things were looking more as Stanner had predicted than as Hasluck had decreed. Aboriginal policy, a backwater when Hasluck had taken office in 1951, was (to mix the metaphors) a hot potato. What to do?

•

Prime Minister Menzies had always been content to let Hasluck answer that question, and Hasluck was always ready with a clear and adamant answer. But he wasn't there anymore. Menzies had rewarded Hasluck with a long-overdue promotion; he was now Minister for External Affairs, presiding over the portfolio from which his splendid career had been launched.[22] Then Menzies was gone as well; in 1966 he retired, trailing clouds of glory. His hand-picked successor, Harold Holt, had a hard act to follow.

Holt promptly did something that Menzies would never contemplate: he took the radical option. He set up an advisory council with teeth.[23] The Council for Aboriginal Affairs (CAA) would be chaired by the eminent public servant H.C. 'Nugget' Coombs, have its own staff and advise the prime minister directly on what was to be done about matters now running out of control. You want us to open the Pandora's box of Aboriginal affairs, the CAA's second member, Barrie Dexter, asked the prime minister. Yes, I do, he said. That's exactly what I want you to do. It soon became clear that Holt meant it: the third member of the council would be Bill Stanner.

To Hasluck, the whole CAA idea was appalling.[24] Even though his long reign in the territories department had ended years before, he was now a senior cabinet minister and widely acknowledged as the father

Barrie Dexter, 'Nugget' Coombs, Bill Stanner, 1968

of his party's assimilationist orthodoxy. Yet he hadn't been informed, let alone consulted, about the CAA or who should be on it. That a gang of three outsiders were able to go over the top of his old department directly to the prime minister was bad enough. But as Hasluck knew better than anyone, one of those three was no longer a little-known academic talking to a handful of colleagues in a distant corner of a scientific conference, able to be brushed aside by a minister riding high. Stanner's appointment threatened a root-and-branch rethink of the whole basis of the policy. In the Boyer Lectures, given a few months after the CAA was established, Hasluck's worst fears were realised.

For Australia, and for Stanner, the Boyers came at just the right moment. Stanner was at the top of his game. His long struggle to make better sense of what he had seen as a young man in the 1930s, those things that had 'set the yeast working', was now completed. The 1958 presidential address had staked out a new way of understanding the Aboriginal response to the Europeans and the Europeans' to them; his reconfigurations of the relationship between the Aboriginal social order and the land and of Aboriginal religion were published in their definitive forms in 1965. Product and producer of all of these was a different kind of science – one that was at once detached, informed and respectful. There was no-one else with Stanner's combination of experience, intellectual force and rhetorical power. Around him was a government in disarray, a policy vacuum, an electorate suddenly aware of 'the Aborigines' but grossly naive about the difficulties ahead, a small but influential urban intelligentsia of newly chastened elders and newly rebellious children of the postwar baby boom, a Western world assailed by the hatreds, resentments and hopes of its collapsing empires, a revolution in much of Western thought, including its social sciences, and, above all, an Aboriginal refusal, widespread but not yet coordinated or comprehended. Stanner's Boyers remain the most celebrated in a series begun in 1959, and represent perhaps the most influential single statement on the relationship between black and white in Australia ever made.[25]

PART TWO

THE STRUGGLE TO DISMANTLE THE SILENCE

Officers of the Aboriginal Tent Embassy arrive, Canberra, 1972

CHAPTER SIX

1971

I n the first of the Boyers, Stanner took his listeners back to the time and the place now thirty-five years and a thousand miles away where he first sensed that there was something fundamentally wrong with anthropology's way of seeing.[1] 'I went overland to central Australia,' he recalled, 'and was there in time to see part of the rush to the gold-strike at Tennant Creek.' There was a tussle between the local Aboriginal people who owned the land (and lost it) and the miners who wanted it (and got it). That was what had the yeast working, he said, not just about the events, which were, after all, much the same as events of the past 180 years, but about a way of thinking about such events, 'a style of thinking that unconsciously ratified that order of life as natural and unalterable'.

The lectures ranged across 'three hundred centuries, of human affairs in this country', drawing on history, epistemology, phenomenology, philosophy and anthropology to do it. In their strenuous formulations and their use of metaphor, imagery and allusion, the Boyers are so brilliantly compressed – just sixty-three pages in their published version, not even a quarter the length of most books on such matters – that any summary or paraphrase will lose much of the original. But one strand of Stanner's argument is central to our story, so I must try.

Stanner explained that anthropology's style of thinking had begun with the 'flowering of intellectual interest in the widest possible world of human customs' in the 1860s and 1870s; wound its way through the 'atrocious muddle' of armchair theorists of human evolution who saw the Aborigines as 'just across, or still crossing, that momentous border which separates nature from culture, and trailing wisps of an animalian past'; to Spencer and Gillen, who, despite their own infection by the evolutionist virus, worked in 'the best tradition of 19th century natural science' to report what was actually there (albeit at the cost of making Aboriginal society seem fragile to the touch and therefore doomed); through the well-intended but fundamentally false assumption that the Aborigines were simply black Australians in waiting; to the eventual realisation that 'there are no natural scales of better or worse on which we can range the varieties of men, culture and society'. The discipline of anthropology had arrived at the 'anthropological principle', from which point it was possible to see something of the innerness of Aboriginal life and how Aboriginal people saw themselves, and to see what *they* had been seeing ever since 1788 and their struggle to come to terms with the hitherto unimaginable.

All that had been there in the 1958 ANZAAS presidential address. Now, ten years later, Stanner took three closely sequenced steps further and they, more than anything else, made the Boyers famous: the true nature of relations between black and white in Australia could only be understood historically, by telling the story; far from telling that story, we had suppressed it; that suppression was itself a central part of the story.[2] The lack of 'historical anthropology', noted in passing in 1958, had now moved from the margins of his analysis to its centre. The Boyers are saturated in history. The first lecture was given over almost entirely to an account of relations between black and white from the first moment of 'settlement'. The second was all about history and the historians.

The third, fourth and fifth moved between current problems and their genesis, problems 'in places now six or seven generations deep'. What the miners were doing to the Yolngu in Arnhem Land even as Stanner was speaking was what they had done to the Warumungu in Tennant Creek in the 1930s, and what they and those great wreckers the pastoralists had been doing long before that.

Stanner had discovered the power of history to uncover what anthropology couldn't, and that in turn revealed a great Australian silence. He trawled through one account of Australia's history after another, finding in every case the same gaping hole. M. Barnard Eldershaw's *My Australia* (1939) had quite a lot to say about the Aborigines (Stanner observed), all of which could be excised without changing the story told. Hartley Grattan's *Introducing Australia* (1942) offered just one sentence on the question; Brian Fitzpatrick's *The Australian People* (1946) one or two pages, 'all backward-turned'. *Australia in the Making* by H.L. Harris included fragments about the Aborigines and Dampier, Banks, Cook and Sturt, 'but there it ends'. The lacunae of Rawson (1948), Crawford (1952), Caiger (1953) and a whole series of authors in a volume edited by Aughterson (1953) are capped by a chapter called 'The Australian Way of Life' by one W.E.H Stanner, 'who can safely be presumed never to have heard of the Aborigines, because he does not refer to them and even maintains that Australia has "no racial divisions like America"'.

Even this partial survey, Stanner continued, is enough to make the point 'that inattention on such a scale cannot possibly be explained by absent-mindedness'. What follows has been quoted so often that it could almost be omitted here. 'It is a structural matter,' he said, 'a view from a window which has been carefully placed to exclude a whole quadrant of the landscape. What may well have begun as a simple forgetting of other possible views turned into habit and over time into something like a cult of forgetfulness practised on a national scale.' Consider the life and times of men like David Unaipon, Albert Namatjira, Robert Tudawali, Durmugam, Douglas Nicholls, Dexter Daniels and many others, Stanner says, '[n]ot to scrape up significance for them but because they typify so vividly the other side of a story over which the great Australian silence reigns; the story of the things we were unconsciously resolved not to discuss with them or treat with them about; the story, in short, of the unacknowledged relations between two racial groups within a single field of life supposedly unified by the principle of assimilation'. The silence had been outed.

•

The Boyers were a culmination of Stanner's thinking and of anthropology's trajectory.[3] For sixty or seventy years a handful of anthropologists and their affiliates had been prominent among the very few Europeans to even notice the Aboriginal people. The more they learned, the more humbled and respectful they became. They helped Australians to pass (as Stanner put it) from depreciation to appreciation of the Aboriginal universe. Anthropology became the most authoritative and influential of white ways of seeing black; much of the evolution of the white gaze can be traced through that one stream of thought.

Stanner expected that history would take up where anthropology was leaving off, that it would press on to tell the story that anthropology couldn't.[4] It was in the work of the scholarly historians that Stanner had found the silence, and in their future work its nemesis. 'I hardly think that what I have called "the great Australian silence" will survive the research that is now in course,' he said. The universities were full of young people 'working actively to end it', and major studies then under way 'will bring the historical and the contemporary dimensions together and will assuredly persuade scholars to renovate their categories of understanding'.

Stanner was right about the silence in that the genie was out of the bottle and wouldn't go back in again, but wrong in several other senses.[5] For one thing, what Stanner referred to as a 'silence' was also a din. The silence about the Aboriginal people and our relations with them went hand in hand with the vigorous production, distribution and exchange of stories about ourselves and our attainments.[6] For another, while it was true to say that the silence was a cult practised on a national scale, a window placed at such an angle as 'to exclude a whole quadrant of the landscape', it wasn't *only* that. From a genesis deep in the frontiers' euphemisms, secrets and cover-ups, the silence embedded itself in social rules and penalties, and in powerful institutions of memory and commemoration, education, the law and scholarship. The genie *was* out of the bottle, but there was more to the silence than that. It couldn't be just 'broken'; it had to be dismantled, in each of its institutional strongholds.[7]

And therein lay a third misjudgement. What Stanner saw as the hope of the side, the discipline of history, was not. There were indeed 'major studies' under way, as he had said – in fact, they were being conducted just down the corridor, as it were, by Stanner's colleagues John Mulvaney and Charles Rowley. Mulvaney's *The Prehistory of Australia*, published soon after the Boyers, attacked the silence from the flank: 'The discoverers, explorers and colonists of the three million square miles which are Australia,' ran the very first sentence of that seminal work, 'were its Aborigines.' Rowley's assault was more direct: the first volume of his great trilogy, published another year on, bore the title *The Destruction of Aboriginal Society*. Both Mulvaney and Rowley were senior scholars, and both were history graduates, but neither was of the discipline's established order. Clever history graduates of Mulvaney's day (he had graduated in 1948) were supposed to go on to Oxford then return to populate Australia's expanding history discipline, but Mulvaney had opted for archaeology and Cambridge before returning to establish his adopted discipline in Australia.[8] Rowley never joined the academy proper at all. A teachers college lecturer when war broke out, he went into the army's education service and emerged to become a senior civil servant; it was Rowley who headed the new college to train staff for service in PNG that took much of Elkin's business. Rowley's encounters in PNG taught him to see what the historians couldn't.

It was also true, as Stanner had said, that a number of young scholars were working on the problem, including my flatmate Mervyn Hartwig (whose brilliant 1962 undergraduate thesis on the Coniston massacres was completed years before almost any other challenge to the silence), Fay Gale, a historical geographer whose PhD was marked by Stanner, and Ann Curthoys, an alumnus of the famous Freedom Ride through outback New South Wales led by Aboriginal student activist Charles Perkins.

But what did all this amount to? The historical work in which Stanner placed his hopes was being done, but it was being done by fringe dwellers and neophytes; in the meantime, the discipline as a whole sailed on, unconcerned. Eight years after the Freedom Ride, seven years after the Gurindji hit the headlines, five years after the Boyers, four years after *The Prehistory of Australia*, three years after *The Destruction of Aboriginal Society* and a year after the Aboriginal Tent Embassy had set up shop on the lawns of Parliament House in Canberra, the prominent historian Geoffrey Serle gave as the ANZAAS presidential address to his colleagues assembled a comprehensive survey of the discipline's disposition, demographics, intellectual interests and current concerns.[9] Serle noted the very low proportion of female historians, took delight in 'the growing number of young specialists who are competing on a world level in numerous areas of scholarship', applauded the relative growth of Asian and American history, and regretted the lack of courses in areas ranging from urban history to the history of ideas. There was no mention of the work being done by tyros such as Hartwig, Curthoys and Gale, or of Rowley and Mulvaney, or of the need for more courses on 'the story of the unacknowledged relations between two racial groups within a single field of life', of the presence or otherwise of Aboriginal historians. The discipline of history was an institution and, like any other, it had its entrenched interests and momentum. It was still less the nemesis of the silence than its custodian and curator.

A fourth limitation in Stanner's analysis followed: he seemed to assume that the central role hitherto played by one scholarly discipline would now be played by another. The anthropologists had blazed the trail for others to follow and so (he seemed to think) would the historians. But when the historians at last realised that Mulvaney, Rowley and the youngsters were on to something, they found that they didn't have this newly discovered province of the past all to themselves. First among the claimants were those who didn't have much discovering to do. The Aboriginal people were, as Stanner had said, 'coming into history' as narrators as well as actors, increasingly telling their story in their own and in adopted ways – through dance, music, ritual and objects, as well as through anthropologists, historians and lawyers and through brilliant propaganda of the deed, such as the Freedom Ride and the Tent Embassy, relayed by the mass media to the wider public. 'Popular' history – stretching from encyclopedias and school texts to films, television shows and novels to monuments, statues and museums to public debate and polemic – rushed into the new field too, much less influenced by the historians than they had once been influenced by the anthropologists. The lawyers were getting involved, often in unequal partnership with Aboriginal peoples and/or the historians, tackling the silence both within the law and around it.

Each of these forms of storytelling came with its own motives and interests, institutional affiliations, capacities and blind spots, its own audiences, its own epistemology, and its own sense of how much each part of the story and the story as a whole really mattered. They influenced and contradicted each other, competed and collaborated with each other, as well as doing battle with those who saw no silence and didn't want to. The struggle over how we came by the continent would become almost as bitter as the struggle over the land itself, pitting white and black against white, conscience against material interests, and southern post-frontier against northern frontier all the way from that most idiosyncratic of Australian towns, Tennant Creek, to the national capital. The lead in this struggle would be taken not by the historians, as Stanner had thought, but by Aboriginal people and their frenemies, the lawyers.

•

One day in 1968 Edward 'Ted' Woodward, a prominent Melbourne QC, took a phone call from a solicitor for the Methodist Church. Was Woodward interested in the Gove case?[10] The national parliament had made a great fuss over the Yolngu's Bark Petitions but it didn't do anything; the government backed the miners, not the Yolngu. But the Yolngu weren't done yet; they proposed to take the government to court.

The scale of this ambition is now difficult to comprehend. The silencing of Aboriginal people (as distinct from the silence about them) stretched back to the very early days of white settlement when they were prohibited from giving evidence in the courts, when 'troublemakers' and 'cheeky blacks' were roughed up or shot, and when police were often a source of harassment rather than protection. Aboriginal people were routinely excluded from consultation about decisions that would shape their lives, let alone involved in making those decisions. When Baldwin Spencer was sent to the Territory by the Commonwealth in 1912 to advise it on policy for the Aboriginal population of its recent

'Not a single Aboriginal person'

acquisition, he consulted with a number of local Europeans but with none of the objects of his recommended policies. Stanner had listened carefully to Charlie Jampin and Zulu Jappangarti in Tennant Creek in 1933 but that was very unusual, and futile. A 1937 government inquiry into the Northern Territory listed the interested parties as the pastoralists, the unions, the missionaries and the anthropologists, this at a time when the Territory's Aboriginal population was about five times that of the rest. The 1950s assimilation campaign was conducted by the Noble Friend of the Aborigines, who knew what was best for them, with the unstated and perhaps unconscious aim of extending the Aboriginal silence in perpetuity. As late as 1961 a national conference to set up an institute of Aboriginal studies (convened by Stanner) included not a single Aboriginal person among its fifty-five delegates, and there were no Aboriginal members of its council until the early 1980s.[11] (The initial conference included just three women, by the way, one of them being Fay Gale.) The equal wage case conducted in the mid-1960s took no evidence from Aboriginal witnesses. So far as I have been able to discover, Harold Holt consulted no Aboriginal people or organisations before he decided to set up the Council for Aboriginal Affairs in 1968, and the council had to fight hard for its first appointments of Aboriginal staff. Aboriginal people were silenced by language, demoralisation and geographic dispersal, as well as by custom, prejudice, policy and regulation.

Woodward, like Hal Wootten, had been involved in the equal wages case (he appeared for the Commonwealth) and, also like Wootten, had learned from the experience. Woodward told the solicitor from the Methodist Church that he did of course know about the matter, that he didn't see how it could be pursued, but he would like to try anyway; it was so obviously unjust that there must surely be an answer somewhere in the law.[12] Just over a year later the Gove case, also known as *Milirrpum and others v Nabalco Pty Ltd*, 'the Yirrkala case' (after the local mission) and 'Blackburn' (after the presiding judge), was under way in the Supreme Court of the Northern Territory. It was a big moment in the long and infinitely complicated relationship between Aboriginal people and European law, and between Aboriginal and judicial ways of understanding our joint and several histories. Readers will not be surprised to learn that Stanner was there.

Stanner was wearing two hats, one as an expert witness, the other as the eyes and ears of the CAA. The council had a close interest in 'the first case of its kind in 180 years of settlement'.[13] So did other arms of the national government. The solicitor-general himself would argue the Commonwealth's case. As well as sending its top man, the government spent up big on research, and worked hand in glove with Nabalco.

The solicitor-general came straight to his point: the judge should throw the matter out forthwith. Stanner's heart sank as he listened to the argument in support.[14] Governments had always proceeded on the basis that from the moment of settlement all land was Crown land. They had done so with a secure foundation in law which reflected, among other things, the fact that there was no Aboriginal system of land ownership. In any event, Aboriginal law and custom was irrelevant unless it was recognised by the law, which it wasn't, and never had been. Apparent exceptions such as the 'reserves' set aside for the Aborigines were not a recognition of native title; they were provided out of benevolence. If indeed the Yolngu had occupied the land in question they had done so as permissive occupants, and if not that then they were trespassers. Much case law was paraded in support of these arguments. 'No German scholar has ever described an elephant more minutely,' Stanner later remarked drily. Counsel for the government and Nabalco saw the Yolngu action as 'a misconceived and most unsettling attack on the laws of property'.

All that was depressing enough. That the Yolngu were equally unable to see why on earth the government didn't understand that the land was theirs – that was worse. In the course of his preparation as an expert witness, Stanner was taken by senior Yolngu men to a secret place to witness an elaborate ceremony involving singing, dancing, the painting of certain designs, and effigies of ancestral beings. At its conclusion one of the men said to Stanner: now you understand. He had been shown what were in effect the clan's title deeds.

Just as it seemed certain to Stanner that those deeds were about to be rendered null and void, the battle turned. From having no idea about whether or how the Yolngu case could be mounted, Ted Woodward had advanced to a very impressive case indeed, and over days of detail piled upon argument he laid it before the court. The Commonwealth and the company had misrepresented both the Yolngu social order (he said) and the conduct of colonial and imperial governments. On the former, the evidence of Yolngu witnesses supported by expert anthropological opinion demonstrated that Yolngu clans did possess a clear, long-recognised way of establishing which tracts of land belonged to which groups. The precedents relied upon by the government and the

company had welded onto the law a fiction which should now be recognised as such. Government legislation, regulation and policy all made
frequent explicit or implied acknowledgements of native title. In the
specific case of the reserves, for example, note the wording of the ordinances concerned: they do not refer to 'Aborigines' in general but to
a specific group with a widely understood relationship with the land
in question. Pastoral leases not infrequently recognised the right of
Aborigines to share use of the land with the leaseholder. In these and
many other instances, Aboriginal rights to land pre-existing the arrival
of the Europeans were in fact recognised and acted upon as a matter
of principle articulated by leading thinkers in London and of policy as
laid down by successive imperial governments. It was true that the law
in Australia had failed to recognise group ownership of the kind practised by the Yolngu, but Canadian and US precedents could and should
be used to repair the omission. The Yolngu's rights to land, Woodward
asserted, are for all these reasons entitled to the protection of the common law and its foundational principle of natural justice.

'Mr Woodward, you have put to me an argument of very great
weight and interest,' said Mr Justice Blackburn. 'If it is accepted a great
deal of received doctrine has to be upset.'

In that event, Woodward responded, the Yolngu claim cannot be
thrown out as the solicitor-general had urged. 'Once you have a difficult point of law, you must proceed.'

And proceed he did, but to no avail. Woodward had invited Mr
Justice Blackburn to take courage and upset received doctrine, but the
invitation was declined, and no wonder. That doctrine had been deeply
entrenched by a variety of legal and historical devices, including the
claim that the land was unoccupied when the First Fleet arrived, either
in the straightforward sense of having no inhabitants, or in the constructed sense of having inhabitants who merely roamed over the land

rather than *used* it, a construction deployed by the Sydney jurist and landowner Richard Windeyer and many others way back in the 1840s. No less an authority than the Privy Council had in 1883 affirmed on those grounds that all land was Crown land from the moment of settlement. The tricky bit for Mr Justice Blackburn was that the Yolngu had demonstrated that they did *not* merely roam the land and that they *did* have a system of land ownership, well understood by all concerned. What to do?

Blackburn got very bad press at the time, and has had ever since, for the legal and historical gymnastics employed en route to his solution. The Yolngu did have 'a feeling of obligation' toward the land, the judge conceded, but that didn't amount to proprietorship – indeed, the land owned them rather than vice versa – and anyway it wasn't clear that they'd had the same arrangements in relation to land from the required date (1788). Leading voices of nineteenth-century British politics cited by Woodward as urging imperial governments to insist upon native title 'might' have 'contemplated' the 'theoretical possibility' of doing what they in fact did. As for the problem of communal ownership of land, Mr Justice Blackburn accepted that it was recognised in Canada and the United States and that in principle such precedents could be drawn into Australian law, but found insuperable legal obstacles to doing so in this particular case. And so on and so forth.

Much more attention has been paid to what Blackburn did than to why he did it. It is at least possible that Blackburn decided that he had extracted as much as he could on behalf of the Yolngu and Aboriginal people generally. He must have known that to go further would be to lose the lot. Woodward had launched the case in the Territory's Supreme Court because it would get a better hearing there than in Garfield Barwick's black-letter High Court, and he subsequently decided against appealing Blackburn's decision for the same reason.[15] Blackburn undoubtedly knew what Woodward knew. Stanner remarked acidly and, I think, unfairly that Blackburn had 'replaced historical fact by a legal fiction'. Perhaps. But against a long history and against the wishes of the government, Blackburn had heard the Yolngu evidence and listened very carefully to it. If he hadn't found that the Yolngu had a system of land title, he hadn't really denied it either. The law had given ground; it had begun to struggle against its own silence.

But what so angered Stanner was there too: the law had insisted that its version of the story would prevail over the Aboriginal one and over comprehensively established historical fact. Blackburn concluded that the Commonwealth was able to lease the land to Nabalco for the purposes of mining. After extraordinary effort, the Yolngu in 1971 had got no further than the Warumungu in 1933. The miners wanted the land; the government gave it to them, and the law complied. The men, the machines, the town, the roads, the grog in Yolngu Country would stay just as they had in Warumungu Country.

•

Stanner's bitter ridicule of the 'Blackburn' decision may have owed something to frustrations elsewhere.[16] In the Boyers he had confessed to a hope that we might at last be turning over a new leaf, but it wasn't long before that hope seemed misplaced. The tables that had turned so dramatically against Hasluck when the CAA was formed were turning back again. The council had been Harold Holt's idea, but he was no longer there. Just months after setting up the CAA, Holt disappeared, presumed drowned. Denied promised resources and access to Holt's prime ministerial successors, the CAA battled for survival against Hasluck's old department, hostile on bureaucratic and ideological grounds, and against Country Party ministers, defenders of mining and pastoral interests as well as of the assimilationist faith. By 1972 Stanner was very nearly fed up, so much so that he risked indiscretion. During the second of his presidential addresses to the anthropologists at ANZAAS, he admitted that the work on the CAA over four years had left him with 'an oppressive sense of a continuing large irrelevance'.[17] He went on to denounce the government's guerrilla warfare against the council within its larger failure to see that its policies were arithmetic responses to problems expanding geometrically. Although he didn't say so publicly, Stanner and his comrades-in-arms Nugget Coombs and Barrie Dexter had several times contemplated resigning in protest.[18]

With the advantage of knowing what came next, it is obvious that these battles by and over the CAA were not so much a sign of bad times as of steepening polarisation in Aboriginal affairs. The Yolngu's petitions had been taken to parliament by Labor MPs. The Gurindji had been supported in their walk-off by well-known communist Frank Hardy, heir to the Communist Party of Australia's many years in the vanguard of advocacy and activism. It was the unions that had outplayed the employers in the equal wages case. Several churches were in support too – it was a Methodist missionary in Yirrkala who had got Labor MPs Gordon Bryant and Kim Beazley Snr involved in the Yolngu campaign.[19] Bryant and Beazley in turn agitated to get their party to support a new approach, which now had a name: self-determination. Neither Aboriginal organisations nor their many supporters wanted to lose assimilation's ideal of equality for all, but they didn't want Aboriginal people to be pushed to un-be themselves either. The claim for land directly affected only that minority of Aboriginal people in the frontier north, but for increasing numbers in the post-frontier south, in the ghettos and on the fringes of the towns and cities, it brought a new sense of themselves. They were no longer outsiders wanting in, but members of a colonised, dispossessed people. Labor and the left adopted the new approach. The Coalition and the right opposed it.

In December 1972 Labor won government. Gordon Bryant, one of the MPs who had presented the Bark Petitions to parliament a decade before, was now minister for Aboriginal affairs in a government that multiplied spending on Aboriginal housing, welfare and representation by a factor of six, and undertook to restore to Aboriginal people their lost power of self-determination. The CAA suddenly found itself reporting to a prime minister who gave same-day service on its many recommendations, including action on land rights (and, before long, the appointment of Charles Perkins, Aboriginal leader of the 1965 Freedom Ride, as head of the new Department of Aboriginal Affairs).[20] There would be a royal commission, and it would be headed by the hero of the Yolngu's struggle, Edward Woodward QC. The government considered whether Woodward should advise on national legislation, or on the less ambitious but also less vulnerable approach of legislation that would apply in the Northern Territory only but serve as a precedent for legislation by the states. It settled for the latter.

Woodward took his royal commission as a chance to avoid the problems encountered in 'Blackburn' and elsewhere. He visited the United States and Canada to see how land rights had been acknowledged there. He compiled a list of no less than twelve traps for young players, then set out to avoid as many as possible.[21] Existing Aboriginal reserves would be made over directly to Aboriginal owners. Other land could be claimed only if it was unalienated Crown land. Title would be freehold, but communal. The land would be held in trust by land councils, funded by government to assist claimants through the process. The whole would be administered by an Aboriginal lands commissioner, based in Darwin. Those Aboriginal people with no land to claim should be compensated by a fund established for the purpose. Whitlam introduced a bill based on Woodward's recommendations to parliament in 1975, not long after he had poured red sand into the outstretched hand of Gurindji leader Vincent Lingiari as a symbol of the transfer of free-hold title, a moment captured in a famous photograph.

Labor's time in office was brief but seminal. Such was the sea change in opinion that the incoming Liberal prime minister and his Liberal minister for Aboriginal affairs were able to resist their Country Party colleagues and introduce the Whitlam bill into parliament, albeit with-out the compensation scheme, and have it carried into law.[22] The royal assent was given by the governor-general, Sir Paul Hasluck. Among the first to lodge a claim under the terms of the *Aboriginal Land Rights (Northern Territory) Act 1976* were the Warumungu.

CHAPTER SEVEN

1985

The land rights option arrived at a difficult time for Tennant and for the Warumungu. Still mutually exclusive categories – the whites lived in the town, the blacks on its margins and in the camps around – they had been getting on badly. The whites resented black intrusion on their dreams of suburban respect-ability, presenting as they did 'an unsavoury picture to the public';[1] the blacks resented white racism and living conditions that ranged from substandard to appalling.

All that was bad enough in the good times, but the good times had disappeared almost overnight. From hope of the side in the 1930s to army way-station in the 1940s to game little battler paying its own way in the 1950s and boomtown in the 1960s, Tennant from the late 1970s ceased to be the exception to the Territory rule. The miners packed up and left (Peko sacked 380 employees in a single go) or switched to FIFO (fly-in, fly-out) workers.[2] Faster roads meant that stations deserted Tennant as a service centre in favour of Alice or Mt Isa. A meatworks was established to the south of the town but it used seasonal workers, in town for six months, elsewhere for the other six, and in any event it collapsed. A smaller abattoir on the northern side went down in a blaze of scandal, selling horsemeat overseas for beef. Tourism? What could Tennant offer to compete with the glamour of the Red Centre or the

Top End? 'Stay a Day', said signs on the outskirts, half plaintive, half resigned. A night in a motel or a caravan park was the best that could be hoped for.

Jammed between economic collapse and racial conflict, Tennant was on the way to becoming Australia's most notorious dystopia. A Canberra consultant hired by the council to suggest how it might arrest the spiral catalogued Tennant's many problems.[3] 'There is a white Australian population and an aboriginal Australian population both occupying Tennant Creek and both regarding it as their town,' the consultant observed with commendable candour; neither has a high opinion of the other, and there is not 'a high degree of constructive interaction' between the two. The consultant recorded the many complaints by residents about the town: too many singles, not enough females, too many stray cats and dogs, too many flies; it was too windy, too dusty and too expensive; there was too much competition from Katherine, Mt Isa and Alice, too much vandalism, too many broken shop windows, too much wanton damage to vehicles, not enough services, not enough get-up-and-go, a 'failure image'. Those who came to Tennant, mostly white-collar staff of government agencies based in the town (no less than sixteen of them by the mid-1980s), came from Down South and went back again as soon as they could. One study of Tennant's plight found that a hospital superintendent who had been in town for just over a year had been there longer than any of his medical colleagues; the high school had a 50 per cent annual staff turnover.[4] At the other end of the social scale were the drifters, the ne'er-do-well, men trying to evade the law or family responsibilities or themselves. Looking for work that wasn't there, they too moved on. A few local businesspeople stayed, sometimes for decades, then used their little pile to escape. Even Mrs Ward, the rock of Banka Banka, spent her last years in Adelaide.

The only people who wanted to stay in Tennant Creek were the Warumungu and the many other Aboriginal people for whom Tennant was a de facto refugee centre. As the European population slowly sank, the Aboriginal population climbed from around 500 in the early 1980s to more than 1300 in the mid-1990s, well over a third of the total. Increasingly, Aboriginal organisations constituted a kind of parallel state.[5] The Warumungu Pabula Housing Association turned itself into the Julalikari Council, a Swiss Army knife of services ranging from housing to employment, aged care and environmental repair. Julalikari's portfolios blurred into those of the Anyinginyi Health Aboriginal Corporation, which opened a primary health clinic and a sobering-up shelter, and offered workshops and other support on child health, diet, cooking, housekeeping and other basics of life in an unfamiliar universe. The Papulu Apparr-Kari Languages Centre set out to keep alive and pass on as many of the Barkly's sixteen languages as it could. The Alice-based Central Land Council set up an office in Tennant. The one institution that wasn't there, or not for most Aboriginal people anyway, was the labour market.

The destruction of the hunter-gatherer economy by the cattle had been bad enough, but in the cattle and later at the mission something had grown out of the ruins. The collapse of *that* economy was a bigger disaster still. Almost all of the Aboriginal people who had jobs worked for one of the Aboriginal organisations but most had no job at all, or intermittent government-subsidised make-work coordinated by Julalikari. Many subsisted on 'sit-down money', the aged pension, the disability pension, unemployment benefits. For many people, there was little to do and even less that they had to do.

One way of filling the vacuum was politics. Everybody – that is, every Aboriginal adult and particularly every Warumungu adult – had a say in the running of the emerging Aboriginal organisations, in their projects, plans, proposals and campaigns. Kimberly Christen, an American anthropologist, spent years in Tennant trying to map and comprehend the complexities of these activities. As the owner of a vehicle she was in demand, but instead of travelling out of town on carefully planned trips she often found herself shuttling between the camps and Aboriginal org offices in the town, getting people to meetings for this or that or sitting in on the meetings as the older Warumungu women marshalled the numbers for projects, decisions or committees and discussed 'everything from the paint color for a new building's bathrooms to the proper boundary lines for mining exploration'.[6]

Another, less optional consumer of time was 'traditional business'. For many Aboriginal people Tennant became a base camp more than a place of residence; they covered often considerable distances in much-prized Toyotas (a generic in Aboriginal English) to maintain relations with kin, attend funerals and sorry business or conduct ceremonies, for the initiation of young men particularly.

And then there was the grog. Of all the European addictives – the sugar, the tobacco, the tea and the alcohol – it was alcohol that did most damage. It was there right from the start, a culture saturated in rum on the one side, a culture with no intoxicants at all on the other. Governor Phillip and his officers introduced Aboriginal men to alcohol. The young Frank Gillen had seen 'tight Niggers' on his journey to the frontier in 1875. John McDouall Stuart was an alcoholic. Spencer and Gillen liked nothing better than a drink, a smoke and a yarn, and Spencer became an alcoholic. That the grog problem came with the cattle is evidenced by Mrs Ward's ban on grog on Banka Banka. Tennant Creek's first proper building was a pub. But it was not until the 1960s that things went downhill fast. That was when Aboriginal people got money, were given the legal right to drink, and left or were pushed off the stations. It was worse in the towns, where white and black lived side by side but radically apart, and perhaps worst of all in Tennant Creek.

'They've got some bloody good drinkers in the Northern Territory', went a ballad by Ted Egan (later the Territory's equivalent of governor).[7] How would Egan's lyrics go for Tennant Creek? Tennant was awash with grog. The two pubs, the Tennant Creek and the Goldfields, were the first – and for decades Tennant's only – substantial structures, standing like cathedrals in a medieval town. By the mid-1980s Tennant had 1.8 per cent of the Territory's population but 3.2 per cent of its per capita grog consumption, effortlessly besting the Territory's own national record.[8] In the mid-1990s an adult population of 2400 was served by two pubs, two bottle shops, four clubs, three private hotels and two restaurants plus home/camp delivery on credit by a taxi driver–cum–loan shark. These many outlets sold prodigious quantities of grog – in just one typical year (1994), 49,000 litres of cask wine, more than 4000 litres of spirits and 243,000 litres of beer, plus sundry other categories of grog including fortified wines, cider and mixed spirits.[9] Those figures exclude amounts sold at seven 'roadside inns' within driving range of Tennant Creek and by pop-ups for events such as the annual rodeo, the races and the show. White Tennant Creek's social machinery just didn't work without alcoholic lubrication. The hospital found that many patients answered a question about alcohol use on the standard admissions form with 'average' or 'not much', then quantified that as eight or ten cans a night.[10]

For the whites the frontier was a man's world, and so was mining. Drinking, holding your grog, holding extraordinary amounts of grog, the hot, noisy intimacy and recklessness of the bar were at the centre of their being. It was another thing that set them apart from the effete southerners. They could drink. Tennant's foundation myth, the one about where the beer truck broke down, was just one of many, some committed to print by (emblematically enough) the town's first barmaid, Margot Miles, in *The Old Tennant*, her compendium of yarns about rollicking times, the brawls, the wonderful mateship, the madcap escapades, all fuelled by grog.[11] At one of the Christmas parties thrown for Tennant's (white) kids by the RSL club, my father won a raffle, the prize for which was a dozen Southwark. When we were packing up to leave Tennant they were still there, covered in dust, tucked away in a dark corner of the pantry. I saw them with something like embarrassment, the inchoate sense of a boy on the cusp of adolescence that my father, in shirts and shorts neatly pressed by my mother, with his rectitude, with that cautious, formal persona, was less manly than my friend Leith's father, the burly Mr McDonald, former boxing champion and reputed monarch of the front bar at the Tennant. It was an unnamed feeling that my parents' teetotal ways were not markers of respectability, of a certain superiority as they managed to convey, but of timidity, a sense that real life was elsewhere. Such was the allure of the frontier and its accounts of itself.

Those po-faced experts from the south told a different story.[12] What they found went well beyond damage to health and dignity. The current blood-alcohol limit for drivers is .05; in one fifteen-month period in the early 1980s, the five drivers of vehicles involved in fatal accidents multiplied that figure by two, three, four, five, even six times, with readings of .124, .216, .230, .248 and .318. Coronial enquires into 100 deaths over four years found that one-third of them – road accidents, fights, suicides, manslaughter, murder and acute dehydration – were alcohol-related. Illness and death came from liver disease, kidney disease, alcoholic psychosis, alcohol cardiomyopathy, cancer of the throat. The drinkers, the Aboriginal drinkers particularly, damaged others as well as themselves. They spent money needed for food and other basics.

Sometimes kids – often sick enough from living in camps with little or no decent sanitation, running water or protection from wet and cold – suffered also from malnutrition, in-utero alcohol poisoning or dehydration. The drinkers were rowdy, disruptive, accident-prone and violent. The hospital recorded 261 'alcohol-related presentations' in a typical period of thirteen weeks, 140 of them injuries from assaults, fractures, heads wounds, lacerations, stab wounds. Most were inflicted on, and sustained by, an Aboriginal population of just over 800 adults.

Some of Tennant's Aboriginal people tried to keep out of harm's way by setting up new camps away from the drinkers or by moving to outstations, tiny settlements scattered tens or even hundreds of kilometres out from Tennant. Another response was to try to cope with the consequences of the grog. In 1985 Julalikari established a 'night patrol', an Australian first. It picked people up and took them to a sobering-up shelter, where in the morning they were given a shower, clean clothes and some tucker, while the Night Patrol volunteers worked with the police to handle offences against regulations, property or people. By the mid-1990s there were almost as many organisations devoted to coping with the grog as there were outlets pushing it: the Night Patrol, the sobering-up shelter, the hospital and the police station, a women's shelter, the Barkly Region Alcohol and Drug Abuse Advisory Group (BRADAAG), the Living with Alcohol program and the Little Sisters of Mercy. An inkling of the scale of the problem and the effort to cope with it: BRADAAG ran a fourteen-bed residential care facility, provided aftercare, follow-up counselling and supervision of home detention (as an alternative to incarceration), and handed out emergency relief funds for people with 'alcohol-related difficulties'.

Embattled and grossly overstretched as the Warumungu and their organisations were, they pressed on with their land claim.[13] And why wouldn't they? There was some hope of material relief, mining royalties certainly, jobs on Aboriginal-run stations possibly, but those were secondary considerations. They had been trying to get an accommodation with the *papulanyi* right from the start, and in that they were representative of Aboriginal people across the continent.[14] Only three or four years after the invasion from the east, the young Cubadgee had tried to make friends of the Europeans and dared to hope that they might come to an understanding about sharing the land. A decade or so on, Spencer and Gillen seem to have been unwitting beneficiaries of that same hope. Then Zulu Jappangarti and Charlie Jampin had tried to negotiate with the government men over their 'reserve', enlisting Stanner in the effort. With many others the Warumungu had worked in the cattle as a way of staying on the land until that was no longer possible. In the 1970s it was still the case that many Warumungu people had been born on Country and had lived most or all of their lives on Country. Why wouldn't they 'claim', in whitefellas' terms, what they had never given up? They knew the country, and wanted to look after it. Ceremonial obligations had to be fulfilled on Country. And running through it all was, as Hal Wootten suggested in respect of equal wages, a demand for dignity. They wanted the whites to know who they were. The claim was made less in spite of all the other things the Warumungu had on their plate than because of them.

•

When I first came across photographs of the land claim hearings, I found them almost as affecting as Spencer's wonderful portraits of Aboriginal life and people. There they are, the white commissioner and the lawyers and their teams sitting at a trestle table under the shade of a tree or a tarpaulin, before them ranks of Aboriginal people, the women in their beanies sitting separately from the men in their cowboy hats, dark faces still and intent as they listen to one of their number, the 'witness'.

Opening address to the commissioner, Gurindji claim,
Dagarugu Station, c. 1981

On the one side are people well into lives lived amidst indifference, contempt and ignorance, reclaiming a world inherited from their parents and grandparents and countless generations beyond by telling of those 'signs of intent toward man' that reveal the doings of the ancestral beings.[15] On the other, the whitefellas, so long deaf and blind to the claims of the Aboriginal people, devoting extraordinary effort to listen and to understand. In the equal wages case in the mid-1960s, the law had failed to even hear Aboriginal people. In the early 1970s, in 'Blackburn', it did listen, and learn, but it went ahead and did what it had always done anyway. But now? First the work of months and years trawling through official records, station diaries and explorers' journals and in interviewing and consulting to prepare the claim book, and then the hearings, more days, weeks, months of work by lawyers, anthropologists, linguists and witnesses, a sustained effort by each side to understand and be understood by the other:[16]

MR McIvor: Billy, the Karlanjarangi – that is Jimmy Jones' country.

BILLY BOY: Yes.

MR McIvor: Wakurlpu country was where your grandfather was.

BILLY BOY: Yes.

MR McIvor: Is that all one group now?

BILLY BOY: One group, yes.

MR McIvor: What do you say about that, Jimmy?

JIMMY JONES: They all one group.

HIS HONOUR: Have you got a word for that, Jimmy?

JIMMY JONES: What?

HIS HONOUR: When you say one group – 'We're all one group' – have you got some way of saying that in your language?

JIMMY JONES: Ankkul nyinta. I forget about that Warumungu.

DR NASH: That is Warumungu – A-N-K-K-U-L new word N-Y-I-N-T-A. The second word just means are, is – the verb 'to be'; the first word is a pronoun. I think it is the first person plural exclusive. In other words, we – but not you.

HIS HONOUR: We are.

DR NASH: We are, exactly.

JIMMY JONES: Yarntingi.

DR NASH: He is saying the word that maybe you are heading for: Yarntingi, he said, Y-A-R-N-T-I-N-G-I, which is Warumungu and literally means one at. The composition together means together, at one. This Yarntingi means together in any context.

HIS HONOUR: Billy, do you know how those three grandfathers came together?

BILLY BOY: Well, he call one group; that mean we say Yarntingi – all in one, Yarnti.

HIS HONOUR: Can you tell me and help me to understand how they came together, those three grandfathers and the children from those three grandfathers?

BILLY BOY: Tribal way you couldn't split; tribal way they both working together.

Deborah Bird Rose was one of many anthropologists to be involved in claims under the *Aboriginal Land Rights (Northern Territory) Act* of 1976. From an initial scepticism, even hostility, she was moved and impressed by what she saw over and again. The law leaned toward the Aboriginal people to really hear them, abandoning its usually ironclad rules.[17] Witnesses heard each other's evidence and passed the microphone around to endorse, support or correct in up to half a dozen languages, including on occasion sign language.[18] They worked out how to get the commissioner to listen their way. Rose recalls one hearing at which the claimants told the commissioner that they would put on a 'show' for him to help him understand. He was instructed when to turn up, where to sit and what to make of what he was being permitted to see. The show was held at night; the dancers used car headlights as spots. Both sides understood the rich humour of this 'ritual inversion'.

The Territory's land claims were 'Aboriginalised', Rose says, in a way that did honour to both sides.[19]

It might have seemed that way to those southern 'experts', but not to the locals it didn't. In Tennant Creek feeling ran against the land claim from the start, in part out of simple ignorance. Unlike the whites on the stations, the townspeople hadn't lived with Aboriginal people and most knew little or nothing about them. When a rock was carted into town on a Peko low-loader and deposited in a park on the main intersection, there to carry a plaque honouring Peko's wonderful contribution to the town, the Warumungu protested; the rock had been taken from Kunjarra, a sacred site on the Dreaming track of the Munga Munga women. Townspeople were nonplussed. 'We just thought that Peko Park's a nice central spot,' one resident recalled years later, marvelling at her earlier ignorance.[20] 'We just wanted to provide something interesting.' For many, the view from Tennant was as in those cartoons of a New Yorker's view of the United States, the foreground crowded with Manhattan's towers, the lesser boroughs behind, then nothing much before the west coast and the Pacific Ocean. What they knew was a bounded world, what they had seen and experienced, and what they had learned from the countless stories they told each other.

Tennant's story and its stories about itself were recorded by two notable women of Tennant Creek, Margot Miles (mentioned a moment ago) and Hilda Tuxworth. Miles was a genuine old-timer. 'I was a very thin girl, the only thing nice about me was my big brown eyes and a youthful, jutting bosom,' she wrote of the younger self who had been delivered to the Tennant Creek Hotel by the mailman.[21] 'I was just eighteen and fleeing the Depression in the city.' Miles lived out her life in the town as a jill of all trades and the life of the party (and is now memorialised by the hotel's Margot Miles Dining Room). Miles' *The Old Tennant* offers one ebullient anecdote after another, yarns featuring sanitary cans (slopping over or empty and blowing all over the place in the ceaseless wind), big-money gambling (illegal but carefully over-looked by the constables), wrestling and bull fighting (drunken miners charging head-on into each other), hanky-panky, suicides, beer-crate coffins, and a blow-up bra that reached amazing proportions in an unpressurised DC-3. Tennant's other chronicler took a later and less Rabelaisian view. Hilda Tuxworth was a postwar arrival in Tennant, wife to a mining engineer at Peko and a serial respectabliser, responsible for initiating no less than three of the town's exiguous associations (history, bridge and Toastmistresses). With the support of a handful of locals and the National Trust in Darwin, she recorded long interviews with old-timers, collected a mass of documents, files, photographs and bric-a-brac, arranged for the old hospital pharmacy building to house her archive, and wrote and published Tennant Creek's first detailed account of itself, *Tennant Creek: Yesterday and Today*. Mrs Tuxworth aspired to record rather than reminisce, and to tell a story of progress wrung from a harsh land by back-breaking work, pluck and determination.

In the mental world of both Hilda Tuxworth and Margot Miles, the Aborigines were fringe-dwellers, just as they were in the town's reality. Neither Miles nor Tuxworth mentions the seizure of Warumungu lands at the behest of the miners, the role of Aboriginal labour in the mining industry, their maltreatment by the newly installed cops (nominally their protectors),[22] the harassment and worse of Aboriginal women by the miners,[23] the impact of Aboriginal people on the life of the town, or why Aboriginal people were there at all. Silence was a matter of psychological comfort as well as ignorance, of course. The many yarns retailed by Miles were mythologising bluster; they distracted and smothered.[24] Miles' and Tuxworth's gaze was averted, their voices wistful, sentimental, a way of not saying what couldn't be said.[25] Miles refers briefly to a sad degen-eration ('in those days they were entirely different from the people you

meet today').[26] Mrs Tuxworth's account closes with the peaceful passing of 'a composite lubra of the Warrumunga [Warumungu] tribe' who
had lived out her imagined life under the stern shelter of Mrs Ward's
Banka Banka.[27] The town's silence,[28] at first enforced – as Stanner had
learned from the delegation of miners who threatened to run him out
of town if he interfered with their business – 'turned under habit and
over time into something like a cult of forgetfulness'.[29]

But something much darker was forming, in Tennant Creek and
elsewhere. In the town, the representative moment was the eventual
return of the rock to Kunjarra – but not before it had been daubed with
'fuck nigers [sic]' and 'kill blacks', or before the carrier contracted to
do the job had reneged after receiving death threats.[30] Up in Darwin, it
was the miners and the pastoralists in thin disguise as the first Northern
Territory government bent upon beating back the land claims, all of
them, everywhere. In both the town and the government, it was Ian
Tuxworth, Hilda's son, Tennant's member in the Legislative Assembly
and minister for many things, including resources and energy. Pressed by
Aboriginal people no longer willing to fade gently away, the Territorians
(as they called themselves) reverted to type. The Warumungu claim
would be the Territory's Alamo.[31] Even the fact of being able to claim
land was a challenge, implying as it did prior ownership, but the claims
also offered the long-silenced a way of recording what was once theirs
and how and by whom it had been taken. When years later it was all
over,[32] the land commissioner savaged the government for its expenditure
of many hundreds of thousands of public dollars in defence of land that
brought it just $11,000 a year in leaseholder fees.[33] Perhaps the commis-
sioner was missing the point. For the Warumungu the land claim was a
demand for dignity; for the Territorians it was a defence of entitlement.

The government's first gambit was to extend the town boundaries
to multiply the area enclosed by a factor of thirty.[34] Then it alienated

nine of the twelve claimed areas, making them available for sale or lease and therefore not claimable. When asked to press on regardless, the commissioner ruled that he couldn't; he had jurisdiction over only the remaining three of the twelve areas. The claimants headed for the High Court to contest the ruling. The High Court found for the claimants and against the Territory; the nine alienated areas could be claimed. The hearings resumed, albeit under a different commissioner, and negotiations over areas adjacent to the town commenced. These were brought to a halt when the Territory appealed to the Federal Court for access to certain claim documents; the court ruled against. In the meantime, the government bought up land containing two sacred sites and then challenged the commissioner's jurisdiction. The commissioner ruled against the government, so off it went to the Federal Court again, and lost again. Yet another appeal to the Federal Court, this time to argue that there were certain errors in the original claim documentation. That lost too. At this point the commissioner expressed frustration at the government's behaviour; the government applied to the commissioner to disqualify himself, which he declined to do. Back to the Federal Court once more. Another loss.

At first the town – that is, the owners of the pubs, the stores, the bakery, the garages, the picture theatre, who controlled things through the *Tennant & District Times* and the council – was at one with its local member and the government up in Darwin.[35] But as things dragged on, white opinion divided and shifted. The boom that had tripled Tennant's population in less than a decade brought a new kind of white into town: teachers, social workers, nurses, doctors, managers and administrators, most on the public payroll. Even as the boom turned to bust and even if the southerners didn't stay long, they were there in force, and so were their southern attitudes. They had the ear of another newspaper, the short-lived *Barkly Regional*, set up in competition with the *Tennant &*

District Times. And they won. In 1985, seven years after the claim had
been filed, the town clerk appeared before the commissioner.[36] 'I have
to say to my shame,' he declared, 'that perhaps the previous council
or councillors were somewhat hostile to matters Aboriginal,' but that
was no longer the case. The town had been working through the difficult and 'confused' issues of the land claim, sacred sites and the camps.
Thanks to anthropologists and other experts, people now had a 'greater
appreciation of the reasons why the Aboriginal community is here'. As
would be expected in a unique and diverse community such as Tennant
Creek (the town clerk continued), there are still some who would not
agree to the land claim under any circumstances but they are now a
small minority. Community attitudes had changed 'dramatically'.

•

Mr Justice Maurice's final report was perhaps the most extensive of dozens from those years, dealing as it does with what is often cited as the
most bitterly fought claim of them all.[37] The report's forty-eight chapters,
sixteen appendixes and three maps comprise a formidable work of foren-
sic enquiry. The commissioner congratulated 'the general population of
Tennant Creek' on its support for the claim, a sharp contrast with many
other towns where black and white lived together. He recommended that
sixteen tracts of land be ceded to eleven Warumungu claimant groups,
denounced the Northern Territory government for its benighted obstruc-
tionism, and offered a capsule history of Tennant Creek.

> In a sense, white Australia has been caught *in delicto* with the
> Warumungu. We have taken all their good land; no watercourse
> remains which does not have some European claim to it. We have
> comforted ourselves with myths about what Aboriginal people
> wanted, what was important to them, what was good for them – all

the while taking more and more of their land, shifting them here, shunting them there; until all that was left was desert wasteland … and when in the struggle for some sort of recognition during the land claim enquiry process, claimants were not always able or willing to recite chapter and verse of a rich litany of sites and mythology for these bleak remaining areas, some were heard to mock them.

Early on in my learning about Tennant's story, I thought that in the person of Justice Michael Maurice and through the agency of the Territory's land rights legislation, conscience was retracing the steps of two hundred years and doing its best to put things right. Years on, those things still seem to be true but other things do too. Maurice's moral ground was not as high as I'd thought, in respect of white or black. Those opposed to 'the whole philosophy of land rights', as the town clerk put it, had been brutalised by the racist legacy of the frontier and enraged by the threat to their property and privilege, but they were also angered by southern sanctimony. The post-frontier was salving its conscience at their expense. It was a re-run of the Conciliation and Arbitration Commission's brave declaration that it would not flinch when it was the one inflicting the blow, not suffering it, and a re-run of Paul Hasluck's insistence on an assimilation that would be done by someone else.

The pastoralists could take particular umbrage. Canberra wouldn't listen when they explained why equal wages would hurt those it claimed to help, and here it was claiming again to be saving the blackfellas from the frontier's baddies. The south – product and beneficiary of the frontier – was happy to use the frontier for its own myth-making purposes, but soothing mythology for the south was hard reality for many in the Territory; its deeply incapable European economy bore hard on those who tried to make it work. Travelling with me on a couple of my trips

north was an old friend and daughter of notable Territorians Sam and
Daphne Calder. The Calders were for many years on Argadargada,
a station 300-odd kilometres north-west of Alice Springs, but were
eventually forced off after years of battling with the toxic leaves of the
gidyea tree that cattle turn to in times of drought. This same Sam Calder,
a lovely and decent man kindly remembered by the Alyawarre people
who had lived and worked on Argadargada, was later the Territory's
man in Canberra.[38] He once told his parliamentary colleagues that they
wouldn't know a blackfella from a barramundi, and after Whitlam had
poured the red sand of Gurindji Country into the outstretched hand
of Vincent Lingiari, Calder asked Whitlam where he'd got that stunt
from.[39] The passionate, mad bitterness of the Territory's campaigns bubbled up from wells dark with racism, but it came also from a sense of
having earned, having suffered for the land.[40]

The Warumungu had a much larger ground of complaint. For a
start, possession was here, as elsewhere, nine points of the law. Much of
the land was ruled out before the process had even started. In essence,
Aboriginal people could claim that which was left over after the pastoralists and others had taken what they wanted. The process was stacked
in several ways and, despite the efforts of those involved, stacked against
women in particular.[41] It was divisive; some of the Territory's Aboriginal
people had little or no claimable land. Then there was the texture and
politics of the process itself, and not just in its conventions of address
(His Honour, Mr McIvor, Dr Nash for one side, Billy Boy, Jimmy
Jones, Topsy Nelson for the other), not just in a form of interaction
and resolution utterly alien to Aboriginal ways which could result in
tears or silence or in the embarrassment of being asked to discuss what
should not even be referred to in the company of men or women or
strangers, or not even in the excessive legalism and expense, but in the
fundamentals. Why were the Warumungu having to ask the people

who had taken their land to give some of it back? Why weren't those dark faces intent on considering requests from the whitefellas to keep some of what they had taken? 'White man got no law,' Kathleen Fitz told the commission.[42] 'They got nothing.'

Michael Maurice belonged to an honourable company of lawyers that included Wootten, Woodward and others, all products of the silence, all taken aback as they realised that their past was not as they had assumed. They struggled to use the law's foundational sense of justice against its equally foundational dependence on legislation and precedent. The justice they wanted was *historical* justice and therein lay the problem. History's account was much the richer and more truthful, but the law couldn't act on it no matter how far it leaned forward to hear and understand. Maurice's slashing account of the European assault on the Warumungu implies agreement with Kathleen Fitz: if justice was to be served, the Warumungu would get all their land back because it had all been taken without permission, agreement or recompense. It was not history that determined Maurice's findings, however, or his sense of justice, but legislation. All he could do was tell history's story then act in the light of what was really just another of those windows placed so as to exclude a whole quadrant of the landscape.

The greatest limitation of the Territory land rights legislation, however, was not in its legal form but its political consequences. Far from acting as a precedent for legislation in other jurisdictions, as Whitlam and Woodward had hoped, it mobilised them against. Over a couple of decades the land rights regime returned a third of the Territory's land and 85 per cent of its coastline to Aboriginal ownership, to the growing alarm of the pastoralists and the miners.[43] The Territory government's inability to stop the rot was more alarming still. It was the Territory land rights legislation that made the miners realise that to win the land, they would have to win the story.[44]

CHAPTER EIGHT

1992

W hat took you so long, Henry, Fay Gale recalls asking
Henry Reynolds, only half in jest, after the publication of *The Other Side of the Frontier*.[1] Reynolds' book
marked the arrival in the history discipline's mainstream
of the perspective pioneered a full decade earlier by John Mulvaney
and Charles Rowley.[2] What *was* the answer to Gale's question? The
historians were, after all, natural whispering hearts material, mostly
Anglo-Saxon liberals who voted Labor, as their president Geoffrey
Serle had noted in his 1973 survey of the discipline,[3] and they worked
in institutions tolerant of critical voices. Why were they so very slow
to get off the mark?

One part of the answer lies in institutional arrangements. Most
historians climbed the ranks from lecturer to senior lecturer to reader
to professor not as intellectual voyagers but as specialists spending long
periods, if not entire careers, doing the equivalent of medieval strip
farming. To till a new field was to abandon an established one, always
risky and even more so if the field to be entered was itself new and
unfashionable. When the youthful Henry Reynolds' appointment to
a North Queensland university college in the mid-1960s led him to
an interest in the Aborigines and their relations with white Australia,
his elders warned against. That was no way to get on, he was told.[4]

Australian history was downmarket but Aboriginal history, like the Aborigines themselves, was beneath notice.

The other parts of the answer are to do with epistemology: Reynolds had been battling his way out of one paradigm and into another.[5] It wasn't just a case of adding 'Aboriginal history'. That was the relatively easy part, although even that wasn't entirely straightforward. Finding out about the Aboriginal experience raised some tricky questions, including how to really listen to Aboriginal people, how to use 'oral history' and how to see what had been hidden by convenient blinkers (the fact of Aboriginal land management, for example) or by the loss or destruction of documents (Aboriginal deaths from white violence, for example). More difficult was understanding the full implications of that *part* of the story for the *whole* story. As late as 1959 a predecessor of Serle's could use his presidential address at ANZAAS to remind his colleagues of our great good fortune in having occupied an uninhabited continent without opposition, bequeathing us a history free of civil war, tyranny and conquest.[6] Now the historians were realising that it wasn't like that at all. We weren't exceptional. We hadn't been exempted from war and conquest. What did that mean for us, and for the story we told about ourselves? How and by whom and in whose interests had the wool been pulled over our eyes? 'It was as if it was about another country,' Reynolds recalled, 'quite unlike the image of Australia I had grown up with.'[7] The work to be done was emotional as well as intellectual. Most difficult of all was learning about a fundamentally different culture, which meant learning from and about another discipline and its way of thinking. Even the most empirical of the anthropological collectors – 'Tinny' Tindale, for example, a lepidopterist when he added anthropology to his quiver – was a theoretician compared with the typical historian. Renovating categories of understanding, as urged by Stanner, was hard, slow work; learning that there are such things was harder still.[8]

The Other Side of the Frontier flagged a classic Kuhnian revolution. Angered, ashamed and excited, the young among the historians constructed a new epistemology as well as a new story. When John Mulvaney and others convened a meeting in 1980 to discuss how historians should go about incorporating this new story within the old one, more than sixty scholars turned up.[9] The discipline's rewards shifted almost overnight from doing 'normal science' to another being formed in the heat of scholarly battle. Newcomers often lurched unsteadily between inherited assumption and shocking revelation. Out of grotesquely misplaced consideration for Aboriginal claims to their own past, one historian (Professor John Molony) just about omitted their part in the story altogether;[10] at the other end of a spectrum was a researcher so shocked and distressed as he uncovered the realities of the Waterloo Creek Massacre of 1837–1838 that he wrote and wrote until his manuscript bulged with 640,000 words.[11] The first learned journal in the field, launched in 1977 (opening article by W.E.H. Stanner), carried the title *Aboriginal History*, suggesting that its founders had not shed anthropology's habit of looking at *them* rather than our relations with them. For many new entrants the impulse was to follow Rowley in angry exposé rather than to try to understand the bafflingly complicated relationship between black and white. For this they were arraigned by those who had been there longer and thought harder. Historical anthropologist (and Stanner's former student) Diane Barwick rebuked writers who 'ignore, or else dismiss as turncoats, "trusties" and "Uncle Toms", those Aboriginal men and women who were apparently willing to negotiate with the invaders',[12] while Henry Reynolds criticised those for whom the worse the story, the better.[13] Some Aboriginal historians – Aboriginal historians! – argued that only Aboriginal people could write their story, a position emphatically rejected by Mulvaney.[14]

Intense scholarly debate belonged to a field that was booming as well as transforming itself. An expanding and increasingly youthful history discipline joined the rush to study the Aboriginal universe and experience. By the mid-1980s the Australian Institute for Aboriginal and Torres Strait Islander Studies (AIATSIS) housed more than 5000 books, 4000 pamphlets, 150,000 photographs, 250 films and 14,000 language and music tapes.[15] Specifically historical publications in the fifteen years to 1984 included nine general histories, ten documentary collections and a large number of biographies, autobiographies and specialist histories. All this belonged in turn to a remarkable upwelling in Australian culture in which an Aboriginal renaissance played an equally remarkable part. Henry Reynolds later recalled meeting singers, composers, painters, poets and filmmakers who told him how much they had learned from his book.[16] When he visited an Aboriginal community in Far North Queensland, an old man there showed Reynolds his copy of *The Other Side*. 'I had never seen a book so worn and so used,' Reynolds said. 'It had been passed around the whole community. Almost everyone had read it or had it read to them.'[17]

An Australian Bicentennial Authority (ABA), formed in anticipation of 1988, was a creature of these heady days. It decided to take a 'warts and all' approach and promote a year-long reflection on the national identity.[18] It earmarked funds for a special Aboriginal program and declined to support a re-enactment of the First Fleet on the grounds it would give offence to Aboriginal people. In the ABA's mind, history would play a central role in the Bicentennial. It supported the historians in their efforts to uncover uncomfortable truths and wanted 'special and extended treatment' given to Aboriginal people.[19] 'I for one would not want to be involved in a Bicentennial that does not address the running sore of black/white relations in this country,' declared the ABA's director, Dr Bruce Armstrong, adding for emphasis that he would have nothing to do with 'a white wank'.[20] The historians signed up for an eleven-volume history, *Australians: A Historical Library*, and were key contributors to an all-encompassing *Encyclopedia of the Australian People* as well.[21] Another four volumes *(A Peoples' History of Australia)* were compiled by younger historians who saw in the Establishment's plans an updated Triumph-and-Progress story, rather than a decisive break with the celebratory and the silent.

In 1983 another star aligned: Labor returned to office in Canberra, full of plans to complete the work begun by Whitlam a decade before.[22] There was talk of new programs for Aboriginal well-being and empowerment, of national land rights and sacred sites legislation, even of a treaty. Things were going so swimmingly that in 1984 the newly prominent historian Henry Reynolds gave an address in London in which he felt able to conclude that the silence had been 'shattered' and that the cult of forgetfulness was being abandoned.[23] 'Slowly, unevenly, often with difficulty,' he said, 'white Australians are incorporating the black experience into their image of the national past.'

'Shattered' is a seductive figure of speech, suggesting a once-and-for-all blow struck by the scholars. In fact, the silence wasn't shattered even among the historians, and it wasn't a single vessel. The story did have to be recovered, told and heard, but it also had to be understood, accepted and acted upon. As Reynolds was declaring white Australians to be incorporating the black experience into our image of the national past, powerful organisations were encouraging us to do the opposite.[24]

•

In July 1984, just months after Reynolds' London speech, two ministers in the new Labor government made the short journey to the annual mining industry conference in Canberra. Their mission was to explain to the miners what the government would be doing about national land rights legislation, sacred sites, national parks, and a treaty with the Aboriginal people. That done, the ministers resumed their seats to listen as Hugh Morgan, immediate past president of the Australian Mining Industry Council (AMIC), delivered a response on behalf of the industry.[25]

'Mr Holding and Mr Cohen have spoken to us today as Ministers of the Crown,' Morgan began. 'They have used language which is conciliatory, persuasive, reasonable. Because of the conciliatory tone of the Ministers I have a heavy duty of care in … response.' Holding and Cohen must have been given pause by the calculated menace of these opening words; Morgan later boasted that as he spoke he could sense the ministers behind him passing from barely contained rage to white-hot anger.[26] The legitimacy of the mining industry had been brought into question by the government and others, Morgan continued. This the industry rejected; it could in fact claim a higher legitimacy from the Christian tradition in general and St Paul specifically. The Territory legislation was perverse and counter-productive; it had brought exploration in the Territory to a complete standstill, a mistake since compounded by the 'cancerous' growth of national parks.[27] The government's support for

'The calculated menace of these opening words'

the legitimacy of Aboriginal claims was profoundly in error. Australian law, which derived from a more humane tradition than the Aboriginal, protected 'Aboriginal girls who seek to escape from the fate of tribal law and custom'. Vengeance killings, said Morgan, citing Blainey's *Triumph of the Nomads*, 'exacted a far greater toll on the Aboriginal population in the nineteenth century than any depredations by the Europeans'. Accounts of clashes between Europeans and Aborigines, particularly in Queensland, 'are quite explicit concerning the partiality of Aborigines for the particular flavour of the Chinese, who were killed and eaten in large numbers'. 'We cannot sanction,' Morgan told the ministers on behalf of that civilising force, the miners, 'infanticide, cannibalism and the cruel initiation rites which you regard as either customary or as a matter of religious obligation.'

Morgan's notorious speech signalled a sustained effort to capture both the high intellectual ground and popular opinion. The latter began with a TV campaign in Western Australia that included an ad showing black hands building a wall across a map of the state and posting a sign: 'Keep Out – this part of Western Australia is under Aboriginal land claim'.[28] The campaign quickly generated a dramatic collapse in public support for land rights. The battle for the intellectual high ground was fought particularly by the Institute for Public Affairs (IPA), a think-tank supported by the miners, and by its *IPA Review*. The *Review* carried one attack after another on the intellectual and cultural underpinnings of policy since Hasluck's time, culminating in a devastating assault on the Australian Bicentennial Authority and all that it stood for. The difference between the ABA's world view and that of ordinary Australians was so stark in the *Review*'s mind that it could be summarised in a two-column table.[29] On one side ('Current Bicentennial Programme') was multiculturalism, religious diversity, Aboriginal culture, women's activities, and the like; on the other ('Themes Ignored') was the Australian achievement, Christian tradition, the Anzacs, our British heritage, the family, private enterprise. The ABA stood for the former and against the latter, the IPA alleged; it should do the reverse.

The miners were joined in their hostility by governments in Western Australia and Queensland, beholden to frontier-zone resources and armed by the tearaway success of the anti–land rights TV campaign. Shocked, the national government beat a humiliating retreat.[30] The prime minister promised that national land rights legislation would not give Aboriginal landholders a veto over mining on their land, and then abandoned the legislation altogether, along with any talk about a treaty. The director of the ABA who wanted no part of a 'white wank' was granted his wish. He was sacked. His chairman followed soon after. In light of this increasingly bitter contention and of the exemplary execution of its former leaders, the ABA took refuge in schmaltz.[31] It ran a mawkish jingle ('Let's lend a hand/And show the world/How great we all can be/All those years/of sweat and tears/It's our Bicentenary'), released a torrent of merch ranging from watches and placemats to a boomerang 'flight-tested and guaranteed to return if thrown according to simple instructions', and decided that the tall ships idea had merit after all. The historians' many bicentennial volumes, along with the year of national reflection, were all overshadowed by a single day. On 26 January 1988 somewhere between one and two million people (estimates vary) and 10,000 boats crowded Sydney Harbour and its foreshores to see the tall ships sail through the heads.

Against the resurgence of the story we had all grown up with, the Aboriginal people struggled to remind us of that other story.[32] Activist Burnum Burnum landed at Dover, hoisted the Aboriginal flag and claimed England for his nation. Another activist suggested that the song 'Celebration of a Nation' might be more accurately called 'Masturbation of a Nation'.[33] Yet another grabbed a copy of Moloney's Aboriginal-lite

Sydney Harbour, Invasion Day (26 January 1988)

history as it was being launched by the prime minister and chucked it into the harbour. And on the big day, somewhere between 15,000 and 50,000 Aboriginal people (these estimates also vary) marched from the ghettos of Redfern to Mrs Macquarie's Chair, overlooking the harbour and the spot where 200 years ago Governor Phillip had come ashore. Every category of that fractured world was represented there, painted-up 'bushies' from the far corners of the frontier north, angry young men from Redfern, the dancers, singers, filmmakers, poets, sportspeople of the renaissance, the national figures, the kids, all there as Aboriginal Australians marching behind the biggest of the many banners: *LAND RIGHTS NOW.*

•

As hopes for the Bicentennial and for national federal land rights legislation began to fade, Eddie Mabo and Henry Reynolds were hard at work on a different line of attack. They wanted to narrow the gap between historical fact and Justice Blackburn's legal fiction. Their work, joint and several, forged one of the great collaborations between black and white in Australia's history.

Both Mabo and Reynolds had been formed by their passage to Townsville. Mabo was twenty-one years old when he left the tiny islands of the Torres Strait in 1957 for Townsville, 1000 kilometres south.[34] He had grown up on Murray Island and lived there under the Queensland government's old-style colonial regime.[35] In Townsville that same regime was fighting for its life against activists, black and white, fired by the contradiction between equal rights talk and the reality of black lives. Equipped with no sense of inferiority whatsoever, a fiery temperament and excellent English, Mabo was incensed by Townsville's virulent racism. A young working-class black man employed successively in the canefields, as a fettler on the railways, as a labourer at the port and as a groundsman at the university, he was soon into everything. He joined a union and the Aborigines Advancement League and quickly became a leader in campaigns for housing, health services, legal services and a school for black kids. With that came meetings, committees and conferences, including in 1967 an 'inter-racial' conference called 'We the Australians: What Is to Follow the Referendum?' Among those involved was a young academic still new to Townsville, Henry Reynolds.

Reynolds' translation was if anything even more dramatic and formative than Mabo's.[36] He had been in London doing postgrad work when he got an unexpected job offer from Townsville University College. After a certain amount of equivocation, he and his wife, Margaret, embodiments of the tender conscience of the post-frontier, decided that they would go to Townsville, not least because it would be a chance to 'do something for the Aborigines'. The exotic and picturesque Townsville of their imagining turned out to be dry, scruffy, violent and dark with hatreds from a terrible past. On a Sunday walk along the beach with their children and the dog, Henry and Margaret were approached by a young Aboriginal man; as he drew level, Reynolds records, the young man took two quick steps toward them and kicked the dog with great force. 'It was a history lesson of the most powerful kind, more telling than any amount of research in the archives,' he later said.

Reynolds had arrived in Townsville in 1965 with his head full of his discipline's reigning orthodoxies, particularly the romance of Russel Ward's *The Australian Legend*, and that was what he taught. But his daily round was taking him back and forth between a post-frontier enclave and the frontier's heart of darkness. Life and activism in Townsville turned him into one of the young historians of Stanner's hopes, working to end the silence. At one of those conferences beloved of activists, Henry Reynolds met Eddie Mabo. And when Eddie took the job as a groundsman at the university, he, Henry and Noel Loos, a postgrad student of Reynolds, often had a brown-bag lunch together. At some point Loos and Reynolds realised that Mabo didn't know that he didn't own his own land. Mabo's attachment to that land was so obvious and so intense, Reynolds recalled, that they didn't know whether they should tell him that it belonged to the government, not him. They decided that they couldn't *not* tell him, and so at another lunch Reynolds did tell him. 'It was as though I had punched him in the face. He looked angry, aghast, incredulous.' And that, Reynolds says, was the first step toward the *Mabo* judgement twenty years later. In 1982 the Murray Islanders' claim began its winding journey back and forth between Queensland's Supreme Court and the High Court of Australia to its eventual and triumphant conclusion in 1992.

In the days following the lunch of legend with Mabo and Loos, Reynolds was almost as distressed as his friend and for the first time started rummaging around in the history of 'native title'. He had a half-recollection from his undergraduate days that the US Supreme Court had recognised native title in a way that might apply to the Murray

Islanders. He'd checked with his head of department, an Americanist, and yes, that was indeed the case. Since Mabo's Meriam people owned land as members of a family, as had native Americans, the US precedent might be applied to the Australian case.

Reynolds reported his findings to Mabo, who was from then until the end of his life, Reynolds says, 'consumed' by the campaign for land rights, but not, it should be emphasised, to the exclusion of all else. Mabo kept working across a remarkably broad range of portfolios: housing, legal aid, schooling, health services, industrial relations, art and 'culture'. He was an intellectual in the precise sense of the term, said Reynolds, and not just because he spent lunchtimes in the university library studying reports of the 1898 Haddon expedition to the Torres Strait islands – his islands.[37] Through his obsessive work with and for his people, Mabo was mastering the whitefella's intellectual idioms and turning himself into an 'organic' intellectual.[38] In this Mabo had a number of predecessors – Stanner had listed some of them in his Boyer lectures, David Unaipon, Douglas Nicholls, Dexter Daniels and others – but many more contemporaries and peers. His work took him first to Brisbane and then to the national capital and beyond. There he met others who were doing what he was doing. No longer more or less isolated figures connected by filaments stretched from one generation or place to another, these Aboriginal and Torres Strait Islander 'activists' now belonged to a dense web of relationships. They were constituting themselves as intellectuals organic to a people-in-formation.

Should Henry Reynolds be thought of as an 'organic' intellectual? He had in common with Eddie Mabo intellectual formation in and through political work – it was activism that led to a changed historical outlook, he later said, not the other way around. But he had come to that change from work and training as a more familiar kind of intellectual, and it was in that mode that he continued. Now alive to the significance and importance of the law in the history of relations between black and white, Reynolds was back in the archives. He had worked his way out of the 'image of the national past' he'd brought with him to Townsville and was settling into a perspective and a method sustained over the rest of a long career. The perspective was very like Stanner's and owed a good deal to it: the story is not of obliteration of one side by the other but of an ongoing, complex relationship, including both extensive collaboration and terrible violence. The method was not to construct a smooth narrative of place or theme in the usual way, but to assemble a mass of documentary evidence on an issue or topic: how 'settlement' looked from the other side; the nature of dispossession; Aboriginal people as Australian pioneers; the character and role of conscience; the question of Aboriginal sovereignty and the even more charged question of genocide; the experience of people of mixed race – and the history of the law of native title, in Australia and in those other anglophone 'settler' societies, New Zealand, Canada and the United States. Reynolds has been accused of several epistemological offences, including 'presentism', the subordination of disinterested discovery to a search for those parts that might serve present-day purposes. It is difficult to see where the conflict or trade-off lies; his questions opened formerly closed historians' eyes as much as his answers prompted action.

In *The Law of the Land* (1987) Reynolds laid out his findings, not altogether different from the propositions put by Woodward QC to a startled Mr Justice Blackburn: international law of the eighteenth and nineteenth centuries did not give the British a licence to dispose of land as they wished; the celebrated claims on the continent made by Lieutenant James Cook and Captain Arthur Phillip were warnings to other colonial powers to keep out, not claims to ownership of the land in question, and applied to only part of the continent anyway; governments in London and in Australia had subsequently acknowledged the reality of Aboriginal ownership of land when they set aside reserves for particular groups (such as the Warumungu at Tennant Creek), or used funds from land sales for Aboriginal welfare, or designed 'pastoral leases' that gave carefully delimited access to both black inhabitants and white leaseholders.[39] British law was, moreover, accommodating of very different forms of title to land. It regarded property as more sacred than life itself, and it claimed to regard Aboriginal people as British subjects entitled to the protection of the law. And yet, and yet: all this notwithstanding, ways had been found to deprive the Aboriginal peoples at a stroke of just about everything they owned.

How? How could it be, Reynolds wanted to know, that from the middle of the nineteenth century or even earlier there had been little disagreement from any point on the legal or political spectrum that 'discovery had delivered to the Europeans not just sovereignty but the ownership of every inch of land as well'; that Australia was a colony 'of settlement not conquest'; that such 'ameliorative measures' as had been taken did not imply any acceptance of land rights?[40] Where had the Crown's case in *Milirrpum v Nabalco* come from? Why were Woodward's counterarguments in that same case so startling to Mr Justice Blackburn?

Reynolds found his answer in 'an amazing achievement' of a specifically Australian jurisprudence, quite different from and often at odds with the jurisprudence of New Zealand, Canada, the United States, South Africa and the Mother Country itself. Under immense pressure from land hunger, from soaring rewards of land ownership, and from fierce resistance to 'outside influence', colonial governments and courts had avoided, overlooked and then forgotten inconvenient laws, precedents and Colonial Office directions. 'In English humanitarian circles,' Reynolds records, 'Aboriginal rights meant native title, in the colonies they meant blankets, rations and protection from the cruder forms of violence ... In England the Protectors were to see that the indigenes weren't cheated out of their land. In Australia their role was seen as controlling the Aboriginal "nuisance" and limiting the spread of frontier violence.'[41] London had been unable to bring the colonial governments into line because the colonial governments couldn't control the squatters. In the late 1880s a case was brought to the Privy Council, at that time the Australian colonies' highest court of appeal, which found that Australia had been 'practically unoccupied [and] without settled inhabitants', thus inserting the silence into the heart of Australian law. It turned colonial practice from Richard Windeyer's day in the 1840s into the legal doctrine later described as *terra nullius*. This was the precedent Mr Justice Blackburn dared not overturn, and that the High Court, twenty years later, did overturn.

One thread in the vast literature on *Mabo*, or in that small fraction of it that I encountered anyway, concerns what it was that caused six of the seven judges of the High Court to do what Woodward had unsuccessfully urged Blackburn to do twenty years earlier.[42] A second thread debates whether and in what way the historians could take the blame or credit. A third, accepting that they could, wonders which aspect of their work weighed most heavily in the judicial mind. Did the story recovered by the historians force a kind of moral crisis in which the judges dared not – or would not want to – follow Blackburn down the farcical rabbit hole? Or were they persuaded by Henry Reynolds' exposé of their own history, advanced as it was in 'a style of reasoning' that they could understand and use?[43]

For a start, Mr Justice Blackburn had to worry about appeals but the High Court didn't. Its decisions were final. For another, this was no longer Barwick's High Court. All seven judges had entered the profession and commenced their ascent during the 1950s and 1960s. Like Hal Wootten and Ted Woodward, they had been formed in the silence then shocked out of it,[44] by the Aboriginal insurgency, by the historians' recovered story, and by the findings of a royal commission into Aboriginal deaths in custody.[45] Two of the six had previously been active in the Aboriginal cause, Gerard Brennan representing the Northern Land Council at the Woodward Royal Commission into land rights, and John Toohey in Western Australia's Aboriginal Legal Service and as the first head of the Territory's Aboriginal Lands Commission. Another, Mary Gaudron, grew up in Moree, as featured in the famous Freedom Ride; her knowledge of discrimination there was subsequently fortified by a rich experience of discrimination at the hands of an overwhelmingly masculine profession. Two others (William Deane and Michael McHugh) were social progressives of long standing. The sixth, the chief justice himself, started out as a conservative but led the High Court's shift away from the strict legalism of the Barwick era.

It appears that individual judges were moved to differing extents by different elements of the historians' work. Justices Gaudron and Deane spoke of 'unutterable shame'; others seem to have found arguments addressing the history of the law more compelling. Whatever the specifics, with *Mabo*, scholarly history moved from the periphery of the legal process – to which it had been relegated in the *Aboriginal Land Rights (Northern Territory) Act 1976* and 'Blackburn' – to its very centre. In the doing, both scholarly history and the law played crucial roles in the incorporation of the Aboriginal account in the new story, the historians through extensive use of 'oral history', the courts by hearing, recording and accepting Aboriginal testimony. Ultimately, the High Court believed Eddie Mabo. It also did what the historians couldn't: it *acted* on what it had heard.

Mabo, like the Commonwealth's Northern Territory legislation, delivered land rights, but did so in a fundamentally different way. The Territory legislation was a form of *noblesse oblige*, implying that rights

'The High Court believed Eddie Mabo':
Mabo with fellow plaintiffs and their lawyer

were being granted where none had existed. *Mabo*, by contrast, found that the rights had always been there and had long been denied.[46] Native title was one of those facts over which the great Australian silence had reigned. Henry Reynolds claimed with justifiable pride (and perhaps a little exaggeration) that *Mabo* changed Australia's story about itself.[47] Before *Mabo*, he said, the 'explorers' and 'settlers' were on Crown land with as much right to be there as the resident Aboriginal population. But after? The entire continent had been in the possession of Indigenous nations. They were entitled in law to defend their acknowledged rights and property. The Aboriginal peoples 'either once were or still are landowners, with … all the protection provided by the common law famous for its defence of private property'.

Mabo was a splendid comeback from the drubbings that culminated in the Bicentennial. But, like the Warumungu claim, it also came with a longish list of drawbacks and compromises: the whitefellas doing the deciding, in their way; a drawn-out, expensive lawyers' picnic;[48] a process of material service only to those Aboriginal people who still had land to claim, with no compensation for the rest; possession as nine-tenths of the law, with the possible exception of pastoral leases; the continent had been discovered and settled, not conquered; the federal government did have the power to extinguish native title; and, looming above all, the question of Aboriginal sovereignty was out of bounds. *Mabo* put an end to one of the greatest of the law's silences, but only one.

There are other scratches on the polished *Mabo* surface.[49] Eddie Mabo and his co-claimants were Melanesian, not Aboriginal; Aboriginal rights to land didn't strictly follow, but were granted by the High Court anyway. As pugnacious as he was courageous and resolute, Mabo was at daggers drawn with a fair proportion of his fellow mainland activists and with many of his fellow Murray Islanders as well. The Islanders were, according to one authority, among the most litigious people in the world, thanks not least to their distinctive system of land tenure (the original thirty-six *Mabo* claims were met by no less than nineteen counterclaims).[50] It should also be said that the extraordinary symbolic importance accorded *Mabo* has overshadowed the achievement of Ted Woodward QC and the Yolngu witnesses in getting Mr Justice Blackburn to concede that Aboriginal peoples did indeed have a system of land ownership, well recognised in Aboriginal law. That was one half of *terra nullius* dispatched. The High Court had only to take the next step, to get the white law to recognise the existence of the black.

Eddie Mabo did not live to see his triumph; he died a few months before the High Court handed down its decision. The headstone of his grave in Townsville was defaced within hours of its unveiling, a perverse tribute to the young man from Mer. Another of *Mabo*'s forebears didn't see it either. Bill Stanner died in 1981, of Parkinson's, but not before he made one last trip to be with the people he first met in 1932, and to return sacred paraphernalia he had been given as a young man. There he was honoured as one who 'had "stood up" for blackfellows about land rights' and as one of last two old men who had witnessed an important sacred, secret ceremony.[51] Stanner's great adversary, Paul Hasluck, did live to see *Mabo*, perhaps to his chagrin. Retired to Perth, he wrote more books, the last his unrepentant *Shades of Darkness*. He died in 1993, covered in imperial honours.

In *Mabo* the High Court pronounced upon the law as it had descended from the past. What that decision would mean for the future had to be settled elsewhere. That it became a signal moment in the struggle to dismantle the silence owes much to another of the great collaborations between black and white.

•

Paul Keating said scathingly of his prime ministerial predecessor that he would weep for the Aboriginal people but he wouldn't do anything for them.[52] It's hard to imagine Keating weeping over the Aboriginal people or anyone else, but unlike his predecessor he certainly went into bat for them and with them in one of the most ferocious controversies in Australia's history.[53] Almost violent disputation over *Mabo* flared within organisations, political parties and governments, as well as between them. It fuelled demands running all the way from Aboriginal sovereignty within a new Australian republic to the extinguishment of any and all Aboriginal claims to any land anywhere. Aboriginal activists threatened to claim the land on which capital cities stood; white activists inveighed against 'reverse apartheid' and special treatment for a racial group and talked about 'Stone Age Abos' who hadn't even invented the wheel. Even the means by which the dispute would be settled – a referendum? more litigation? legislation? – was itself hotly disputed.

Months into the fight, Keating announced that there would be a legislative resolution; he would deliver the national land rights legislation that had been squibbed by Whitlam, Fraser and Hawke. More months of meetings, forums, assemblies and conferences – and a federal election which against all expectations Keating won – all came down to a sitting of a knife-edge Senate that went deep into the night. Keating's bill was passed. Two hundred years after the Europeans started taking Aboriginal land, a hundred years after Cubadgee had hoped for an understanding with the whitefellas, sixty years after the government had tipped the Warumungu off their 'reserve' at the behest of the miners, twenty years after 'Blackburn' let it do the same to the Yolngu, the government had turned against its own history. The new law differed in several respects from the Territory legislation, and it left unresolved the status of pastoral leases (later settled by the High Court's *Wik* decision), but Aboriginal rights to land – albeit limited, hedged and qualified in myriad ways – now applied across the country. Within six years of *Mabo* more than 1200 agreements had been struck between Indigenous groups and miners, pastoralists, industry bodies and governments; by 2002, ten years on, the total exceeded 3000.[54]

That victory for the Aboriginal people was also a victory by them. They could never have succeeded without the 'sympathetic' whitefellas, the voices of the post-frontier conscience, the academics, the lawyers, the churches and unions and community organisations, most of the politicians of the Labor Party and a few from the Liberal Party (but none from the National Party). But the converse is also true. This time the Aboriginal people weren't just noises offstage. They had organised political strength and sheer intellectual horsepower. Their organic intellectuals, many close to being household names – Pat Dodson, Mick Dodson, Marcia Langton, Lowitja (Lois) O'Donoghue, Noel Pearson, Galarrwuy Yunupingu – could go toe to toe with the miners, the pundits of the conservative parties and the Murdoch media and, when needed, with the federal government and its prime minister. Years later Keating spoke with his usual eloquence of his collaboration with these people in *Mabo*. It was markedly less tumultuous in his recollection than it had been in fact. He had been stung and taxed by their demands and refusals. But it was these demands and refusals, as well as their support, that allowed Keating to sail closer to the line of his own convictions. He was of their cause.

Keating made three great speeches between early 1992 and late 1993: the first before the *Mabo* decision, one not long after it, and a third as the controversy approached its almost melodramatic denouement.[55] On Anzac Day in 1992 Keating was at Kokoda, in Papua New Guinea. There in the course of his speech he abruptly knelt and kissed the ground on which Australian soldiers had died in 1942 in the battle to arrest the Japanese advance. On Remembrance Day of the following year, he spoke at the funeral service for the Unknown Soldier. 'We do not know this Australian's name ... We know that he was one of the 45,000 Australians who died on the Western Front ... He is all of them. And he is one of us.'

These two speeches bracketed the third, at Redfern, the most celebrated of them all. One passage from early on has been quoted over and over again, and in delivery it switched his audience from being present to being riveted. It was all a matter of recognition, Keating said, 'recognition that it was we who did the dispossessing. We took the traditional lands and smashed the traditional way of life. We brought the diseases. The alcohol. We committed the murders. We took the children from their mothers. We practised discrimination and exclusion ... And [it was] our failure to imagine these things being done to us.' The fifteen-minute speech used the words 'history' or 'historic' eight times, 'justice' or 'injustice' thirteen times. It listed the injustices done by our histories as well as our history – the fictions that the continent had no owners before us, that it was we who did the exploring and the pioneering all by ourselves, that the Aboriginal people had given it all up without a fight. There were no qualifications in Keating's speech, no weasel words, no blame-shifting. They were words without precedent or, sad to say, sequel.

In these speeches as well as in the *Mabo* legislation, Keating was trying to herd the four cats of Australia's storytelling – the legal, the scholarly, the Aboriginal and the popular – toward a broadly common understanding of the national story. Three of those four had collaborated to make *Mabo*; he would use the fourth to go one crucial step further. Among the many furious disagreements that swirled around *Mabo* was whether its resolution should focus on land or be broadened to include 'reconciliation'. Keating insisted on the larger view. He had also concluded that there could be no reconciliation of peoples while they told unreconciled stories about themselves and each other. At Kokoda, at Redfern and at the tomb of the Unknown Soldier, he tried to weld the foundational story of the Australian 'nation' to the story that it had excluded and suppressed. Even had he stayed in office, the struggle between those trying to dismantle the silence and those defending it would have rolled on. But he didn't stay in office.

CHAPTER NINE

2000

Howard was, like Keating, a history buff and, like Keating, acutely aware of the political uses of history. Keating wanted to draw the story of relations between black and white into the heart of the national story, knowing that it would make the Tories – a pejorative he loved to employ – look hard-hearted, out of touch and lacking in vision. Howard wanted to keep the history of race relations on the fringes of the national story, knowing that would diminish Labor and sustain his political base. Howard, like Keating, had all the resources and powers of office at his disposal, but he had them for eleven years, not four. Keating had enjoyed the broad support of the Aboriginal leadership; Howard expected its opposition, but halfway through his eleven years the leadership split and Howard made an ally of the most prominent of Aboriginal leaders, Noel Pearson. Keating had a house historian, and so did Howard. Through his historian-speechwriter Don Watson, Keating's lineage could be traced back through Henry Reynolds and many others to Stanner. Howard's guru was Geoffrey Blainey, heir to Hasluck.[1]

I sometimes see Blainey on Saturday mornings in Melbourne's Queen Vic market, his corona of wispy white hair and hint of a quizzical smile making him look like a panto wizard who has wandered onto the wrong stage, often chatting amiably with a stallholder with no hint of condescension on the part of Australia's greatest living historian.[2] It is hard to reconcile this diffident figure, 'approachable, supportive and entirely without affectation', as one of his former colleagues wrote,[3] with the author of often strident polemics for right-wing causes, including restricted Asian immigration and opposition to Aboriginal land rights, the environmental movement, trade unions, 'judicial activism', and an Australian republic.[4] In 1993, in the wake of *Mabo*, Blainey gave a speech to an august audience in which he argued that two versions of Australia's history now contended: the 'three cheers' version, which had been too favourable, too self-congratulatory, and the 'black armband' version, 'an opposite extreme that is even more unreal and decidedly jaundiced'.[5] That phrase, 'black armband', provided the once and future Leader of the Opposition John Howard with his compass.[6] Blainey's low-key authority and unrivalled prestige lent weight to Howard's campaigns and gave him the confidence to assert that the story he'd grown up with *was* the story, but Blainey's most important contribution was the idea of 'balance'. Yes, the treatment of Aboriginal people was a blemish, but a blemish on a story overwhelmingly of progress and triumph.[7]

Howard's drive as prime minister to control the story ranged even more widely than Keating's. He seems to have taken a leaf out of the Territory's book. There conservative governments had promoted 'Territorianism' via a government History Unit, a History Award, an oral history program featuring Territory old-timers, the Museum and Art Gallery of the Northern Territory, and the preservation of Heritage Sites such as Tennant Creek's Battery Hill and the old telegraph station. The Territory's conservatives understood that the story had to be won on every field, and so did Howard.[8] But for all its length and breadth, Howard's war was, like Keating's, dominated by a single issue. For Keating it had been the taking of land; for Howard, it was the taking of children.

•

On a winter's afternoon in 1947 a green Bedford truck, driven by an officer of the Native Affairs Branch and carrying an officer of the Aborigines Inland Mission (AIM), arrived at Phillip Creek.[9] What had it brought, or come for? The following morning sixteen children – all 'half-caste', none older than nine years, one not much more than a baby – were loaded onto the truck. There had been talk of a picnic, but somehow the children and the small crowd of adults and 'full-blood' children knew or had realised that the truck was taking the children away. Terrible scenes ensued – children howling, women wailing and beating themselves with digging sticks until the blood ran. 'They didn't tell us they were gone [forever],' Edith Graham Nakamarra told me. 'There was a lot of crying for that. After that the dormitory, the half-caste one, that one just empty.' The children were taken from Phillip Creek to another AIM establishment, in Darwin, 700-odd miles away. Some returned to live in Tennant Creek years later, others never. Among those who did not return was Lorna Nelson Napanangka.

Almost fifty years later Lorna Nelson, now Mrs Lorna Cubillo, was among the 500 people, many of them raised in institutions, who attended the Going Home Conference in Darwin. There they heard a leading QC suggest that those who had been taken as children in the Northern Territory might have a claim on the Commonwealth. Two years on, Mrs Cubillo was one of two complainants in a case filed with the High Court and referred by it to the Federal Court. The case concerned a great injustice done by the Commonwealth of Australia to two of its citizens, Cubillo's counsel told the court.[10] '[They] were removed as young children from their families and communities. They were taken hundreds of kilometres from the countries of their birth. They were prevented from returning. They were made to live among strangers, in a strange place, in institutions which bore no resemblance to a home. They lost ... the chance to grow among the warmth of their own people, speaking their people's languages and learning about their country. They suffered lasting psychiatric injury. They were treated as orphans when they were not orphans ... Decades later, the Commonwealth says ... that it did them no wrong at all.'

Less threatening to material interests than *Mabo*, *Cubillo* was more threatening to most Australians' sense of themselves. To take children from their families was to trespass on the most fundamental of human relationships. For many Aboriginal people, the taking of land belonged to a half-remembered past; the taking of children was a living memory, widespread and intensely painful.[11]

The case was conducted on an almost epic scale.[12] Preliminary proceedings determined that, yes, the case should go ahead. Hearings in seven centres (including Tennant Creek) occupied a total of 106 sitting days between March 1999 and May 2000. Mr Justice O'Loughlin's summary and reasons for judgement ran to 485 pages of close narrative, analysis and argument. It was, an appeals court later said, a 'case of great factual and legal complexity'. It was of even greater import. Waiting on the outcome were more than 2000 claims from people who had been removed as children and from *their* children, to a total estimated in the hundreds of millions of dollars.[13] Assimilationism was on trial and so therefore was its patron saint, Paul Hasluck, even though the events in question came before his time as minister. As in 'Blackburn' nearly thirty years earlier, the Coalition government did everything in its power to defeat the Aboriginal claim.[14] It outlaid $11 million on the case, around five times the amount available to the Cubillo team. Three-quarters of a million of the Commonwealth spend went on private investigators to 'dig up the dirt on the claimants'. The Commonwealth engaged to lead its case a QC strongly identified with the right. Sentiment on the Labor side was with the claimants; one of Cubillo's two QCs was later a senior member of the Rudd and Gillard governments.

Media coverage in Australia and overseas was extensive.[15]

By the time Cubillo at last came to judgement, its symbolic and political freight had multiplied thanks to the sensational *Bringing Them Home* report.[16] Over twelve months from late 1995, the National Inquiry into the Separation of Aboriginal and Torres Strait Islander Children from Their Families visited more than fifty centres from Broome to Redfern, from Cape Barren Island to the Torres Strait, to hear more than 500 people tell of their own removal and their subsequent lives. The inquiry delved into the history of child removal, attempted to estimate its scale and impact and made recommendations for a substantial national response, including acknowledgement and apology, guarantee against repetition, measures of restitution and of rehabilitation, and monetary compensation. Its findings triggered an emotional outpouring.[17] The Leader of the Opposition wept as he addressed the parliament; hundreds of thousands of people signed 'sorry' books.

The government was in a quandary.[18] This wasn't its inquiry. To the contrary, it had been commissioned by the preceding Keating government, reason in itself for a cool response (which included refusing to top up the inquiry's miserable funding). Another difficulty lay in the government's own contradictory feelings on the matter. Some of its members were distressed by the report's revelations, others were sceptical or straight-out hostile. Unsurprisingly, the government wanted to do as little as possible while being seen to do something, but even that solution contained difficulties.[19] Pauline Hanson had come into parliament along with the Howard majority. There were now a million truculent white votes up for grabs; the frontier north was reminding the post-frontier south that it was still there.[20]

For the right-wing intelligentsia, the *Bringing Them Home* report was incendiary. One aggravation was the government's insufficiently hostile response. Another was the widespread sympathy for the 'Stolen Generations'. A third was the sensational finding that under international law and conventions Australia had been guilty of genocide.[21] That finding would have exposed the inquiry to attack even from its many sympathisers, but it was further exposed by the several limitations of its proceedings and report.[22] Cautious in emphasising that removals had been made in a variety of ways and for a variety of reasons, and in stressing differences in the treatment of children and the impact on their lives, the report was exceedingly incautious in its estimate of numbers taken, and in its failure to distinguish clearly between prewar and postwar removals – the former eugenicist in motive, the latter with the child's welfare as the stated principle. The inquiry relied mainly on the testimonies of those who had been taken, no substitute – no matter how truthful and heart-rending – for evidence from others involved such as public servants, patrol officers, police officers and missionaries. That the inquiry was grossly underfunded and pressed to a very tight deadline was no defence against conservative outrage. One of several theatres of combat was the centre-right journal *Quadrant*. Editor Robert Manne was accused of running a leftist, pro-Aboriginal line and resigned. Under new management, *Quadrant* came to serve the anti–Stolen Generations campaign as the *IPA Review* had served the land rights blitzkrieg.

As the sometimes-hysterical controversy raged, Mr Justice O'Loughlin was threading his careful way through a mass of evidence and argument. Three years on from the release of *Bringing Them Home*, Cubillo was the hope of both sides. So much hung upon the outcome that when the judge had at last arrived at his conclusion, he took the unprecedented step of allowing its announcement to be televised. At the outset the facts had seemed obvious, but as the trial unfolded, much less so. Months before final submissions *Quadrant*'s new editor had the case 'point[ing] inexorably in the direction of a dismissal'.[23] The judge's opening lines gave the plaintiffs no cause for comfort. 'The applicants ... are said to be members of "the Stolen Generation",' Mr Justice O'Loughlin began.[24] 'Neither the evidence of this trial, nor the reasons for judgement, deny the existence of "the Stolen Generation". Numerous writings tell tragically of a distressing past.' Anyone familiar with the Warumungu land claim could see that Mr Justice O'Loughlin was following Mr Justice Maurice's example: unable to do historical justice, he was doing some history before doing what the law required. 'But this trial has focussed primarily on the personal histories of two people ... each of the claims that have been made ... must be dismissed.' Mrs Cubillo had not established that she was removed without the permission of a parent or guardian. She had been taken to Darwin out of consideration for her welfare and not because she was a 'half-caste' destined for assimilation.[25] And in any event it was the Northern Territory authorities who did the removing, not the Commonwealth. The case of Mrs Cubillo's co-claimant was quite different in key respects, the judge said, but conclusions as to the merits of that case were the same. Neither claimant was entitled to compensation or damages. The decision was appealed to the full bench of the Federal Court and lost; the High Court declined to hear a further appeal.

•

Cubillo was a defeat on several fronts. Aboriginal people had already seen the *Bringing Them Home* recommendations for an apology, for rehabilitation and for compensation watered down, ignored or refused. Now the hope that the law might acknowledge and compensate was gone as well.

For those wanting to dismantle the silence, *Cubillo* meant more than a loss of confidence and momentum. The triple alliance of Aboriginal,

legal and scholarly forces established in *Mabo* collapsed in bitter recrimination. Historians, who had done so much over decades to document
child removal, alleged that the lawyers couldn't see what was in front
of their noses *and* had refused to listen to those who could.[26] By what
sophistry had the court failed to appreciate the reality of Lorna Nelson
Napanangka's removal? White officials seeking, and Aboriginal mothers
giving, *permission*? When many of Phillip Creek's parents were refugees from the Coniston massacres less than twenty years before, and
when Aboriginal people were so afraid for their kids that mixed-race
children were darkened with charcoal whenever a 'government man'
was rumoured to be nearby? Sixteen children taken to a home purpose-
built for 'half-caste' children out of consideration for their *welfare*? By
a regime that took orders directly from the minister in Canberra, and
was so racialised that it maintained a system of 'welfare officers' for the
'half-castes' and 'patrol officers' for the 'real' Aboriginal people? As for
'the child's best interests' – as determined by people incapable of imagining anything but a white future, and as practised ever since Baldwin
Spencer appealed to the fig leaf of 'best interests' in his 1913 report to
the Commonwealth government – words fail!

Historian Peter Read, a pioneer in the use of 'oral history' to uncover
the grim history of child removal (and co-coiner of the phrase 'the Stolen
Generations'), was incensed by the law's wilful ignorance.[27] He had been
engaged by Cubillo's legal team to prepare an expert report, which he
did. It laid out in detail the historical circumstances that explained what
happened at Phillip Creek. That, he was told, was not what we need.
He redrafted his report, and that wasn't it either. It's not the historical
context we're after, he was told, just the facts. A second historian commissioned by Cubillo's team fared better, but to her cost. Ann McGrath
was asked to report on the extent to which the removal of Aboriginal
children was supported or accepted by the white Australia of the day.

McGrath compiled extensive evidence suggesting widespread community disquiet.[28] The flat opposition by Mrs Mary Ward at Banka Banka, and the distress of officers who actually had to do the removing, was cited. McGrath's reward was to be grilled for three days by a hostile QC on her discipline's dubious epistemology and its negligible claims to objectivity. The judge subsequently accepted her report, but nonetheless determined that child removal *did* reflect the values of the time, on which we should not presume to sit in judgement.[29]

McGrath and Read both published accounts of their experience, and McGrath co-edited one of four substantial volumes on how it was that two disciplined, evidence-based ways of establishing the truth could arrive at such divergent conclusions as to where it lay.[30] The historians argued – and this is a free translation – that the problem wasn't in *their* epistemology but in the law's, and particularly in its rigid rules of evidence and its unwillingness to accept expert reports in matters historical as it routinely did in, say, medical matters. We believe that the law should do better, concluded the editors of one volume. For the editors of another volume, *Cubillo* was an elegy for both 'a redemptive legal historiography', and for the stolen generations who relied upon it in their quest for justice'. The law and redemptive history, they concluded, are 'epistemologically incompatible'.[31]

The most informed of the lawyers' responses came from Hal Wootten. Thirty-five years on from his initiation into the realities of Aboriginal lives during the equal wages case, Wootten was as deeply engaged with the Aboriginal cause as with the law. We do not need to suppose defects in the legal concepts of truth, proof and evidence to understand why things have gone wrong, Wootten told the historians.[32] The problem is more institutional than epistemological, and more political than either. The Aboriginal search for redress in the taking of land and of children should never have been subject to adversarial judicial determination in the first place. The courts and their servants, the lawyers, are not equipped by background, experience or training to comprehend the issues brought before them, to which we can add that most such cases revolve around events decades in the past, leaving judges to grapple with lost records, faded memories and witnesses dead before the case is brought. The problem, Wootten concluded, lies not in the law but in the use to which it has been put, the 'relegation' (his term) of 'the search for an acceptable outcome to our country's relations with its Indigenous people' to the courts.

The estrangement of allies in the wake of defeat was bad enough. Worse was an all-out attack by those for whom *Cubillo* was a victory. Pauline Hanson took *Cubillo* as demonstrating that the *Bringing Them Home* report was a fiction; the prime minister thought that it vindicated his government's policies; and *Quadrant* organised a conference on the theme 'Truth and Sentimentality' to prosecute the historians for encouraging 'those Aboriginal leaders and white self-flagellators who prefer to tell a story of victimisation and blame, and demand a kind of ritual abasement of the white community before a version of history which is simply not supported by the evidence'.[33]

The evidence referred to came – or was represented as having come – from *Cubillo*, not the historians. In *Mabo* the law had been guilty of 'adventurism' and gross irresponsibility, but now it had returned to the one true proof against sentimentality, the facts and nothing but the facts. This epistemology was taken to its extreme by the most notorious (or celebrated) of the history warriors, Keith Windschuttle. Windschuttle had emerged from Sydney University in the 1960s as a first-class-honours history graduate and a member of one of the most dogmatic of the left's many sects, the Trots. He subsequently exchanged one closed intellectual system for another, nailing his new colours to the mast in *The Killing of History* (1994).[34] Far from renovating categories of understanding, as Stanner had urged, Windschuttle polished up the old ones and followed Hugh Morgan in scorning the very idea of cultural equivalence. Gifted by the historians with a handful of misquotes and misreadings of documentary evidence – errors in each instance favouring their own case – Windschuttle asserted that the story as 'recovered' was in fact 'fabricated'.

In the first of a projected three volumes on this theme, a history of relations between black and white in Tasmania, Windschuttle discounted any evidence other than written accounts by reputable eyewitnesses; represented cattle-spearing as the senseless destruction of property by criminals; and saw so-called warfare as the necessary defence of vulnerable settlers. A second book, on child removal, relied heavily and selectively on *Cubillo*. Windschuttle took the exact opposite course to that urged by Mr Justice O'Loughlin, conflating the verdict on the 'personal histories' of just two people with the history of child removal as a whole. Where the judge insisted that 'neither the evidence of this trial, nor the reasons for judgement, deny the existence of "the Stolen Generations"', Windschuttle used *Cubillo* to assert that 'there were *no* Stolen Generations' (emphasis in the original).[35] 'The real Australia would never have stooped so low as to try to eliminate the Aboriginal race by stealing its children,' he declared. 'Australia is not and never has been a country whose people would condone such practices.'

With few exceptions the history warriors were pundits rather than historians.[36] They had the heavy artillery of the Murdoch media at their disposal as well as high-level cover from the national government. But the historians had much the better ammunition. The conservative arguments for assimilation, cultural superiority and an enlightened sense of racial responsibility, given such intellectual and moral force by Hasluck back in the 1930s, had been tainted in defence of the pastoralists and miners who wanted open access to the reserves, much more than Hasluck had been prepared to allow, and further diminished by a refusal to confront a mass of evidence accumulated in the decades since Hasluck first reached his assimilationist conclusions. In Windschuttle's eventual assertion that racially based child removal didn't happen because it couldn't have happened, we're just not that kind of people, the conservative argument arrived at a preposterous dead end. But it took millions of words in conferences and seminars, in scholarly books and articles and in media polemic, to demonstrate that that was in fact the case. The historians were forced to go over and over again issues in evidence and interpretation settled in debates among themselves in the 1970s and 1980s before the attack on their account fizzled out. Fifteen years later, Windschuttle's third volume (volume two) is yet to appear.

With *Cubillo*, the law's contribution to dismantling the silence, beginning with 'Blackburn' and then the Northern Territory land rights legislation and culminating in *Mabo* and *Wik*, came to an ignominious end.[37] Four or five years on, the history wars fizzled to a close and the historians followed the lawyers into the wings. The pressing task now was not in recovering or defending the story but in getting it widely understood, accepted and acted upon. There was not much more the scholars could do about that. The people who had started it all with their bark petitions, and had driven it ever since with the help of their many allies, were left to do battle with official public history.

•

With Blainey as his guide and warrantor, John Howard was having a good war. He took every opportunity to assert that the events on which the 'black armband' historians liked to dwell were indeed mere blemishes on an overwhelmingly positive story of progress and achievement. Following Blainey in his call for 'balance', Howard spoke as if from the sensible centre, apart from both the right-wing maddies of the history wars and the gloom merchants of the left. He argued against those on his side who wanted to fight the High Court's *Wik* decision, but negotiated legislation that weakened its impact. He conceded, with apparent feeling, that the taking of children was the worst of the blemishes in our story, but used the considerable resources of government to thwart *Cubillo* and to delay, fudge or refuse the recommendations of the Stolen Generations inquiry. And he made solid gains in the ongoing campaign by conservative national governments to reassert Australia's official story, not only defending its symbols and rituals (the flag, the anthem, the national day) but also updating the national story and a national infrastructure of memory and commemoration.

I had thought that the kind of thing that got my dander up on the 'heritage highway' was an extraordinary concentration of winners' history, but that says more about the workings of an unnoticed curriculum than about reality. Not long after my first trip north, I did an audit of public history in Sydney's Hyde Park and found there dozens of monuments, memorial gardens, fountains and the like. Almost all were to do with our loss, sacrifice and valour in war, the struggles of our explorers and pioneers, and the sagacity of our civic leaders. Of the 97.8 per cent of human affairs conducted in that place, or the many hundreds of generations who made their lives where Hyde Park now stands, on what happened in our obtaining of it, and on what became of the 'dispossessed', not a word or stone was spent.[38]

Hyde Park (like the heritage highway) is intensely concentrated but nonetheless representative. Australia boasts tens of thousands of obelisks, statues, plaques, headstones, cairns and honour boards – 34,232 of them, according to the estimable Monument Australia website[39] – in which Aboriginal people and relations between 'them' and 'us' get scarcely a nod.[40] Just 190 of those 34,232 markers of the past concern

Indigenous people, places or events, and less than a quarter of those (41) remember violence between black and white. Those who died in wars overseas, stretching from the Maori Wars to Afghanistan, do vastly better; what the Australian War Memorial calls 'places of pride' comprise one-quarter (8395) of the total.[41] The explorers and pioneers do better still (Lieutenant Cook alone gets 600-odd markers of one kind or another).

Explorers and pioneers were bumped aside by the Howard governments; they promoted warriors. They spent hundreds of millions on new and upgraded monuments and museums in Australia and overseas, turning the Anzac legend in a quasi-cult.[42] The Australian War Memorial emerged as a strange combination of theme park and temple. Anzac Cove, the site of the Gallipoli landing, became holy ground, complete with pilgrims. The other side of this coin was a discounting of the Aboriginal story and its telling. The Aboriginal voice was muffled when representative institutions were weakened or, as in the case of ATSIC (the Aboriginal and Torres Strait Islander Commission), abolished. Proposals for a major monument in Canberra were scaled back.[43] And reconciliation was redefined as a 'practical' rather than 'symbolic' matter: it should focus on the many disadvantages endured by Aboriginal people in the here and now, rather than on the unfortunate events of a now-distant past. In this shift, Howard received assistance from an unlikely direction.

Noel Pearson emerged from the *Mabo* controversy as the most brilliantly equipped of the new generation of Aboriginal organic intellectuals. He began the Howard years as might be expected: when Howard attacked the 'black armband' historians, Pearson attacked him.[44] But Pearson was a thinker before he was an ideologue or political partisan, and the hard fact that his thinking kept returning to was that things weren't getting better.[45] Why *was* it that during the period

of 'Indigenous policy enlightenment and recognition', of the resto-
ration of homelands, of the expenditure of billions of government
dollars, and of much improved housing, infrastructure and government
services, there had also been a 'corresponding social deterioration'?[46]
Pearson's answer, soon reached: an 'overwhelming reliance on passive
welfare', flowing from a well-intentioned but deeply patronising 'progressive left' that had dominated Aboriginal policy and politics since
the demise of assimilationism.

Suddenly every door was open to a young Aboriginal man.[47] In a
series of high-prestige lectures and densely argued articles, most in *The
Weekend Australian*, Pearson made the case for a complete rethink of
policy, political alignments and the administration of 'Aboriginal affairs'.
In the doing, hostility between Pearson and Howard turned into a marriage of true minds.[48] It was a politically formidable combination, but
an expensive one for Pearson, and for the previously common front
presented by the Aboriginal people. For every headline suggesting that
Pearson had 'sparked a revolution that emboldened the PM to act' and
the like, there were others accusing him of being 'drunk with power'
and of 'telling whites what they want to hear'.[49]

For Howard, the problem was less in being seen as a rat than as a
diehard. For all his powers and resources, Howard was increasingly on
the defensive. The old white men of official Australia and their symbols and rituals and institutions were being demystified and derided
by younger people, many of them Aboriginal, operating in the distinctly non-official (and often anti-official) world of 'expressive' public
history. There, different rules obtained. Howard's 'official' public history resisted change from below through controlling public process.
'Expressive' public history, by contrast, was driven from below, by a
market-like openness to newcomers and by collaboration, competition
and rewards to the new. 'Aboriginal-themed content' was getting a run

'"Expressive" public history, by contrast, was driven
from below': Yothu Yindi in concert

at last, and Aboriginal actors, directors, novelists, sports stars, painters,
photographers, musicians – and intellectuals, politicians and national
leaders – were collaborating with thousands of non-Aboriginal cultural
and political workers to reach audiences in the millions.

For these people, Howard's refusal to countenance any apology to
Aboriginal peoples came to stand for the whole of his line and policy. A
few months before the 2000 Sydney Olympics, another John Howard –
John Howard the actor – delivered an apology on a high-rating national
TV show: 'At this important time, and in an atmosphere of international
goodwill and national pride, we here in Australia – all of us – would like
to make a statement before all nations.'[50] The opening ceremony of the
Olympics featured Midnight Oil wearing 'Apologise' T-shirts and Cathy
Freeman lighting the Olympic flame on behalf of 'all of us'. Even that
was topped by a jubilant Freeman carrying both the national and the
Aboriginal flags after winning the big race. But John Howard – prime
minister John Howard – never budged, and nor did his image until at

last, in 2007, came an awkward moment of disclosure. 'The challenge I have faced around Indigenous identity politics,' Howard said, 'is in part an artefact of who I am and the time in which I grew up.'[51] Had he *really* budged? Some Aboriginal leaders, including Marcia Langton, thought that perhaps he had; others, including Lowitja O'Donoghue, thought that he hadn't. Howard's disclosure had come in the run-up to an election in which his Coalition government was in deep trouble and the 'Apology' issue loomed large. Howard lost both the election and his seat. For the incoming prime minister, the Apology was the first order of business.

•

The National Apology to the Stolen Generations on 13 February 2008 was a great moment in the story of relations between two racial groups within a single field of life, but only the most recent in a line of great moments stretching all the way back to the Referendum of 1967. It did not mark the eventual triumph of the struggle to dismantle the silence. Still less did it undo all that Howard had done.

Prime Minister Kevin Rudd with Indigenous leader Lowitja
O'Donoghue, Parliament House, Canberra, 13 February 2008

One measure of Howard's impact is the distance between the recommendations of the Stolen Generations inquiry and what was actually
delivered. The inquiry had wanted compensation, restitution, rehabilitation and an apology; all it got, eventually, was a limited program of
services and an apology. Another measure is what was apologised for. On
Keating's Redfern list was dispossession, the smashing of the traditional
way of life, the diseases, the alcohol, the murders, the discrimination
and exclusion, the taking of the children. By the end of Howard's term
in office, only the last of these was to be apologised for.

Rudd's speech was, among other things, an announcement by
Howard's successor as prime minister and Keating's successor as Labor
prime minister that Labor would accept the terms of an unspoken ceasefire. As between nuclear powers, there would be local skirmishes in the
long struggle over the silence, but no more set-piece battles. Neither side
had got what it wanted. Stanner and then the historians and Keating
and the Aboriginal people had wanted to fuse two very different parts
of Australia's story into one; Hasluck, Blainey and Howard wanted one
story to drown out the other. Each of these positions had its strongholds and exponents, but in between, for most people most of the time,
was a mash-up.[52] More attention would be paid to the appreciation of
Aboriginal culture than to telling the story – us learning about them,
rather than us learning about us. To the extent that the story was told,
it would tell of the Aboriginal experience rather than our role in making that experience – the camera would still ride with the cowboys. The
duration, scope and implications of much white conduct toward black
would be shrunk for comfort, the use of armed violence particularly.
Just don't mention the war.

CHAPTER TEN

2005

After sandwiches in Paradise Square we were back on the road – not the new road, the old one. I was heading for Tennant via memory lane and in many footsteps: John McDouall Stuart's, of course, and hence the whole ragtag cavalcade of the invasion that followed, the sheep and cattlemen, the telegraph linesmen, the policemen, the sadly deluded farmers, the Afghan cameleers, the fettlers, the scientists of the Horn expedition, the world-famous anthropologists Baldwin Spencer and Frank Gillen and, in the fullness of time, my family and me. My gathering indignation at the info boards and the monuments and their plaques had to compete with memories and imaginings, hundreds of them summoned up over and again.

After Melrose came Quorn. Once the first staging post for the Adelaide–Alice railway but now historic, it was still almost exactly as I'd remembered it. The winter sun shafted down on the empty marshalling yards, but I saw again clouds of steam billowing from the doubleheader, uncoupling from the train that was taking us back to the Territory from Christmas holidays after the steep climb through Pichi Richi Pass. As the engines puffed gently toward the coal bunker and a steel water tank (square, high on a cross-braced stand, still there), passengers wandered about the yard and my brothers and I stood with our parents in the heat of the late summer's afternoon, staring at the grand hotels where, in the days before sleeping carriages, passengers had overnighted – the Transcontinental, the Overlander, the Criterion, their broad verandas fringed with timber fretwork. They too were still just as I remembered them. Back on board, we kids had gazed from open windows as the Ghan's smoke drifted across the greyish saltbush of the Willochra Plain, the little narrow-gauge train rattling steadily into the desert night as we sat down to a four-course dinner at a table laid with white linen and heavy EPNS cutlery.

In 2005 we were rattling along too, often beside the old railway, sometimes on it. Rails and sleepers gone, it was now a road, sort of. The old Ghan was said to average around 13 miles an hour on its shaky narrow-gauge tracks laid straight onto the sand and rocky dirt, but we were slower still, held up over and again by Historic Sites and Historic Markers and Historic Ruins which had to be fumed over and photographed, and by memories. At Marree I remembered leaning out of the window to watch an Aboriginal man in ragged trousers with his torso bare, a clutch of spears on his shoulder, stroll past the train, followed at a distance by a heavily laden woman and two or three children. Further along, on the banks of the mighty Finke, was a cairn (of course) but a welcome one for a change: it marked the great floods of 1930, 1953 and 1967. 1953! That was our flood! The bridge-cum-causeway that had taken us across the sandy riverbed a month before on our way down south had in the meantime disappeared. From the bank where the train stood, engine wheezing and puffing, we looked at half a mile or more of track supported by sleepers stacked crisscross on top of each other. It looked about as stable as a pile of fiddlesticks. The river had subsided but was still running freely. As the train edged its way forward at less than walking speed, we hung out of the windows watching ripples spread from the wheels under us out into a brown lake.

On the slow road back fifty years later I fell for the country, as so many do, for its extraordinary variety and beauty. After one long day on a rough road under a windy, whitish sky, a cheerless camp threatened, but with no warning at all we were suddenly in sandhills. Turning off the road, we floated softly around islands of clustered trees and shrubs and across sandy bays and inlets and passages in between. The wind fell away; as the slanting light set the low vegetation against sharp shadows, the blue-white glare faded to pastels of pink and aquamarine and blue. It is a commonplace that there are no averages in the Australian deserts, only extremes; they record, apparently, the highest variation in and lowest predictability of rainfall and temperature of any region in the world.[1] Drought is followed by flood, days over the old Fahrenheit century by nights near freezing, barrenness by fecundity, desolation by beauty. Of all the contrasts of the desert none is more complete than that of night with day. Camp pitched, there was an hour or two between sunset and moonrise and in the interval appeared an opulent night sky so improbable that the eye kept trying to see it as white clouds as the mind slipped in and out of grasping it: the Milky Way. Another couple of days on, we ran along a valley formed by north–south sandhills while heading for an east–west range of flat-topped hills, blue in the distance and separated from each other by sharp V-shaped notches. In light scrub the sky was less encompassing and the world below was dense, almost crowded, detailed and intricate with low grasses, often thick with yellow or white or purple flowers, masses of shrubs and bushes arranged against an earth that seemed red until contrasted with neat little mini volcanoes of almost scarlet sand brought to the surface by ants. To the north across dark olive-khaki plains were the MacDonnell Ranges, its notches flanked by cones and pyramids and mesas, as crisp as a cardboard cut-out.

In Alice, more footsteps to be followed, including a great density of them at the old telegraph station, where I figured out what must have

been the spot on which Spencer and Gillen had built themselves a shelter and recorded the great Engwura ceremonial cycle that made them
famous, and where I sat at sunset on the hill at the back of the station
compound where they'd often repaired for an end-of-day smoke and
chat. They had done their bit to mythologise what countless novels,
docos, feature films, memoirs, colour pieces, paintings and photographs
have since made the most mythologised stretch of country in the entire
continent: the imagined world of the Red Centre.[2] North from Alice, a
detour to Coniston, where the body of trapper had been stuffed down
a rabbit burrow and the miseries of the Warlpiri had begun, then back
to the main road and Barrow Creek, where the old telegraph station
still nestled against the hill that had carried the Kaytetye warriors to
a surprise attack and those terrible reprisals. More monuments, info
boards, cairns and plaques, a few registering uncomfortable facts and a
few more having two bob each way, but most taking Spencer and Gillen's
advice that all things considered it might be best to pass a veil over
unwelcome memories.

•

My second entrance to Tennant, like the first, was disheartening. On
that September afternoon in 1952 my parents and brothers and I had
climbed down the two or three steps at the back of a DC-3 onto the
hot black tarmac of the Tennant Creek aerodrome. Twelve hours earlier
we had taken off at dawn from the still-misty green of Parafield, now
1300 miles away. When my teacher back in Adelaide had learned that
I would be going to Tennant Creek, he asked the class if anyone had
ever been to the Northern Territory. No, none. How many had been to
another state? Not many. Nearly half, it turned out, had never been to
Adelaide, a 12-mile trolley-bus ride away. None had ever been on an
aeroplane. The prospect was exciting almost beyond bearing. But staring

from the shade of a tin and flywire building across the tarmac, past the DC-3, to a bare, shimmering vastness, I was like the bride who has looked forward to nothing but the wedding only to find themselves landed in a marriage, forever.

In 1952 Tennant had stopped at the schoolyard fence. On one side, the town, on the other, spinifex. Fifty years on, Tennant Creek blurred into being: first some hobby farms, blank-looking rectangles of a few scrubby acres with a kit house in the middle and cars, sheds and machinery scattered about, then depots and trucking yards, a motel, a servo, a flash silvery, swooping-roofed structure then, at last, houses. Where was the school? Our house? The other government houses? Were they still up ahead somewhere or had they gone? At last something I recognised, the Australian Inland Mission building, the Very Reverend John Flynn's forlorn alternative to the pubs. We used to pass the AIM building on our way down to the shops. So: our place had gone, along with the other govvie houses, the school, the post office and the police station. For all my dislike of the Tennant Creek I'd lived in, I still resented this vandalism.

Taking my bearings from the old AIM building, I began a survey. That highway, that thin, shimmering strip of bitumen flanked by stretches of reddish dirt, was now a dual carriageway divided by a green (green!) median strip. Of the buildings I remembered, only a few were left: the picturesque Catholic church up on a little hill above the town, the two pubs (flourishing), the Pioneer Picture Theatre (derelict). Kittle's Garage, Cavanagh's cool drink factory, Armstrong's Bakery and the two general stores had all gone. In 1952 Tennant was harsh, makeshift, dusty. Now, the green and the trees and the new houses and offices notwithstanding, it had a failed, depressed air, faded For Sale signs hanging from sagging fences, gardens populated by weeds, shopfronts boarded up.

I couldn't claim to be surprised; national headlines had by then turned Tennant into Australia's most notorious dystopia, headlines about the kids taken to a boarding school in Queensland because the local school couldn't handle them and then more headlines about their expulsion 'for disobedience and gross disruptive behaviour', stories about government child bonuses being blown on gambling and grog and shiny new bikes, stories telling readers that 'getting smashed is a way of life in Tennant Creek', and the story about the house block offered for sale at a dollar.[3] All those dreams of a population surge, all those plans and strategies and programs, had come to nought. Tennant had gone bust in the 1970s, it was still bust, and showed no sign of ever being anything else. Irony of ironies, had it not been for the influx of Aboriginal people, Tennant's population would have collapsed rather than risen a bit, and without the welfare money that came with them its economy would have collapsed too. Nearly a quarter of Tennant's 'industry' was in 'Public Administration and Safety', another quarter in 'Health Care and Social Assistance' and 'Education and Training'.[4] 'Wholesale and Retail Trade' contributed just 9 per cent, 'construction' 8 per cent. Decades after the end of the mining boom, Anyinginyi Health told a royal commission that 'the major industry in Tennant Creek is welfare support'.[5] Most of the town's adults, it said, are on welfare 'with limited employment', which in 2011 meant jobs for one in four or five young adults and around 50 per cent employment at the most for the rest.[6] It was Noel Pearson's bitter paradox in distilled form. Apartheid had gone, the feudal regime on the stations had gone, there was political equality and wage equality, there were legal rights, land rights, welfare rights, human rights, but with what result? Across the road from the Food Barn, Aboriginal people sat cross-legged on the median strip, every day. Every day there were Aboriginal people dozing in parked cars, or walking slowly along the footpath, just being there. Still there was nothing to do, and still there was the grog.

In the late 1980s, the interminable land claim process over at last, Julalikari turned to the grog problem. The Night Patrol, the sobering-up centres and the rest weren't enough; Julalikari wanted a 'holistic' approach that tackled the problem from several directions with the support of all involved, white as well as black. After years of agitation and negotiation, including successful campaigns for a Grog-Free Day and against a strip club which encouraged alcohol-fuelled audience participation, a Sunday lunch specialty, the Liquor Commission accepted Julalikari's proposal for a three-month trial of restrictions on the sale of grog by the big four outlets (two pubs and two bottle shops), on pension day particularly.[7] White opinion on the grog trial was mixed. There were rock-solid supporters, and not all of them blow-ins from Down South. 'I'm prepared to stick my neck out,' said the owner of the Dolly Pot restaurant, 'and say that in five or ten years, Julalikari will be seen as a fine example of how an Aboriginal community has taken a white mining town and turned it into a model of an Aboriginal town developing as a viable community.'[8] There were also those who still talked about 'gins' and 'bucks' and who had put up a mock gallows for the pushy blacks and their patsy, the chair of the Liquor Commission, and there were still the vested interests (including the owner and editor of the *Tennant & District Times*, owner also of the strip club). The trial began in 'an atmosphere of intense controversy' but ended in grudging admissions that it had worked.[9] The restrictions would stay. It was a win, but a win like the win on land; the grog would be restricted but only a bit, as was obvious to even the most casual observer. On a late-afternoon constitutional I passed a stretch of bare spinifex beside one of the town camps. There the drinkers, barred from taking grog in, had gathered outside the fence, marionette-like figures reeling, flailing, screeching.

After three or four days in Tennant I couldn't wait to leave. I'd come hoping to meet those strangers of fifty years ago, but what I was getting was the current reality. I had made no contact with any of my Aboriginal contemporaries, and I didn't know whether or how I would. I'd come thinking that I would just follow my nose, which I did, but it took me to a dead end. I started with Paul Ruger, former classmate, son of a miner from the early days and sometime mayor. We chatted for a while then he passed me on to Alf Chittock, also a former mayor, a cheerful, bird-like figure who yarned at length about the old days and referred me to Jasmin Afianos at the *Tennant & District Times*, who suggested asking Dave Curtis, the driving force of the Anyinginyi Council. The council's office was just across the main street. It was late afternoon; the office was closed. Next morning I was told no, he's not in at the moment, but call Helen Kane, she'll know people. No, Helen is away at the moment, out bush, but try the people up at the Stolen Gen office. They were away too, on a field trip, but Patrick Ah Kit over at the health centre might be able to help. Patrick was at the health centre and was happy to chat for a while – a lovely man, alternately determined and despondent about his work. His mother was about my age, he said, she was at Phillip Creek, at the mission, but she's passed away now. You should try at Nyinkka Nyunyu, ask for Trisha Frank. So, to Nyinkka Nyunyu, that silvery swooping-roofed building up the other end of town. There a young woman behind the flash reception desk in an elegant foyer listened patiently to my explanation. I'm not sure if Trisha's available, she said. I'll just check for you. She disappeared through a door behind her. I wandered around the shop, off to one side of the foyer, collecting postcards and a couple of books. The young woman returned. Trisha's tied up at the moment, she apologised. Could you come back tomorrow? I did. Trisha was then in a meeting – perhaps I could email her? With hopes sinking and time on my hands,

I set out to see if Tennant's stories about itself were any better than all that highway history I'd seen on the way up.

•

Tennant's story, or fragments of it anyway, had been recorded in print right from the start, thanks to John McDouall Stuart's journals, the journals and memoirs of later 'explorers' and 'pioneers', reports to and from governments, Spencer and Gillen's celebrated work and, from the 1930s, 'outback' tales by popular authors such as Ion Idriess, Ernestine Hill and Bill Harney. With the entry into history of the Aboriginal people in the 1960s and 1970s, this trickle turned into a flood:[10] official reports, reviews and plans, as well as shelves of documentation from land claims and *Cubillo*, and scholarly books, articles and monographs drawing on anthropology, linguistics, political science, sociology, archaeology and history to tell the story of the previously unacknowledged relations between two racial groups within this particular field of life and/or its tangled pathologies, notable among them Diane Bell's history and anthropology of Warrabri/Ali Curung (1983), David Nash's 1984 history of the dispossession of the Warumungu, Patricia Davison's 1985 survey of the short life of the Phillip Creek mission, Mr Justice Maurice's trenchant final report on the Warumungu land claim (1988), Maggie Brady's investigation of the grog and its ravages (1988), Mary Edmunds' analysis of the shifting racial politics of the 1970s and 1980s (1995), and Alexis Wright's *Grog War* (1997), commissioned by Julalikari.

It didn't take long to discover that as far as Tennant's public history is concerned, most of this work by self-righteous blow-ins from Down South was just so much wasted ink. At Attack Creek of vivid memory – that frisson of excitement on coming to this famous place en route to Darwin in the single spinner – I found a cairn bearing a plaque unveiled by the Minister for Territories, the Honourable Paul

The Minister for Territories, Paul Hasluck MP,
remembers the day when 'hostile natives' attacked

Hasluck MP, on 25 June 1960, the centenary of the day when 'hostile natives and illness' had forced the redoubtable John McDouall Stuart and his companions to return whence they had come. There was more of the same at Threeways, about 50 kilometres down the highway. There stands another monument, a *huge* monument, a 10-metre tower of crazy-paving rock surmounted by intersecting crosses, honouring the memory of John Flynn. This I'd seen before. I was there, along with a fair proportion of Tennant's population, when it was unveiled in 1953 by His Excellency the Governor-General, Field Marshall Sir William Slim KG, GCB, GCMG, GCVO, DSO, MC in full ceremonial fig. 'His vision encompassed the continent,' said the plaque of John Flynn. 'He established the Australian Inland Mission and founded the Flying Doctor Service. He brought lonely places a spiritual ministry and spread a mantle of safety over them.'

Perhaps these archetypes of winners' history could be excused, or explained at least, as belonging to their time, well before all those exposés of the 1980s. But where do we say so, now that we know better? Looking about at Attack Creek I noticed a second cairn, much newer-looking than the one unveiled by Hasluck in 1960. Ah, I thought, an update, a comment on obsolete sentiments? It turned out to mark the death long ago of a member of the Northern Territory police force. At Threeways an info board provided some local colour but left passers-by unaware that Flynn's mantle of safety did not protect most of the Territory's populace, just those who happened to be white, and unaware that the monument, this massive embodiment of dominion, stood at the point of intersection of two of the Territory's invasion routes, the one up from Adelaide (now the Stuart Highway) and the one across from Queensland (now the Barkly Highway).

At the old telegraph station I found that the buildings had been fixed up a bit, but remained much as I remembered them and as described by

'Another monument, a huge monument'

Spencer and Gillen in 1901 and, no doubt, as they had been ever since 1872 when they caused the Warumungu to call the whitefellas '*papulanyi*', people who stay in one place. It was easy to imagine away, as instructed by the NT Parks and Wildlife Service info sheets: 'Imagine being here when the Overland Telegraph Line was first constructed,' they urged. 'Except for members of construction parties and Aboriginal inhabitants of the region, you and your team are isolated from the rest of the world except by the link with the Telegraph Line. Your supplies would arrive 6-monthly via camel train from Port Augusta. You and your team are responsible for manning the telegraph equipment 24 hours a day ...' And so on and so forth.

The visitor is not invited, however, to imagine other aspects of life at the telegraph station. The passing reference to Aboriginal inhabitants in the passage quoted above was one of four in as many densely filled pages. The second was a remark in the course of a sentence about John McDouall Stuart, that the creek had long been a reliable source of water for the local Aborigines; the third records that those same Aboriginal inhabitants were studied by Spencer and Gillen; and the fourth notes that station officers handed out rations to the Aborigines. And that's it. We were not invited to imagine why it was that those Aboriginal people needed or wanted rations, or the impact on their 'reliable water supply' of the station's goats, horses and cattle. Nor were we told that 'Tennant Creek' had for centuries, millennia, been known as Jurnkurakurr, crowded with experience, stories and spiritual significance, or asked to imagine losing all that to these people who came from nowhere and refused to leave, or for that matter what it would be like to be one of the 'half-caste' children picked up by the police when they set up shop near the telegraph station in the early days of the gold rush. And there is certainly no mention of Mr Justice Maurice's rage:[11] 'Nothing symbolises the high ascendancy of Western Traditions and culture,' he had written in his final report, 'more than the fact that ... Jurnkurakurr was acquired by the Northern Territory to preserve as a monument to white settlement.'

In the town itself, Heritage was hard to miss. The biggest wall in the main street carried a giant mural of Tennant's Progress, wheelbarrows at one end, trucks in the middle and jet planes zooming at the other. On the next block was the collapsing facade of the old Pioneer Picture Theatre, on which were fixed info boards and grainy photographs from yesteryear. In a park on one corner of the town's main intersection was a plaque in praise of Peko Mines – *not* mounted on one of the sacred Kunjarra rocks – from which point Peko Road heads out of town, passing through a kind of avenue of honour formed by little rail-borne dump trucks before climbing a gentle rise to arrive at the Battery Hill Mining and Visitor Centre.

The old battery that used to keep us awake at night had been co-opted to the cause of Territorianism by the Minister for Mines and Energy, the Honourable Ian Tuxworth. It turned out to be quite a little village in itself, the many buildings of its heyday, the generator shed, the assay building, a workshop, a drill rig and cyanide vats, all there still and in good nick, and a museum containing several exhibitions, including one on Tennant's 'social history'.

The social history exhibition seemed to have everything going for it, coming as it did years after the land claim and its revelations and all those scholarly studies and histories and analyses, and it had the professional services of a curator as well.[12] The exhibition was lively, but it wasn't different. The random leavings of the past, which in most country-town museums end up as piles of dusty junk, were here organised to tell an interesting tale.[13] But which tale? The title gave the game away: 'Freedom, Fortitude and Flies'. This was old-timer's history, quite directly so, based on the recollections of Kevan Weaber (whose son, also Kevan, sat just a couple of rows away at school). Where were the Aboriginal people? As in Hilda Tuxworth's *Tennant Creek: Yesterday and Today* and Margot Miles' *The Old Tennant*, they had walk-on, walk-off parts (gold is said to have been discovered 'by an Aborigine known to history as Blue Moon Frank'), but relations between them and the miners, the primary engine of Tennant's history, were barely mentioned. Here, as in the Tuxworth and Miles accounts, the dispossession demanded by the miners, the labour of Aboriginal people in the mines, the miners' relentless pursuit of Aboriginal women, the many impacts of the miners' town on Aboriginal people up to the present day and no doubt well beyond, the failure to pay royalties or to even *think* of paying royalties – none of these was mentioned. In Tennant, as in Sydney's Hyde Park, public history was telling very much less than history knows.[14]

•

I found just three moments of dissent from the dismal rule of winners' history.[15] The first took the form of graffiti on the back of the door of a toilet, thoughtfully provided next to the Attack Creek carpark by the NT Parks and Wildlife Service. *Who were the 'hostile natives' that forced Sturt [sic] to turn back?* asked a dissenter. *Where is the cairn celebrating their defense* [an American?] *of THEIR country?* Below, in emphatic caps and a different hand: *WHO INITIATED THE ATTACK?* Then, below that, in a third hand, were some answers, taken from Alexis Wright's *Grog War*: the Warumungu had followed Stuart for some time before warning him, even giving him food and medicine; then they attempted to frighten him off, at which point Stuart ordered his men to fire on the *wumparrani*, who finally retreated after a brave stand. Here, on the back of a toilet door, I told myself, was a refusal to take white Australia's word for it, a tiny insurrection, a pursuit of truth! On a later visit I found that it wasn't there anymore; it had been painted over.

A second exception turned up almost by chance. I'd wanted to see that mysterious place, 'the mission', but it was marked on neither map nor land. On the way back to Tennant from Attack Creek and Threeways, I happened to see a sign pointing to Phillip Creek Station. On the other side of the road was a gate; it seemed worth a try. Driving slowly along a track used often enough to be clear and smooth but not so often as to become a road, I came to a fork and a small arrow-shaped sign that said, inscrutably: 5 kilometres. Soon another sign, this one announcing 2.5 kilometres, then another, 250 metres. This last took me around the end of a long, shallow lagoon to a scattering of concrete slabs with stubby bits of mudbrick walls. This was the other side of Tennant Creek's apartheid, the place whence came the men in greatcoats standing on the back of the truck, the kids at sports day, the people at the open-air pictures. A mudbrick cairn carrying a brass plaque, shining new, had been unveiled just a couple of months before.[16] It recorded that here stood from 1945 to 1956 the Kumanjai Creek Mission and that from this place sixteen children were 'removed from family, country and culture to the Retta Dixon Home in Darwin'. Each of the sixteen names glittered in the sunlight. There were no words of recrimination, scarcely an implication that things were done *to* people *by* people, only that things were experienced, as if in our absence. We have monuments that bandy about terms like murder and treachery, but this one didn't even mention 'stolen'. Perhaps a fog of loss and misery descended to blanket any spark of anger? Perhaps they knew that they know but we don't and that trying to tell us, to teach us, is just too hard? Perhaps they feared our response? In the couple of months between the unveiling and my visit, the monument had been encased in a lock-wire cage.

The third exception to the dismal rule of winners' history I found at Nyinkka Nyunyu. A striking place, the grandest edifice in town, a museum, a shop, a café and offices, set in a garden of native flora (with a space for dance and other performances) on a prominent site on the main street, Nyinkka Nyunyu has few if any equivalents elsewhere. It is the fourth and newest of the Warumungu's key institutions, a keeping-place for precious things, headquarters for the 'culture work' essential to the long struggle of recovery.[17]

At Nyinkka Nyunyu is told the story of life before the *papulanyi*, and the story of what life became after they arrived. 'Returned histories' – Nyinkka Nyunyu's term for those beautiful things in the magical photographs of a century ago – are mesmerising: the boomerangs, shields, belts and headbands, firesticks, spears and spear-throwers, coolamons, axes and picks and adzes and digging sticks, gifts from the people of that vanished world per kind favour of Spencer and Gillen. As arresting are Nyinkka Nyunyu's 'bush TVs', dioramas the size of an old-style TV set made by Warumungu people, each illustrating one of a series of themes determined after extensive discussion with the old people. Thus 'The Dearest Place' depicts Jurnkurakurr, 'an important sacred place and one of the few permanent water sources' in the region. Bush TVs on singing and dancing and food-gathering evoke the old ways. A diorama on Cubadgee Jappangarti relates the life of 'a young Warumungu man who acted as a guide, interpreter and go-between for explorer Dick Lindsay in the 1880s'; 'The Pastoral Industry' tells how Aboriginal people 'adapt[ed] their skills and knowledge of the land to their work in the cattle'; a diorama on mining represents the role of Aboriginal people in the industry and the industry's impact on them. There are bush TVs on the mission, the stolen children, the Pioneer Picture Theatre, and the efforts of the Night Patrol to stem the ravages of the grog.

Like the list of the long dead in Melrose, Nyinkka Nyunyu's stories were affecting, but somehow troubling. It was a moving riposte to all that winners' history I'd seen elsewhere, but there was something wrong, harder to grasp than that silence in the middle of the Paradise Square info board. One problem, I eventually realised, was that *this* version of the story was locked up inside, while *that* version was told everywhere else. The whitefellas had a head start, of course, beginning at Threeways in 1953 and the 1960 monument on the banks of Attack Creek. When the Warumungu 'came back into history' in the 1960s and 1970s, their first priority was to tell their story to the land commissioner, not to Tennant's residents and tourists. Then there was so much else to cope with, including the grog and the whole issue of the Stolen Generations. It was not until the late 1990s that the Warumungu turned their minds to the idea of a cultural centre, and not until 2003 that it was accomplished. All this while the whitefellas were turning just about every available space and place to their own storytelling purposes: the park at the main intersection, the roadsides and streetscapes, the telegraph station, Battery Hill, all supplemented by info boards and guide sheets, tourist brochures and annotated maps and websites.[18]

'Don't be frightened, come in', said the sign at Nyinkka Nyunyu. Like the 'Stay a Day' billboard pleading at tourists as they drove into Tennant, it was a dead giveaway. In peak tourist season the carpark at Battery Hill was never empty and often close to full, but at Nyinkka Nyunyu one or two cars was the best that could be hoped for. At least part of the fault is with the architects – they won a prize, of course – who managed to require visitors to drive off the highway into a carpark, walk 30 or 40 metres to the main building and from there find a café that ought to have been on the roadside but is actually another 30 or 40 metres on.[19] It takes time, effort and intention. And once you get there, the entrance, while impressive, is also a bit daunting. If you get past all that and then pay ten dollars, you'll see a story that belongs out in the streets, in the parks, on the walls of the cafés and pubs and servos,

but is here muffled by the hush of carpet and the hum of air con, by
the soft lighting and by those almost unreadable captions favoured by
white museum curators.

There were problems in the message as well as in the medium.
For one thing, Nyinkka Nyunyu tells a Warumungu story. There are
no bush TVs on Tennant Creek as a refugee centre, or on the specific
experiences of the Warlpiri, Alyawarre, Kaytetye and others, or on the
violence inflicted on them, not even at Coniston. For another, it is a
denatured story. The bush TV on the Pioneer Picture Theatre does not
mention that the old people didn't go to the pictures because they were
frightened of guns. The bush TV on life in the cattle is silent on the
maltreatment and cruelty that were often part of the deal. There is no
reference to the excision of the Aboriginal experience from Tennant's
public history. Perhaps the Warumungu needed to report more success in their struggles than is in fact there? Or perhaps they wanted to
avoid ruffling white feathers, as indeed they had been doing ever since
the Kaytetye were hunted down in 1874. At Phillip Creek they had put
their monument in a lock-wire cage; here, at Nyinkka Nyunyu, they
told of their experience, but not where it came from.

Even had that not been the case, had the Warumungu opted (for
example) to tell the story as told by Mr Justice Maurice – there would
still be a fundamental problem in Tennant's accounts of itself: there
would still be two stories, the European story out there, the Aboriginal
one in here. The consultant who in the 1980s had remarked so can-
didly on Tennant's racial divisions suggested that the town might go
for a research centre that would serve as 'an inter-cultural "bridge"', and
'a museum and gallery for art and artifacts from both cultures'? It didn't
happen then, and it hasn't happened since.

•

I went back to Tennant again a year or so after my first trip. I hadn't met Trisha Frank or any of my Aboriginal contemporaries, but I had been given some carefully phrased encouragement, first by email and then by phone. You'd have to meet Mr Jones and explain what you want to do, Trisha told me. No promises, but if you can come back I'll do my best. This time when I presented myself at Nyinkka Nyunyu's sweeping reception desk, I was a known quantity. A few minutes' wait and then a young woman with dark, diffident eyes – a dead ringer for one of the women photographed by Baldwin Spencer in 1901 – appeared through a door off to one side of the desk.[20] This was Trisha, with an apology. She'd expected Mr Jones to be here but he'd had to go to a meeting. Could I come back tomorrow morning? As I recall this pursuit I flush with embarrassment. I read recently a memoir by a woman who had grown up at the Cherbourg mission in Queensland,[21] just as my contemporaries had grown up at Phillip Creek. Busloads of tourists came to Cherbourg to stare. What was the difference between those tourists and me?

The next day I followed Trisha through the door behind the desk, past an open-plan office, through another door to a large, light-filled room that looked out through a cinemascope window to the green of a playing field where once our house had stood. A handsome man, with a stylish razor cut and in a crisp open-necked shirt, was talking on a mobile in language. We waited. I was introduced to Mr Jones and made my pitch. Trisha and Mr Jones retired to the far end of the room and talked for some minutes. I was put at my ease by a cheerful woman a couple of desks along who introduced herself as Rose Graham. She could have been Trisha's sister; it turned out they were cousins. Mr Jones left, and Trisha returned to put the deal.[22]

Yes, she could help. There were some old people in town at the moment who would agree to talk with me. She would join the

conversations where possible but because of a funeral she was organis-
ing she wouldn't have enough time to do all of them, so Rose would
be there instead. I would need the help, Trisha said, because some of
those old people, they spoke a lot of languages but their English was
not too good. I should pay each of the old people a small amount to say
thank you. Also, it would be good if I would write up the stories and
put them in Nyinkka Nyunyu's resource centre. When they've passed
away, Trisha said, their grandchildren and great-grandchildren will be
able to read their stories. If I did write anything else about the conversations, I'd have to send it to her so they could check it. Also, Trisha or
Rose would take me to these old people's houses or would pick them
up and bring them here, to Nyinkka Nyunyu, to talk.

The next afternoon we sat at one of the tables under the spreading
awning attached to Nyinkka Nyunyu's café, Trisha, Rose, me and, at
the top of the table, Edith Graham Nakamarra, who was Rose's mother
and Trisha's aunt. I look now at a photograph and see a whitefella, pen
poised above a clipboard, chin on fist, looking across a table flanked by
two thirty-something Aboriginal women to a dark, full figure in a tur-
quoise dress, stringy hair streaked with orangey-pink, a strong, strong
face, an imposing figure, intimidating even.

I explained myself. Trisha and Rose translated bits of it, switch-
ing from Warumungu to Creole and back, a phrase or two in standard
English along the way. Edith, quite still, listened, then, I think, decided
that she would help. She told me where she was born, not far from here,
about her family, her early life, the years at Phillip Creek mission, the
years after, a life told tersely and abruptly. As we talked, a few people –
tourists? locals? – passed by with their cake and coffees, some sitting
nearby listening and trying to look as though they weren't. Two girls, six
or seven years old, appeared, one clinging to Trisha, the other to Edith.
There is something I'd like to ask about, I told Trisha and Rose. I'd been

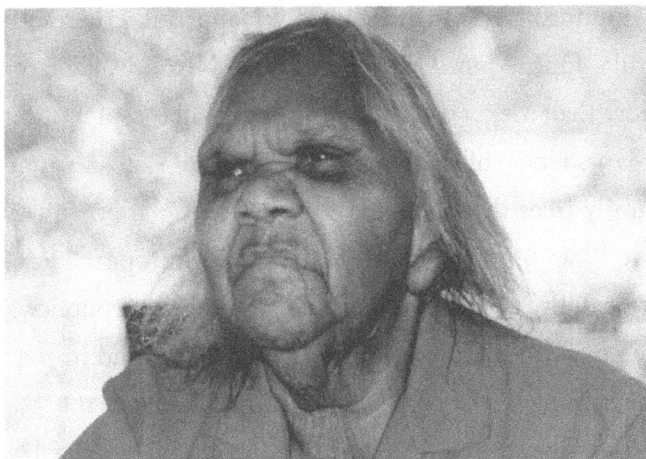

Edith Graham Nakamarra, Nyinkka Nyunyu, September 2006

told what not to ask ('Don't ask about anyone who might have passed away,' Trisha had said, 'family especially') but not what would be okay. I want to ask about a memory, I told them, at least I think it's a memory but I can't be sure. I've asked my family and they can't remember it; they think I must have imagined it. But what I think I remember is that when we used to live here, just over there (I pointed toward the green playing field), in those days the spinifex used to start just there, where the back fence was. And sometimes I used to see, or think I did, people, Aboriginal people camped out there in the spinifex. They would come for a while and camp there, I don't know for how long, maybe a few days or it might have been weeks. Do you know, I asked, if that would be true? Rose, Edith and Trisha talked, translating and discussing what I was saying and asking.

'That was me,' Edith said. 'That was me and my mum. My family. We come sometimes. See my dad. Nat Williams. Tracker. Police station, just there, just down there.'

On the days that followed I met another six of the people whose world I had briefly glimpsed fifty years before: Kathleen Fitz Napanangka,

Rosie Thompson Nakamarra, Bunny Napurrula, Therese Patterson Napurrula, Jimmy Jones Jampin and Judy Nixon Nakamarra.[23] Some were older than me, two a little younger, but all except Mrs Fitz (about twenty years older) of the same generation. All were Warumungu but with family trees that included various combinations of Alyawarre, Kaytetye, Wambaya, Warlpiri, Garrwa and European, testament to the permeability of the boundaries of those little republics on Tinny Tindale's map, to the power of the Warumungu, and to the way that with the coming of the *papulanyi* and then Tennant's role as a refugee centre, 'the tribes get all mixed up', as one put it.

All but one had worked on the stations, some for a pittance, others for keep. Most recalled long days of hard, unremitting labour. Rosie Thompson Nakamarra's working day on Rocky (Rockhampton Downs) started at five in the morning and sometimes extended to eleven at night, preparing and cleaning up after three meals a day plus smokos. Even when the men were away on stock work, there was cleaning, polishing, washing and ironing to be done, 'all the old way' – copper, wringer, irons containing hot coals – as well as 'men's work' like cutting wood and fencing. 'We dug that holes,' Bunny Napurrula told me. 'You know that boundary crossing at the highway? I done that, like with my mother-in-law and my sister-in-law.' All had been taken or pushed from one place to another: the stations, Seven Mile, the mission, Warrabri and eventually Tennant Creek. Several had close encounters with child removal. Most had been at the mission when the sixteen 'half-caste' kids were taken away on the back of a truck. None had any illusions about the violence that had underwritten the white regime. Therese Patterson's parents were Coniston refugees, as were Rosie Thompson's neighbours. Those people over there, Rosie said as we sat in her front yard in the winter sun, they Warlpiri. Coniston. Bad time. That mob they walk up here. All way in bush. Not come out till

here, Seven Mile. And that was all she said about the Coniston massacres. Edith Graham and Judy Nixon Nakamarra were daughters of
Nat Williams, whose many roles included stints as a tracker; he'd told
them about the old days when their people were chased by white men
on horseback and shot.[24]

Did they crank it up for the whitefella? Tell sob stories? Not that
I could tell. None was discourteous, or offhand even; just for the most
part subdued, undemonstrative. They neither sentimentalised nor
demonised. They talked about the fun as well as the hard times (the
girls sneaking out through the windows of the locked dorms for late-
night assignations, singing hymns on Sundays, the big get-togethers
out in the bush over the stations' Christmas break). They talked about
the kind and decent whitefellas (Mrs Ward, a couple of the missionaries) as well as one who shot all their dogs, and the one who would
take the girls swimming but not the boys, and the ones who demanded
hard, harsh work in return for miserable rations. For the most part
they spoke of their lives in a matter-of-fact way with no analysis, no
striving for effect, no moralising. There were moments in those conversations that shone (for me anyway) in the way of that instant when
I learned that Edith had been out in the spinifex while I had been in
the house by the school; moments at which the coordinates of our
lives had briefly crossed. The Pioneer Picture Theatre and sports day
were particular favourites for all of us. There were also moments when
emotions showed.

One was when Kathleen Fitz described her own narrow escape
from a cop on horseback looking for 'half-caste' kids, and talked about
her half-sisters and half-brother (to use our terminology) being not so
lucky.[25] Another was in Bunny Napurrula's vivid account of that morning nearly sixty years before when the truck took the kids away. Bunny
would be a star in any company. Round-faced and round-bodied, she sat

Bunny Napurrula, Nyinkka Nyunyu, September 2006

back in her chair, arms folded, self-possessed, on the edge of scepticism. It was Bunny and her sister who had given the local DAA case-loader a hard time when he tried to move people out of the camps. When a researcher came to study the old Phillip Creek mission site it was Bunny who listed the name of every kid at the school and identified dozens of varieties of flora. It was Bunny who taught Warlmanpa to David Nash (and offered Wambaya as well if he liked). Mr Justice O'Loughlin found Bunny to be 'a most impressive witness'. When Bunny told me what she'd told the judge, she leaned forward in focused indignation about that terrible morning in 1947. Another moment of sharp intensity, if I read it correctly, was provided by Edith Graham. Her grandfather, Jacob, had been at Attack Creek. *He turn them back!* she said. I was just about breathless at the nearness of that distant age, as well as thrilled by the splendid rebuke to my Grade VI Social Studies book, to that plaque at Attack Creek and to the camera that always rode with the cowboys. For Edith Graham it was, I think, a statement of anger as well as pride, anger at the arrogance of the *papulanyi,* pride that her people had stood up to them. These were stories unmuffled by Nyinkka Nyunyu's carpet and air con and circumspection.

•

Was there more known about Jacob, Edith's grandfather, Rose's great-grandfather? I was as fascinated by the telescoping of time as by the fierce rebuttal: *he turn them back!* I'd done the arithmetic and it worked. Aboriginal men often had much younger wives, so had Jacob been, say, twenty years old when Stuart came through in 1860, he might have had sons up to 1900 or thereabouts, and a son might have had children in the 1940s or beyond. Trisha and Rose thought that Francine McCarthy might know more. Francine (another cousin) worked at the Central Land Council and had a close knowledge of Spencer and Gillen's work (a tool of the trade at the council) and a keen interest in the history of the region. She sketched a genealogy for me and found some gaps in her own knowledge. Her interest was piqued. Perhaps her mother, Jean, might be able to help? A day or two later Francine, Jean and I pored over links spreading up, down and across the butcher's paper. The names emerged like credits for a movie. Among Jacob's sons was Nat Williams Warano (born around 1901), Edith's father, key man at Phillip Creek, the 'black tracker' visited by his daughter and others who camped in the spinifex at the back of our place. Among Jacob's nephews, older than Nat Williams, were Zulu Jappangarti and Dick Cubadgee. Among their contemporaries but on another line of descent was 'King' Charlie Jampin; among Jampin's grandsons were Jimmy Jones Jampin, one of the 'old people' I'd talked with, and his younger brother Michael Jones. Mr Jones! But Jacob remained just a name on butcher's paper.

Had Jacob, like Zulu, worked with Spencer and Gillen? Jean thought that her older brother Day Day might know.[26] On a mild winter's evening, we headed out through country that was at that moment the antithesis of Spencer and Gillen's desolate wind-blown plains to Day Day's outstation. Over chicken and chips that I'd brought and surrounded by young relatives and their children, Day Day wrestled with his memories. He had an uncertain childhood recollection of his grandfather; he did not know whether he had worked with Spencer and Gillen.

Back in Sydney, where I then lived, I went back to *The Northern Tribes of Central Australia* and to both Spencer's and Gillen's journals in the Mitchell Library. A total of five references to old Warumungu men turned up, two of which suggested that the old man in question had been at Attack Creek. As well there were pen sketches and photographs of old men, sometimes named, often not. When identifiers were given they came in different forms, some as names given by the *papulanyi* ('Cockney'), some Warumungu. And the Warumungu identifiers came in different forms (*Murramunti*, or 'a Thakomara man of the white cockatoo totem'). There was no reference anywhere that I could find to a 'Jacob'.

After wasting a good deal of Francine's time, and after contact with several scholars and institutions that might settle the matter, and after wrestling with information and documentation provided by them (including land claim transcripts and Hasluck's infamous 'stud book'), I accepted that I was out of my depth. And why should it matter anyway? I don't know, but it did. It mattered as a way of corroborating Edith's knowledge and combating the discount often applied to Aboriginal 'oral history'. It mattered to Francine and the others, Jean, Day Day, Trisha and Rose, and hence it mattered to me as a way of providing a small return for their generosity. It mattered also as a way of imagining that when I'd passed the old men sitting cross-legged on the veranda of Williams' general store, I was in the presence of Zulu Jappangarti and 'King' Charlie Jampin and in touch with Stanner and

Spencer and Gillen and Jacob, and with that day when a world began
to vanish.

•

You have to stay for the Harmony Week parade, Trisha and Rose said.
It'll be a good night. Prep for the big event had been going on in and
around the conversations with my age-mates at the Jajjikari Cafe, Trisha
and Rose coming and going between phone calls, making paper lanterns
and helping to turn a truck into a spinifex bed for a king-sized papier-
mache Nyinkka, the spiny-tailed goanna. If you want to do spinifex,
Bunny Napurrula told the spinifex installers in the middle of our conversation, you better talk to me. I was born in the spinifex! So, I stayed
for the big night.

Looking at photos years on I see a blue highway patrol car rolling
slowly up Paterson Street, trailing a fleet of kids on decorated bikes, a
big contingent of mums, dads and more kids strolling along behind a
'Tennant Creek Child Care' banner, a clown or two, yet more kids with
balloons and hoops, me clutching a supply of paper lanterns and wonder-
ing where the candles were, an elderly couple sitting among the spectators
on the median strip in fold-out chairs, and Nyinkka borne along on its
float of spinifex, all heading for Nyinkka Nyunyu. There, hundreds –
black and white, old and young – milled around food stalls and trading
tables. As twilight splendour turned to night, rock groups took turns on
a pop-up stage to belt away more and less tunefully at a thinning crowd.

Harmony Week parade night belonged to the long struggle of
the Warumungu to hang on to a sense of themselves while finding
an accommodation with the *papulanyi*. How far they had come! The
great-grandparents of the painted-up Aboriginal kids now racketing
around the milling crowd had been 'bucks' and 'gins' dragooned into
a 'corroboree' for the miners and the minister from Canberra and the

reporters from southern newspapers. Their grandparents, pressed into dormitories, had been forbidden to use their own language. Their parents had seen a sacred rock stolen and dropped in the main street to honour the miners. Now the world was coming to them, at their place! But parade night was time-out, really. Here there was no grog, no violence, no nothing to do. As the sun went down, the heat, the wind, even the flies were gone. Here, in this brief moment, black and white were together, on Aboriginal land, not apart in a white world.

•

Tennant Creek is unlike almost any other town in Australia and, on the face of it, quite unlike Australia as a whole. It is small, isolated and impoverished, racked by misery, home to nearly as many black people as white; Australia is big, urban, prosperous, confident and overwhelmingly not Aboriginal. And yet in both has been waged a decades-long struggle over telling the story, differing in weight and emphasis but with much the same ingredients. In both, the struggle began when the Aboriginal people, supported by many others, refused their allotted position. It continued through battles over land and then on to the Stolen Generations and conflict over the story itself. In the town and in the nation, the struggle was conducted within and between Aboriginal, scholarly, legal and popular forms of storytelling. In both, governments used public history to counter unwelcome accounts, trying to smother them with stories of the Territorians' triumph over hardship and adversity in one case, and of the coming of age of an Australian nation at Gallipoli and Flanders in the other. A stalemate, a ceasefire on much the same unspoken terms emerged in both: there would be two stories, the dominant and the subordinate.

I often puzzled over how there could be such similarities in two such different places. Of course there was cause and effect – mostly

Australian cause, local effect – but it wasn't just that. My best solution was to find under the differences a fundamental similarity in the organisation of life and power. In that respect Tennant is as like Australia as it is different from most other places in Australia, in the presence there of black and white, of the miners and the pastoralists, and of the southerners and the Territorians. Tennant, like Australia, is a field of life on which have played and interplayed relations between two racial groups, between material interests and conscience, and between frontier and post-frontier.[27] In Tennant as in Australia, no combination of those poles was sufficient to overcome any other. On Harmony Week parade night, as in Australia as a whole, was the wish, longstanding and heartfelt on one side, recent, contested and erratic on the other, for something undefined and not quite graspable currently called, for want of a better name, 'reconciliation' between peoples with unreconciled stories about themselves and each other. Tennant did try to tell its story and so did Australia; neither failed, and neither succeeded. The silence was not dismantled, but it wasn't restored either.

AFTERWORD

In the years that followed my last trip to Tennant, I came to assume that the strange career of the great Australian silence had arrived at its terminus. The 'history wars' had fizzled out, John Howard and his 'black armband' crusade were gone, and his successor had apologised for 'the profound grief, suffering and loss inflicted on ... our fellow Australians'.[1] What I failed to notice was a new contest, fought on the ground of public history. There, the guardians of the official national story struggled to contain a story very different in kind, content and creation.

The official storytellers were Howard's progeny back in office. Dropping Howard's campaign against 'black armband history', they pressed on with 'practical' reconciliation (for Them) and lots of the 'symbolic' (for Us). They followed Howard in defending the flag, the anthem and the national days, and in turning the Anzac legend into a cult through big spending on the infrastructure of memory and commemoration. Among myriad makeovers, and representative of them, were the hills above King George Sound in Albany, Western Australia. This was for many young men the last sight of Australia before Gallipoli, perhaps forever. I learned this fact sixty-odd years ago from the inscription on a simple obelisk on a hill overlooking the sound. The emotional force of that unforgettable moment came from the contrast between

the grandeur of the setting and the gravity of the events commemo-
rated with the simplicity of the memorial. And now? On one peak is
an Avenue of Honour, an Apex Lookout, a Memorial Place, a memorial to the Desert Mounted Corps and the Padre White Lookout. On
another is the National Anzac Centre, a refurbished Princess Royal
Fortress, and Convoy Lookout. There are dozens of info boards and
dozens more markers detailing each and every troopship departing the
sound. Poetry is etched in marble ('I chant this chant of my silent soul
in the name of all dead soldiers'); soldiers' letters home, in facsimile,
are etched in marble too. There is a grand marble staircase, a statue in
bronze of a mounted corpsman and his horse, life-sized. There are guns,
a Naval Discovery Trail, a Memorial Garden and an upscale restaurant.

Such official chest-thumping has been subverted by the rise and
rise of distinctly non-official 'expressive' public history. Thousands of
Aboriginal artists, writers, dancers, actors and directors, activists and
intellectuals have combined with thousands more non-Indigenous cultural workers to give the Aboriginal world an astonishing prominence.[2]
It is this work, not the contrived solemnities of official public history,
that has seized imaginations beyond Canberra, including the imaginations of state and local governments.[3] In one of the many nooks
and crannies of cultural life, a gathering of Catholic school principals
opens with a prayer that truth will make possible a reconciliation with
Australia's First Peoples. In another, the Sutherland Shire Council wres-
tles with the problem of provocative signage at Botany Bay ('Welcome
to Kurnell, Birthplace of a Nation'). In yet another, SBS On Demand
offers a long, long list of Indigenous-themed movies to mark NAIDOC
week (National Aborigines and Islanders Day Observance Committee),
and rock star Peter Garrett puts out a Top 20 playlist of Indigenous
performances. Meetings, conferences, events everywhere begin with
an acknowledgement of traditional ownership (on one occasion by the

prime minister, in parliament, in language), often with a 'welcome to country' as well. The Aboriginal flag flies on local government offices. Most states and territories are discussing or even negotiating compensation and a treaty with their Aboriginal peoples (in fact, in Victoria a brand-new commission has started doing this work). Athletes black and white object to the national anthem, a premier suggests changing the words, Cricket Australia drops the term 'Australia Day' from its promotion of a big competition, an NRL final opens with the national anthem sung in Eora and English by a young Wiradjuri woman, and not one but two full-length documentaries are made about the racist tormenting of AFL star Adam Goodes. Aboriginal people are now routinely referred to as members of a specific group or 'nation'; Australia Post is encouraging the use of 'traditional place names' in addressing postal items. Most remarkable of all, in Tasmania Indigenous elders and the RSL are working together in the commemoration of the Anzacs and those who died in the frontier wars.[4] The cumulative effect of this explosion in expressive public history is to make the official national symbols and rituals look like whitefella throwbacks.

But expressive public history has its limitations too. It has had more to say about Aboriginal life before 1788 and about Aboriginal culture of the present day than about what happened in between. It has been more successful in taking us from depreciation of the Aboriginal world to appreciation (to borrow Stanner's apposition) than in telling the story of relations between two racial groups within a single field of life. This limitation the Uluru Statement from the Heart has confronted.[5] Up there as a top priority with a Voice to Parliament is 'truth-telling'.

•

Australia is just one of many nations – from Poland to Japan, France to Turkey, Indonesia to England – that make certain realities unwelcome and prefer mythology to truth-telling. But Australia is unusual in having a very small group that cares a great deal about the telling of the story, as well as a very large group that cares somewhat. If we do manage to press on with dismantling our silence, it will be because that small group has been able to seize the moment to mobilise the large one to get behind truth-telling.

But which truths?[6] Told how? Will truth-telling mean just the truths of the experiences of the living, perhaps given as testimony in the way of the *Bringing Them Home* inquiry? Truths told by Them, at Us? Or, to avoid ruffling white feathers, just the historical truths of the Aboriginal experience since 1788 but not truths about who inflicted it and how? Will it mean truths found and documented by yet another commission, soon forgotten? Or just those truths that might at last deliver reparation and compensation? Simple truths, or complicated ones?

The first and hardest of many truths is that of organised violence. In scale alone it is hard to confront: an armed conflict between peoples, the invaders and the invaded, spread over an entire continent and 140 years and costing tens of thousands of lives, almost all of them Aboriginal, a total in excess of the 63,000 lost in the First World War and getting up toward double the number of Australian casualties in the Second World War.[7] Harder still is the use of overwhelming power against people who were both innocent and relatively powerless. No wonder we don't like mentioning the war. But this, the truth about organised violence, has to be told first because until it *has* been faced, other and sometimes very different truths can't be told either.

One of those other truths: something like half of the killings of Aboriginal people were at the hands of Aboriginal men, the troopers of the Queensland Native Police. How can that truth be explained? What should be thought and felt about it? More difficult truths follow: if not everything done by Aboriginal people in the face of invasion was 'good', however and by whomever that is defined, then not everything done by the invaders was 'bad'. There are few moments in the story of white wants in which white conscience was entirely absent, and there are even some moments in which it prevailed. The 'bad' was so often so bad that it can be difficult to remember the good, but it is crucial that it *is* remembered. The 'balance' that Blainey wanted exists, to some degree at least, *within* the story of relations between black and white as well as between it and the rest of the Australian story. Were that not the case, there would have been no great Australian silence nor such prodigious efforts to dismantle it. Even Stanner, that most reflective and self-aware of thinkers, never really acknowledged that the moral position from which he assailed our conduct was as much part and product of our history as the conduct he assailed.[8]

Another truth: not all of that conduct lies in some distant past. It's not just that in Tennant Creek in 2005 there lived people who as children had fled the Coniston massacres, or that the terrible consequences of organised violence and all that it brought roll on through the generations. For all the massive effort at putting things right (and the rather less massive successes), there remains much in the present that is continuous with the past.

The truth to which all these truths belong is that the story to be told is both very simple and very complicated. Simply put, the continent was theirs, we wanted it, and we took it. But in the patterns of events, in the content of relationships, in the interaction of two social orders as different in their ways of being and moral systems as any such interactions in human history, it is a story of baffling complexity.

Then come the difficulties of 'telling'. Yet more 'telling', in the usual sense of that term, is the last thing we need. Aboriginal people have told their stories to commissions of enquiry and courts of law and oral historians, in hundreds of memoirs, autobiographies and biographies, as well as through the political theatre of agitation, strikes, walk-offs, demonstrations. Historians, anthropologists, linguists, archaeologists, journalists, public intellectuals and many others have told the story, in broad and in almost microscopic detail, in tens of thousands of books, monographs, theses and articles, as well as in speeches, conferences, debates, seminars, public meetings and protests, as well as in film, theatre, literature and all the rest.[9] What 'the truth' needs is not more 'telling' but more comprehension, more absorption and more acting upon. That cannot be done by trying, yet again, to convert millions by preaching at them.

For one thing, most Australians don't *need* to be converted. Most would like to see it put right. In May 2020 the multinational mining company Rio Tinto blew up a sacred Aboriginal site in Western Australia.[10] Nothing new about that, but the consequences have been astonishingly different from those that followed the miners' assault on Warumungu Country in 1933 or the invasion of Yolngu lands in the 1950s or countless other vandalisms. In the face of escalating media coverage, Rio hoped at first that it might get away with eating humble pie. Then three top executives, including the CEO himself, had to go. And now both compensation and new legislation threaten. Compare this humiliation of the miners with the days when they explained to the Hawke government how things stood or when Hugh Morgan's hysterics about *Mabo* could be taken seriously. Very large numbers of people felt angry and shamed. Rio hadn't just blown up a cave somewhere up north; it had desecrated something sacred. Hearts are mostly in the right place, and to the extent that heads are the problem it is not in hostility or even ignorance – of which there is plenty – but in *confusion*, that constant in the history of relations between two racial groups within a single field of life, currently sustained by the contest between the official story and the expressive.[11]

For another, heads and hearts that *aren't* in the right place won't be converted by being preached at either. As Tennant Creek's town clerk told the land commission in 1985, there are some people who wouldn't have a bar of land rights under any circumstances as a 'matter of principle'. Others have long since been turned off by words and yet more words.

And, for a third, the 'problem', whether of confusion or recalcitrance or apathy, might exist in hearts and minds but that's not where it comes from. The fraction of the silence that is gone wasn't 'shattered', it was battled out. The fraction that remains is embedded in rituals and symbols and institutions of memory and commemoration, stretching all the way from those 34,000-odd statues and obelisks and plaques to the Australian War Memorial. These leavings of the past are the rarely noticed history curriculum of everyday life, the means by which the past attempts to perpetuate its own account of itself. Dismantling is a wholesale business, not retail; it is about the power of and over institutions, not preaching. In this, those who want truths absorbed and acted upon have much to learn from Tennant Creek – more, alas, from what it didn't do than what it did.

•

The first thing that Tennant didn't do is name the problem. In and around the town I saw just one protest, that half-hidden graffiti on the back of the Attack Creek toilet door. Elsewhere? No graffiti, no red paint, no headless statues, no toppled obelisks,[12] not even an uprooted info board, no sign whatever of so-called 'cancel culture',[13] unless we count that cage constructed around the monument at Phillip Creek out of fear that it would be cancelled. Nor did I see anywhere any provision for visitors to comment on the truths told and not told. There is little if anything in Tennant's official public history that should be demolished, but much that needs to be shown for what it is. Why no

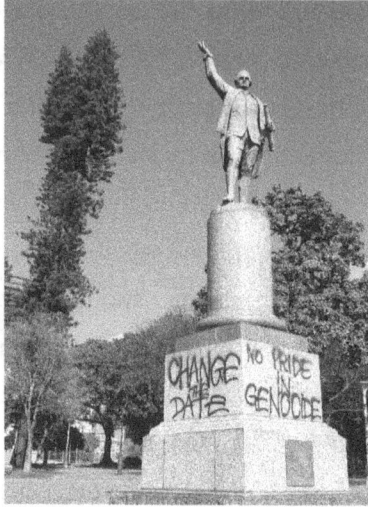

'The first thing that Tennant didn't do is name the problem': comment
on the 'discoverer' of Australia, Hyde Park, Sydney 2017

digital graffiti, a website ('www.dunnydoor.org.au'?) for images, anec-
dotes, memes to out the many silences in the telling of Tennant's story?

A second thing that Tennant didn't do: it did not rewrite the info
boards and guide sheets and annotated maps. It didn't add plaques or
info boards to the monuments at Threeways and Attack Creek to explain
how the 'attack' looked from the other side, or to explain that John
Flynn's mantle of safety did not extend to most of the Territory's population. It didn't erect new monuments to Mary Ward and the people
of Banka Banka, or to Nat Williams and Engineer Jack, or to Charlie
Jampin, Zulu Jappangarti and Bill Stanner. It didn't offer visitors to the
Battery Hill mining museum and to Nyinkka Nyunyu a chance to have
a say about how Tennant's story was being told there. And it didn't ask
whether and how the stories told by those two institutions might be
made more complete, more truthful.

All these things that Tennant Creek didn't do, a few communities
across Australia *are* doing, and many more could do, given the right

kind of help and encouragement.[14] A nationwide program would not aim to 'cancel' artefacts from the past, but to place them in it. It would need to be systematic but not directive; hearts and minds that won't be instructed can be informed. Many towns and communities would welcome a chance to decide whether and how to tell a more truthful story about themselves; the Makarrata Commission proposed by the Uluru Statement would get much more truth told by providing the occasion and the support (or perhaps by pressing for something like a reincarnated Heritage Commission to do so) than by yet more proselytising.[15] Why not enlist Australia's 1000-odd local history societies to work with Indigenous groups and with historians and their research students to help communities tell their story more fully and truthfully? What better training in the skills of the trade, and what better education in the purposes of history? A nationwide project could easily generate a nationally cumulative account. It could link to websites such as the national heritage database, the Monument Australia site, the University of Newcastle's

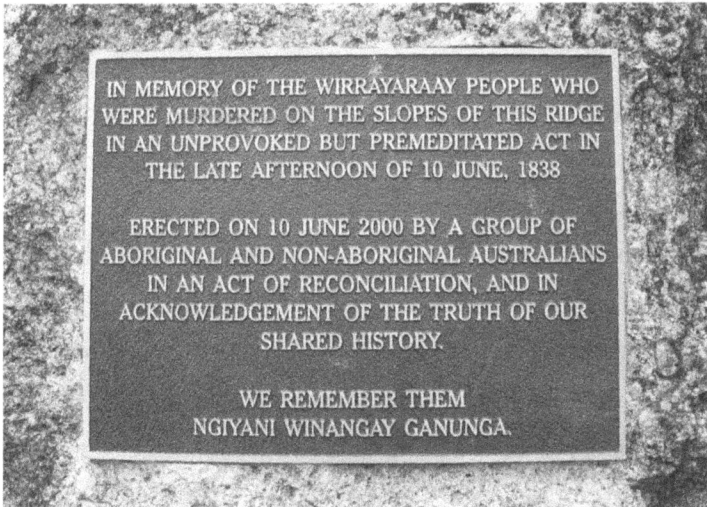

IN MEMORY OF THE WIRRAYARAAY PEOPLE WHO
WERE MURDERED ON THE SLOPES OF THIS RIDGE
IN AN UNPROVOKED BUT PREMEDITATED ACT IN
THE LATE AFTERNOON OF 10 JUNE, 1838

ERECTED ON 10 JUNE 2000 BY A GROUP OF
ABORIGINAL AND NON-ABORIGINAL AUSTRALIANS
IN AN ACT OF RECONCILIATION, AND IN
ACKNOWLEDGEMENT OF THE TRUTH OF OUR
SHARED HISTORY.

WE REMEMBER THEM
NGIYANI WINANGAY GANUNGA.

'A few communities *are* doing': plaque commemorating
the Myall Creek Massacre

colonial massacres site and the AWM's register of war memorials, gradually building up a double-sided record of the extent and depth of the silence that Aboriginal people have had to endure, and of the grassroots achievement in overcoming that silence.

A third lesson from Tennant: in settling for two major storytelling institutions, rather than the one suggested by the Canberra consultant way back in 1984, Tennant allowed the mining museum to go on telling one part of the story as if that was the whole story. Something like that has happened in the national capital too. There the National Museum of Australia (NMA) does try to tell the recovered story (much as Nyinkka Nyunyu has tried to do), but the bigger, grander, more influential Australian War Memorial does not. Moreover, it doesn't want to. It has repeatedly insisted that the so-called 'frontier wars' are covered elsewhere, including at the NMA, so there is no need or place to tell the story at the AWM as well.[16]

Of the many counterarguments put over and again, only one is fundamental: the AWM, like Tennant's mining museum, is telling only part of the truth. It sustains the myths that the white Australia of the War Memorial's imagining is always and everywhere the goodie, and that collective grief and tragedy have been only occasional visitors to our history, myths so pervasive that they pop out of a prime minister's mouth unbidden: our history, said Prime Minister Rudd not long after delivering the Apology, is free of 'wars, revolution [and] bloodshed'.[17]

The AWM has immense symbolic power. It is among the world's most recognised sites of memory and, as it keeps saying, repository of 'the soul of the nation'. There is no more important place for a more truthful national story to be told; my own feeling is that 'truth-telling' won't have been done unless and until the AWM tells a fuller truth, simply because successive governments have made it the St Peter's of the national religion. To try to get around the problem by building another institution to tell and commemorate what the AWM won't, as was suggested recently by Henry Reynolds and others, would leave Australia's apex institution of memory and identity telling a fundamentally misleading and untruthful story.[18] In all likelihood, any workaround would be left in the shade, just as Nyinkka Nyunyu lives in the shade of the mining museum. Separate coverage of frontier conflict would imply that it didn't really amount to 'war' because real wars are recorded in the AWM, and it was mainly to do with Aboriginal people anyway.

By these same tokens, there is no place in which telling a more truthful story would be more difficult. Could a Makarrata Commission hope to succeed where many have failed? That might depend in part on the story the AWM is asked to tell. The frontier wars are not only or even mainly a matter for conventional military history. The truths to be told are of armed conflict inseparable from 'life', in its conduct and its consequences. Some of these truths are unpalatable in the extreme, but the AWM should not be asked to tell a story that demonises us (or sentimentalises them). The story should include the controversy and disagreement over whether and how the story should be told, the AWM's role in that not excepted. The splendid example of the Attack Creek toilet door should be followed: those for whom the story is being told should be encouraged to say what they think and feel about the telling.

Appeals in these or any other terms to the AWM leadership would fall on ears that have been deaf for a long time. It is now nearly fifty years since none other than Geoffrey Blainey was the first to suggest that the AWM should consider incorporating the frontier conflicts. Powerfully defended by its military-dominated council and by strident Coalition governments (and a gun-shy Labor Party), the AWM is nonetheless increasingly exposed to change.[19] It is anachronistic. Its many critics include some of its own, and the wider supports of its stance on the frontier wars are shifting.[20] The frontier zone is now much less inclined to brawl with the post-frontier and its conscience than it was in Hugh Morgan's day. Pastoralists and miners alike have found that they can work with Aboriginal people, and in the aftermath of the destruction of Juukan Gorge will be increasingly willing to do so. Thirty years on from their spectacular clash with Keating over *Mabo*, perhaps they are ready to switch from attempting to win the story to *reconciling* stories, as Keating was trying to do?

A public campaign to press for change would almost certainly fail. It is a task for quiet diplomacy, in which that frail vessel, the Labor Party, would necessarily be central. Perhaps with the help and provocation of the Statement from the Heart, a Labor government could be persuaded to return the AWM to its stated mission: to 'assist Australians to remember, interpret and understand the Australian experience of war and its enduring impact on Australian society'?[21]

•

However pursued, truth-telling is a big undertaking. Does it really matter? The question has been answered in many ways. One is that we must heal the wound at the heart of the nation, or free ourselves from deep-seated fears about its 'legitimacy'; we must 'come to terms' with our 'unresolved past'. Another: we will go on being the Americans of our neighbourhood, blind to the way others see us and the past we try to hide, unless and until we 'face up' to the truth about ourselves.[22] Or, on a less lofty plane: this whole issue has consumed far too much of our political time and attention; let's get it sorted so that we can 'move on'.

There is something to be said for each of these, but none is compelling. Big words about the Nation and its Soul and so on appeal only to the converted, and implicitly point the finger at Australians rather than at the disposition of power in Australia.[23] The more instrumental thinking about 'moving on' or presenting a less bumptious face to the world might be right, but is it inspirational? For me, only two of many arguments offered are compelling.

The first concerns those who have been most directly and extensively damaged by the great Australian silence. Aboriginal 'disadvantage', 'closing the gap' and the like are trivialisations, and exculpatory ones at that. The harm inflicted on the continent's 500 or so little republics and their peoples in the years following 1788 is scarcely a blip in the history of organised human cruelty, but it looms large in Australia as incomprehensibly destructive of what existed when the British arrived. No-one, including the many generations of victims, has really grasped how far the consequences reach, or how, at last, to bring them to a halt. For many Aboriginal people, a problem in everyday life more common, less detectable and as damaging as overt 'racism' or 'discrimination' or 'disadvantage' is having to live with a half-comprehension of who they are and where their circumstances have come from, a half-comprehension (and worse) that appears in the public realm when Aboriginal people are spoken of or treated as just another minority group or lobby group or ethnic group, or even as having opted for a certain (unaffordable) 'lifestyle'. Contrary to John Howard, the 'symbolic' *is* practical. After one of my visits to Battery Hill's social history annexe, I went back into town to continue work with Francine McCarthy to find 'Jacob', first doing a bit of hyperventilating about what I had just been looking at up on the Hill. I know, she said. I can't bear to go up there.

The second of these arguments is to do with truth and its place in our culture. The pursuit of truthfulness through disciplined enquiry and evidence, tested and contested, rather than through revelation or gut feel or general agreement (or the internet), is not exclusive to Western countries such as Australia but it is foundational. It was the thrill of the hunt for what was *actually* the case, and the rewards for finding it, that fuelled Gillen's excited letters to Spencer about his latest discoveries.

The pursuit of truth was the taken-for-granted when Stanner asked his colleagues: have we truly understood the process by which Aboriginal people are transforming themselves? Hot on the trail of the truth in a London archive, Henry Reynolds exulted when he found evidence that Australian law had been lying to itself and everyone else for a century or more. The justices of the High Court were chastened and shamed by the evidence presented to them in *Mabo*. Windschuttle paid unintended tribute to the pursuit of truth when he accused the historians of fabricating evidence, and it was the further pursuit of the truth via evidence tested and contested that effectively put him out of business.

That way of pursuing truth is central to our culture, but so are other impulses. For reasons good and bad, many influential figures have opted for a policy of least said, soonest mended (or Best We Forget, as Aboriginal activists have put it). That is what Spencer and Gillen did when they proposed that a veil be drawn over unfortunate events; what Hasluck did when, out of fear that Australia would follow the US into racial conflict, he attacked anything that might stir up 'racial feeling'; perhaps that was what Blainey was doing when he deployed the pejorative 'black armband'.

As the struggle between these two impulses shifts from the scholarly disciplines, the law and public disputation to a contest between white 'official' and a collaborative 'expressive' public history, there is room for concern about both the possible outcome and the extent to which it is influenced by the pursuit of truth. Neither official nor expressive public history care as much about truthfulness as their antecedents did; both lack institutional penalties for ignoring the truth and rewards for respecting it. In racial politics that is a dangerous thing, as recent events in the US and elsewhere illustrate.

We might have got away with the silence had Aboriginal people not declined to disappear from history, as they were once expected – in two senses of that term – to do. The past should indeed be 'put behind us' but it won't be until it has been properly acknowledged, not by fessing up, or by telling just those parts of the story that suit particular purposes, but by telling our shared story as fully and truthfully as possible. How to persuade those with control over our institutions of that case? We're on an offer to make it joint business.

ACKNOWLEDGEMENTS

In pursuing a preoccupation off and on over two decades I have accumulated many debts.

For the title: 'The strange career' is from C. Vann Woodward's classic *The Strange Career of Jim Crow* (1955); the 'great Australian silence' is from W.E.H. Stanner's 1968 Boyer Lectures.

I thank particularly the people of Tennant Creek who appear in these pages: Trisha Frank Narrurlu, Rose Graham Namikili and Francine McCarthy Namikili, who in 2005 and 2006 helped me meet and talk with a number of my contemporaries: Edith Graham Nakamarra, Jimmy Jones Jampin, Rosie Thompson Nakamarra, Bunny Napurrula, Therese Patterson Napurrula, Judy Nixon Nakamarra, Kathleen Fitz Napanangka, Jean McCarthy Nakamarra and Day Day Frank Jakkamarra, all of whom have since passed away.

As will be obvious to anyone who has read any of these pages, I am indebted to many scholars in several disciplines and sub-disciplines. Many of those people are no longer with us; among those who are, and to whose work I am particularly indebted, are Henry Reynolds, Ann Curthoys and Tim Rowse.

Officers at a number of agencies and institutions gave expert assistance in locating materials and providing images for reproduction: Anna Gilfillen at the Office of the Aboriginal Land Commissioner, Darwin, Eve Terry at the National Archives of Australia, Nancy Ladas and Mary

Morris at the Museums Victoria, Lea Gardam at the South Australian Museum, Mathias Richter at the Australian Institute of Aboriginal and Torres Strait Islander Studies, Joann Hamilton at the National Museum of Australia, Elke Wiesmann at the Central Land Council, Kent Watson at Monument Australia, and Pam Hodges, curator of the For Tennant Creekers website.

Among the many friends and allies of the Indigenous people of the Barkly who gave generous assistance I must make special mention of David Nash, who read the manuscript, responded promptly and uncomplainingly to dozens of queries, and put me in touch with his friends and colleagues – many of whom, I discovered, are also beneficiaries of his half-century of work on the languages, history and anthropology of the region, and of his exceptional generosity.

The manuscript was read by Jim Ashenden, Ken Boston, Erika Martens and Ian Temby, by Chris Feik at Black Inc. and, through Chris, by Robert Manne and Mark McKenna. Their corrections, suggestions and encouragement did much to turn a manuscript into a book. Rebecca Bauert, senior editor at Black Inc., saved me from many errors and infelicities, and was a pleasure to work with. Needless to say, responsibility for what emerged is mine.

Others who helped, in many ways, include Brian Abbey, David Alexander, Max Angas, Diane Bell, Paul Brown, Peter Browne, the late Anne Deveson, the late Fay Gale, Helen Garner, Olaf Gherkin, Bill Hannan, Lorna Hannan, Natalie Kam, Dick Kimber, Arthur Beau Palmer, the late Merv Pattemore, Sam Newman, Harriet Olney, Jay Winter, Neil Williams, and the late Hal Wootten.

My lifelong friends David Woodgate and Erika Calder Woodgate supported and were involved in the project at every stage. Without my partner in all things, Sandra Milligan, the project would never have started or finished.

IMAGE CREDITS

119   Members of the Council for Aboriginal Affairs, 1968. From left: Barrie Dexter,
      'Nugget' Coombs, Bill Stanner, courtesy of Australian Institute of Aboriginal and
      Torres Strait Islander Studies. With kind permission of Jocelyn Dexter.

123   Officers of the Aboriginal Tent Embassy welcomed, Canberra, 1972 (Jim Green),
      The Sydney Morning Herald.

133   Delegates to the National Conference on Aboriginal Studies, University House,
      Canberra, 1961. Stanner is front row, centre, almost invisible between Minister in
      charge of Aboriginal Affairs Bill Wentworth (to his right), and A.P. Elkin (to his
      left). Fay Gale is further along in the front row, the second of the three women.
      Norman Tindale is on the left of the row of three men at the back. Courtesy
      of Australian Institute of Aboriginal and Torres Strait Islander Studies, Stanner
      Collection (N872-15).

150   Opening address to the commissioner, Gurindji claim, Dagarugu Station, c. 1981
      (Arthur Beau Palmer), courtesy of Arthur Beau Palmer.

166   Hugh Morgan, President of the Australian Mining Industry Council, Canberra,
      1982, David Bartho / Fairfax News Archive.

169   'Sydney Harbour, Invasion Day', 26 January 1988 (Huw Davies), courtesy of
      Jocelyn Davies and Branwen Davies.

177   Eddie Mabo: *Mabo* plaintiffs Father James Passi, Eddie Koiki Mabo and James
      Rice with their lawyer Bryan Keon-Cohen, Supreme Court of Queensland, May
      1989 (Trevor Graham), courtesy Yarra Bank Films.

198   Yothu Yindi, 1997 (Michael Amendolia), courtesy of Newspix.

199   Prime Minister Kevin Rudd with Indigenous leader Lowitja O'Donoghue,
      13 February 2008 (Gary Ramage), courtesy of Newspix.

210   Paul Hasluck, Minister for Territories, unveiling the memorial to John McDouall
      Stuart and his companions at Attack Creek, 25 June 1960, the 100th anniversary
      of the day on which 'hostile natives and illness forced the party to return'. John
      Edwards Collection, by permission of the For Tennant Creekers website.

211   Flyer for the unveiling of the John Flynn Monument, courtesy of Pam Hodges
      for the For Tennant Creekers website, http://fortennantcreekers.com/places/
      landmarks/john-flynn-monument.

221   Edith Graham Nakamarra, September 2006 (Erika Calder), courtesy of the
      author.

224   Bunny Napurrula, September 2006 (Erika Calder), courtesy of the author.

238   James Cook statue graffitied, Hyde Park, 26 September 2017 (Dave Swift),
      courtesy of Newspix.

239   Myall Creek plaque, Heritage, Community Engagement, Department of Premier
      and Cabinet, courtesy of the National Museum of Australia.

NOTES

Note on Usage

1   This much-quoted formulation is from W.E.H. Stanner's celebrated Boyer
    Lectures, given in 1968, and published as *After the Dreaming*. Stanner plays a
    central role in the story told in this book.

Chapter One: 1860

1   Tindale's map is barely the tip of a colossal iceberg. It summarises findings laid out
    in detail in Tindale's magnum opus, *Aboriginal Tribes of Australia: Their Terrain,
    Environmental Controls, Distribution, Limits and Proper Names (1974)*. Individual
    entries for hundreds of tribes detail their location (including cartographic
    coordinates), area of land occupied and alternative names, and list references
    to each from a wide range of scholarly and informal literatures. That in turn
    was a distillation of one part of a phenomenally productive research career that
    spanned seventy-odd years. For an overview, see Philip Jones' obituary for Tindale
    (December 1995). Tindale's now-famous map can be found at the South Australian
    Museum website: http://archives.samuseum.sa.gov.au/tribalmap. For a revised
    semi-official version, see the Australian Institute of Aboriginal and Torres Strait
    Islander Studies website: https://aiatsis.gov.au/explore/map-indigenous-australia.
2   Alan Powell (2009, p. 13) reports that by Tindale's count 126 tribes had most or all
    of their country in what was marked as 'the Northern Territory': some small and
    densely populated, others (such as Warlpiri Country) larger than many European
    states of the day. Referring to these as 'republics' and applying a term developed
    in one time and place to a very different one is problematic, but the similarities
    are there: a territory with known and recognised (if permeable) boundaries, with
    which the inhabitants identify; independence; and the absence of a monarchy or
    similar political authority. Tindale's map and the descriptor 'Aboriginal' have been
    criticised on similar grounds – that is, as impositions of Western concepts on a
    different reality.
3   A problem arising in the writing of this book: which spelling to use when
    paraphrasing, quoting from or drawing on texts and documents (such as Tindale's
    own map) that predate the now generally accepted spellings? Here and elsewhere

I have followed the spelling used by the source in question, and have indicated its obsolescence by adding the now-common form in square brackets. In 'Blunders, Excusable Errors, and Discarded Ideas', a chapter of his magisterial *Aboriginal Tribes of Australia*, Norman Tindale bemoans chaos in the spelling of tribal names. In addition to frequent typographical errors (he writes) must be added 'the vast corpus of variant spellings engendered by the hit and miss methods of transcription practiced by the usual English speaker' (1974a, p. 154). Tindale set himself to eliminating this chaos by prodigious scholarship; he included in each of his profiles of hundreds of tribes a list of the various spellings of that tribe's name. The very first of those profiles (of the 'Antakarinja') includes more than twenty other spellings, ranging from 'Antakarindja' to 'Unterrgerrie' as well as nine different names (as opposed to spellings) used for the same group. Tindale's amazing efforts notwithstanding, spellings are still not completely stabilised, although there are generally accepted conventions in most cases.

4   The story of reactions to Tindale's map is told by Philip Jones in Tindale's obituary (December 1995). Billy Griffiths (2018) records the archaeologists' excitement as they chased further and further back into an extraordinary cultural continuity.

5   Berndt and Berndt (1999).

6   Speaking in 1986, the founding father of Australian archaeology, John Mulvaney, could report that in the space of just twelve years 'archaeological research [had] added thirty thousand years to Australia's human past. No parallel exists elsewhere.' Mulvaney (1986) p. 53.

7   A long debate about the possible role of humans in the extinction of the mega-fauna appears to incriminate them. See Frederik Saltre, Christopher Johnson and Corey Bradshaw (December 2019).

8   This account draws particularly on Berndt and Berndt (1999), Gammage (2013), Broome (2019) and Blainey (1982). The phrase 'the biggest estate on earth' is from Gammage; 'Australia was groomed' is from Reyburn (June 1993) (see note 10 below).

9   Gale (1998) p. 9.

10 The formulation 'Zen road to affluence' was suggested by US anthropologist Marshall Sahlins in the mid-1960s to contrast societies that limited their desires to what was available with societies (such as ours) that have not. Anthropologist Bruce Reyburn has worked harder than most to comprehend a mental and cultural world so fundamentally different from our own. Of the Warumungu he says: 'The Wirnkarra [Dreaming] dimensions of the country ... exist like harmonic resonances beyond the material world as conceived in European terms. The manipulation of these resonances to produce a humming universe is the business of senior initiated men. The excellent condition of Australia at the time of the arrival of the desperate Europeans was not the result of the mindless workings of nature, but the result of the successful integration of human practice with the forces of the ecosystem. Australia was groomed by people who dedicated their lives to the task of life's priests. The practical wisdom accumulated over eons was refined into chants and other "ritual" practices which, when properly carried out, sent out messages which tuned life ... The messages of experience are combined in a compacted form which

exceeds those provided by the modern miracle of electronic engineering. Metaphor and metonymy are employed to achieve fractal arrangements which solve problems of information compression and transgenerational communication which would defy linear means' (June 1993). The 'variety' in Aboriginal cultural forms was much greater than is often assumed, as can be illustrated by the number of languages and language types. Europe has just four language families; Aboriginal Australia's 400-odd languages comprised twenty-seven families. See Bowern (March 2018).

11   See Chapter Ten.

12   Spencer (1901) p. 187.

13   The phrase does not suggest that Aboriginal women were crushed under an oppressive male thumb. As Spencer and Gillen pointed out more than a century ago, women's lives were 'far from miserable as they are so often depicted' (1912, p. 33). But much of Aboriginal women's knowledge and power remained half-understood at best for many decades to come. 'Women's business' is not meant to be revealed to men, let alone white men (even if they thought to ask), and almost all anthropologists were both white and male. Accounts of the 'Aboriginal world' were as told by old black men to old white men. See note 7 for Chapter Two and note 20 for Chapter Three.

14   Phillip was shocked by violence different from his own, as were Aboriginal people shocked by his (hangings, for example) and his kind's (hitting children, for example).

15   Another anthropologist estimated that in one small part of Arnhem Land, around 200 men died during organised warfare over a twenty-year period (1909–29), amounting to one person in 300 per year. 'Aboriginal men quarrelled and killed over prestige, religion and women,' says a historian in reference to these estimates, 'they were like men the world over.' See Powell (2009) p. 16.

16   To state the obvious, this is unavoidably an assessment by one culture of another. Anthropologists, including those whose work I have tried to understand, have made a sustained effort to see how things might look from the other direction.

17   Gillen (1968) entry for 14 December, p. 262.

18   Stuart's account of events ('I told my men to get their guns ready, for I could see they were determined upon mischief') differs substantially from a relatively recent Aboriginal account (see Wright, 1997, Chapter 2). It is worth tracking down a facsimile copy of Stuart's journals for the illustrator's imagining of Attack Creek as a Scottish glen. Hardman (1975) pp. 214–21.

19   More plainly, he was an invader who 'opened up country' both directly and indirectly. At least five subsequent 'expeditions' departed from and/or returned to Stuart's route: Giles (1872–74), Gosse (1873), Warburton (1873–74), Barclay (1878) and Forrest (1879–80). See Powell (2009) p. 70.

20   See Cross (2011). The 'Northern Territory' was carved out from New South Wales in 1863.

21   Spencer and Gillen (1904) p. 11.

22   Peter Taylor (1980) gives a detailed – a *really* detailed – account of the line and its construction. The irony in his book's title, *An End to Silence*, appears to have been unintentional.

23 Cross (2011) p. 42.

24 Attack Creek was the site of a second violent clash just over a decade later, when a member of the first droving party to use Stuart's route north was clubbed to death. Further north, beyond Warumungu Country, that same party sooled dogs onto Aboriginal men, killing at least one of them. A third – and last – fatal conflict involving the Warumungu followed when they attacked a subsequent droving party about halfway between Tennant Creek and Attack Creek. At least two Warumungu men were shot. Reid (1990) pp. 49–52, 62.

25 My account paraphrases and quotes from Spencer and Gillen (1912) p. 320, which in turn draws on their 1901 journals. Reid (1990, pp. 62–7) and Mulvaney (2003) also give detailed accounts of the attack and its aftermath.

26 Spencer and Gillen (1912) p. 320.

27 See Mulvaney (2003) and Edmunds (1995) p. 12. Edmunds reports an estimate of around ninety deaths.

28 Many historians have written about the QNP. Henry Reynolds was among the first to do so and to pay particular attention to contemporaneous controversies over its methods (Reynolds 1989, 1998, 1999, 2013). Our understanding of the impact of the QNP has been virtually transformed by the work of three Queensland historians, summarised in Evans and Ørsted-Jensen (2014).

29 Reid (1990, p. 11) lists others.

30 Broome (2019, pp. 47–50) ponders the conduct and motivations of the 'native' troopers. The question has been a difficult and painful one among Aboriginal people; see note 24 for Chapter Ten.

31 Day's summary (1996, pp. 129–30) of these various estimates brings him to make his own estimate of around 50,000 casualties, a much higher number than was then accepted. Twenty years on, he has been more than vindicated – see Evans and Ørsted-Jensen (2014). Broome (2019) summarises evidence about sources detailing Aboriginal deaths and population decline, although his estimates relating to violence are outdated.

32 For others in the popular 'overlanders' sub-genre, see Buchanan (1933) and Birtles (1946), the latter being the book of the 1946 film *The Overlanders*.

33 This account of events in the Gulf Country draws on Bottoms (2013); Broome (2019) pp. 109–11; Cross (2011) pp. 328, 359, 362–4; Powell (2009) pp. 59–61, p. 66, p. 77, pp. 98–9; Reid (1990) pp. 52–62, 158–63, 171–4; Roberts (2005, August 2009, November 2009), who draws on Read and Read (1991). On the factors that made the northern frontiers particularly violent and lethal, see Broome (2019) p. 109.

34 These and other details of the invasion are from Roberts (August 2009, November 2009).

35 See Roberts (August 2009).

36 Roberts (November 2009).

37 Gillen's remark was made in his journal entry for 17 June 1901 (1968, p. 126). See also Roberts (August 2009, November 2009).

38 Abbott (1950) p. 5.

39 Powell (2009) p. 13 and Reid (1990) p. 196.

40   The story is told in detail by Jones (2007) pp. 186–223. Another of the many
     whose remains were treated as artefacts was the so-called 'last of the Tasmanian
     Aborigines', Truganini. See Pybus (2020) p. 282. Among the efforts by white
     people to repair some of the terrible damage was the return of Cubadgee's remains
     to the Warumungu, in a ceremony held on 4 June 1991, the hundredth anniversary
     of his death.

41   See Roberts (2005, August 2009, November 2009). On mining, land speculation
     and corruption in South Australia's governing circles, see Cross (2011) pp. 7, 125,
     152, 230–1.

42   Roberts (August 2009).

43   Quoted by Reid (1990) p. 163, emphases in the original.

44   See Chapter Ten.

45   The first meeting of the Society for the Abolition of the Slave Trade was held in
     London on 22 May 1787, nine days after the First Fleet sailed from Portsmouth.
     (Reynolds, September 2017).

46   Phillips's instructions can be seen at https://www.foundingdocs.gov.au/resources/
     transcripts/nsw2_doc_1787.pdf, accessed 20 December 2020.

47   From Reynolds (1998) pp. 18–21.

48   Evans and Ørsted-Jensen (2014) p. 6.

49   See Reynolds (1998) *passim*.

50   Reynolds (1998) p. 115, quoting a contributor to the debate sparked by *The Way We
     Civilize*, an 1880 critique of the frontier.

51   In Chapter 1 of *Imagined Destinies*, McGregor (1997) describes the construction of
     'race science'.

52   The division between frontier and post-frontier Australia was established by
     differences in the circumstances of life as well as by chronology and geography. As
     early as 1891, three-quarters of the colonies' population lived in cities and towns,
     the highest proportion in the world at that time, and most of that three-quarters
     were in a handful of coastal capital cities. Day (1996) p. 178.

53   The definitive history of the idea – for some, perhaps even the hope – that
     Aboriginal peoples would 'become extinct' is McGregor (1997). McGregor's index
     lists no less than thirteen factors suggested at one time or another to explain
     'extinction': Asian contact, cultural fragility, disease, Divine Providence, drugs and
     alcohol, inability to adapt, interracial sexual relations, miscegenation, missionaries,
     primitivity, tourism, vices of civilisation, and violence. On estimates of population
     and population decline, see Rowse (2004).

54   The formulation is Stanner's (1968). It sets the question pursued in this and
     many other books and articles. On Stanner and his 'great Australian silence'
     thesis, see chapters Four and Five, and notes 1 and 5 for Chapter Six. The most
     comprehensive and astute of many commentaries is Curthoys (2008).

55   The views and activities of John Downer and his colleagues are detailed by Roberts
     (August 2009, November 2009).

56   These and other ways of concealing and avoiding the truth, including the
     destruction of records, have been documented by many historians, including

Griffiths (March 2003) and Roberts (August 2009). The examples relating to Barrow Creek are from Mulvaney (2003) p. 46.

57 Foster and Nettelbeck (2012) refer to 'the great Australian whispering' and point out (p. 166) that local histories were often less silent than more general studies.

58 'Jurnkurakurr' is sometimes used to refer to Tennant Creek the creek, and occasionally even to the town as well. Properly used, it refers to a particular and sacred rock formation in the creek.

59 See Dewar (1997) p. 27. Jeannie Gunn was making the most of not very much. She was on Elsey for just two years; the purportedly remote station entertained 250 guests in one of those years; it was only an hour's ride from the telegraph line and got mail eight times a year. Dewar (1997) pp. 19–20. Dewar credits Gunn with being among the first of the Territory's many writers to see Aboriginal people as individuals rather than instances of a category. Elsey is perhaps the most storied of the northern stations; for detailed accounts of its history, see Merlan (1978, 1996) and Gleeson and Richards (1985).

60 Merlan (1996) p. xviii.

61 Tindale (1974a).

62 Peasley (1983).

63 Blainey (1982) p. 254.

64 The Pintupi experience is described and analysed in exhaustive detail by Myers (1991). For accounts (and some wonderful photographs) of first contact in the vast Western Desert region, see Batty (2006); Davenport, Johnson and Yuwali (2005); Lowe with Pike (1990); Richards, Hudson and Lowe (2002).

65 Many anthropologists, historians and others have made the point, but Rowse (2017) was the first, so far as I am aware, to show how relations between that 'other country' and the post-frontier south explain much in Australia's history. See also note 27 for Chapter Ten.

Chapter Two: 1901

1 Spencer and Gillen (1912) p. 361.

2 See Spencer and Gillen (1912), a travelogue based on their journals, the journals themselves (Spencer, 1901–02; Gillen, 1968), and their two anthropologies (Spencer and Gillen, 1901; Spencer and Gillen, 1904). The authoritative account of their work is Mulvaney and Calaby (1985). My account also draws particularly on introductory chapters to the collected letters from Gillen to Spencer (Mulvaney, Morphy and Petch, 1997), one by Mulvaney and a second by Morphy.

3 Spencer (1901–02) entry for 25 July, p. 134.

4 This is the European view of those relationships and is used only to suggest for non-Indigenous readers the closeness of the affiliations.

5 Some, perhaps many, of these people lived to see this ground become a racetrack, vivid in my mind from the day I saw there men silhouetted against hessian screens as they pissed into a galvanised iron trough rigged up for race day.

6 Spencer and Gillen (1912) p. 399.

7　Only a fraction, that is, of the Warumungu men's repertoire. On the complicated relationships between male and female anthropologists and their access to and understanding of the worlds of women and men in Aboriginal society, see note 13 for Chapter One and note 20 for Chapter Three.

8　Nash (1984) pp. 2–3.

9　'I like these blacks much better than the Kaitish,' Spencer's journal records. 'Some of them are quite 6 feet high and there are even one or two women taller than myself.' Spencer (1901–02) entry for 31 July, p. 146.

10　Spencer and Gillen were shocked by the intensity of these rituals and the pain that people inflicted on themselves, the women by striking their heads with digging sticks, the men by cutting, so much so that Gillen presumed to interfere. 'Our Walunkwa assistant [Zulu] … slashed himself across both thighs in my presence one wound extends to a depth of three inches cutting deeply into the principle [sic] muscles and extending across the whole outer surface of the thigh. The whole scene was one of horror, blood everywhere. Women with their scalps divided along the whole length of their heads and blood running over their faces looked like "ghouls escaped from the infernal regions". One young woman picked up an iron tomahawk and was just about to lay open her scalp when I snatched it from her and threw it away she then snatched a yamstick from another woman and hacked away at her head until there was a wound five inches long down the centre of her scalp, this wound she will probably sear later on with a firestick as a further measure of her grief.' (Gillen, 1901, p. 223.) I found it difficult to read their accounts – or to look at Spencer's photograph of a man with a massive leg wound lying on his blanket (Batty, Allen and Morton, 2005, p. 101). Entries in Gillen's journal for 12 and 15 August suggest that the man in the photograph was Zulu.

11　Gillen (1901) entry for 27 August, p. 244.

12　Gillen (1901) entry for 27 August, p. 244.

13　Their discovery is detailed in Chapter 10 of *Native Tribes of Central Australia*; its importance in anthropology and elsewhere is suggested by a still-growing literature of exegesis, appreciation and debate. For an excellent introduction and contribution to the debate, see Morphy (1988).

14　The diary was edited for publication (Gillen, 1995) by his grandson.

15　His mates, Mounted Constable Ernest Cowle and line operator Pado Byrne, became Spencer's mates too – see Mulvaney, Morphy and Petch (2000).

16　See Mulvaney and Calaby (1985) pp. 117–72 and Spencer (ed., 1896).

17　Much of the credit for recovering the story of Spencer and Gillen and establishing the importance of their work belongs to John Mulvaney, author of all except one chapter of the biography of Baldwin Spencer (Mulvaney and Calaby, 1985), and editor/co-editor of two volumes of letters to Spencer (Mulvaney, Petch and Morphy, 1997, and Mulvaney, Petch and Morphy, 2000). Sadly, Spencer's letters to Gillen were burned by Amelia Gillen after her husband's death. In the years since Mulvaney's biography was published, Spencer and Gillen have become a sizeable academic industry; for an overview and case in point, see http://spencerandgillen.net.

18   For short biographies of Gillen, see his *Australian Dictionary of Biography* entry,
      introductory chapters to Mulvaney, Morphy and Petch (1997), and Spencer
      Gillen's introduction to the published version of his father's 1901 expedition
      journal (Gillen 1968). Spencer Gillen was born while his father was on the
      expedition with Spencer, on 28 April 1901. 'The news came to me by wire a little
      after 9 a.m. and I am greatly relieved to hear that Minnie and the little chap are
      doing splendidly.' One guest at the wetting of the baby's head 'in good whisky'
      expressed the hope (Gillen's diary continues) that 'the little fellow may grow up as
      good a man as his father'; Spencer followed, hoping that he may grow up better,
      'while the modest father hopes that he may grow up as good a man as Spencer
      whose name he is to bear'.

19   Anthropology emerged from the study of the natural world through the
      immensely powerful new lens of Darwin's theory of evolution. In this view,
      Aboriginal people were often assumed to be an evolutionary stage or two 'lower'
      than fully modern man, aka Europeans, or even a species of natural fauna. Spencer
      found against that assumption, but nonetheless failed to rid himself of it – see
      pages 61–3.

20   The fifty-one surviving Alice Springs letters by Gillen to Spencer are collected in
      Mulvaney, Morphy and Petch (1997). Ranging in length from just a hundred or
      so words to 6000 or more, they are bursting with energy, fluent and lucid, the
      frequent absence of punctuation notwithstanding. The passages quoted or referred
      to are as follows: I can imagine you (letter 1, 8 September 1894, pp. 51–3); anguish
      at his own and others actions (letter 30, 30 July 1897, p. 178; letter 23, 14 July 1896,
      p. 127); flares in anger at pastoralists (*passim*, but see for example letter 21, 1 May
      1896, p. 116); like the wanderings of the Children of Israel (letter 30, 30 July 1897,
      p. 177); gratuitous attack on my countrymen (letter 17, 31 January 1896, pp. 93–4).

21   Mulvaney, Petch and Morphy (1997) p. 161, Gillen to Spencer on 6 May 1897
      (letter 28).

22   Byrne to Spencer 29 February 1896, in Mulvaney, Petch and Morphy (2000) p. 232.

23   Spencer and Gillen (1904) p. xiv.

24   Spencer and Gillen (1901) p. 50.

25   See McGregor (1997) pp. 21–59. Spencer and Gillen had a lively sense of fun; they
      named their horses after various European pundits (Frazer, Tylor, Lubbock) and
      Australian anthropologists (Howitt, Fison).

26   Quoted by Mulvaney and Calaby (1985) p. 180.

27   Australian anthropology was first put 'on an institutional footing' by its inclusion
      as Section G of the inaugural meeting of the ANZAAS in 1888 (McGregor, 1997,
      p. 33), by which time it had a number of significant publications to its credit.
      Furphy (2013) lists R. Brough Smyth's *Aborigines of Victoria* (1878), Lorimer Fison
      and A.W. Howitt's *Kamilaroi and Kurnai* (1880), James Dawson's *Australian
      Aborigines* (1881), and E.M. Curr's *The Australian Race* (1886). Rowse (2017, p. 64)
      adds authors including Taplin, Roth, Ridley, Fraser, Worsnop, Mathew, Parker,
      Basedow and Matthews.

28   Mason (1998) pp. 6–7.

29   Robert S. Gillen (ed., 1995) p. 126.

30   Gillen (1968) p. 297.

31   Quoted by Spencer Gillen in his epilogue to the published version of his father's 1901 journal (1995, pp. 366–7).

32   Mulvaney and Calaby (1985), see particularly chapters 12, 13 and 16.

33   Ahead of the publication of the great work, Gillen was interviewed for the *South Australian Register*. It reported that 'Mr. Gillen speaks generously of the despised native. He does not deem him treacherous, and says he can be faithful when he is well and firmly treated … One cannot expect a mirror of chivalry in a mere savage.' ('Our coloured kindred', 12 September 1898, retrieved 18 August 2020 from http://nla.gov.au/nla.news-aticle54389622.)

34   In *The Arunta,* the last of the books written by Spencer but published under joint names: 'Australia is the present home and refuge of creatures, often crude and quaint, that have elsewhere passed away and given place to higher forms. This applies equally to the aboriginal as to the platypus and kangaroo.' (Quoted by McGregor, 1997, p. 40.)

35   A selection of Spencer's photographs has been published in a handsome volume (Batty, Allen and Morton, 2005). The photographs have often been criticised as a kind of con, passing off as genuine what was in fact staged. That was true of some photographs but not all. Both – the staged and the not – belonged to anthropology's fascination with What Was There Before rather than the contemporary reality of Aboriginal lives.

36   That inconsistency can be seen in their various publications but is particularly obvious in their expedition journals (Spencer, 1901–02; Gillen, 1901). Gillen's conduct in relation to the churinga is another case in point

37   Spencer and Gillen (1899) p. 18.

38   Gillen (1901) entries for 30 and 31 October, pp. 310, 312.

39   Spencer and Gillen (1912) p. 189.

40   Wright (1997) p. 36.

41   Spencer and Gillen (1904) p. x. Mulvaney and Calaby (1985, p. 175) report that Spencer and Gillen downplayed their offence, and point out that since full initiation involved sub-incision, the 'fully' was an exaggeration.

42   Apart from their influence on international anthropology, Spencer and Gillen amassed what is perhaps the most influential collection of Australian ethnographical material ever assembled. It is composed of approximately 4000 objects, 2000 glass plate negatives, 750 photographic prints, 35,000 pages of field notes, diaries, letters, drawings and some of the earliest ethnographic sound and film footage ever recorded. This vast output has been 'haphazardly scattered throughout the world as a result of exchanges, sales and happenchance … in over thirty institutions as far afield as St Petersburg, Oxford, Vienna, Rome, Manchester, Geneva, New York, Chicago, Wellington, Melbourne, Sydney and Adelaide'. A collaboration between Museum Victoria, the South Australian Museum, the Australian National University, the Northern Territory Library, Australian Capital Equity and the Barr Smith Library turned this 'haphazardly

scattered' treasure trove into a digital collection, *Spencer & Gillen: A Journey through Aboriginal Australia*, which can be accessed at http://spencerandgillen.net.

43   The museum is described and discussed in Chapter Ten.

44   Spencer and Gillen placed themselves on a spectrum of opinion. At one end was the eponymous sponsor of the Horn Expedition, who viewed Aborigines with contempt (see the last paragraph of this chapter). At the other was Gillen's old mate (and Spencer's new mate) Pado Byrne of Charlotte Waters, who in the last of his letters to Spencer (16 December 1925) wrote: 'Whatever the past hides, the present of the unfortunate Aborigine is sufficiently miserable ... our Missionaries undermine their authority, and ridicule their traditions, we take from them everything that makes life worth living, work them until they can work no longer, and then hand them over to the police, whose main endeavour is to work things as cheaply as possible, and thus please a Gov't that has neither Knowledge nor conscience. It is a despicable crime.' (Mulvaney, Petch and Morphy, 2000, p. 258.)

Chapter Three: 1933

1   Stanner recalled these events in the first of his Boyer Lectures – see Stanner (1968) pp. 15–6. He later gave a witty account of the long journey from Sydney via Broken Hill, Oodnadatta, Alice Springs and Tennant Creek, and so eventually to the Daly River in the far north-west (Stanner, 1979a). Stanner played a central role – perhaps *the* central role – in the political, legal and intellectual events described in this book. His remarkable life and seminal work are outlined in the introductory chapters to Barwick, Beckett and Reay (1985) and Hinkson and Beckett (2008). See also the entry on Stanner in the *Australian Dictionary of Biography.*

2   One of the first policemen to arrive on the field recalled many years later what he found: 'She [sic] was in a raw state. There were bag humpies and tin shanties around the place. Living conditions were very tough. A lot of coves they didn't have tents or anything like that. They were camped in the open – just made bough shades for themselves to sleep and cook under. They were arriving there in droves all the time too. See it was Depression time, more or less ... there were some very decent coves amongst them and, of course, there were some scum among them too ... we'd let the pubs go till 11 o'clock, pm, but then they'd buy a quantity of grog and get out, two or three of them, and have grog parties, away from the pub ... there'd be these undesirable types where they'd be watching these drunken coves that had their parties and if they lay down where they were in the bush, they'd sneak up and try and rob them, roll them as we called it, sleeper rolling' (Transcript of recollections of Tony Lynch, Northern Territory Archives Service, NTRS 2261, TS 480, pp. 261–2. See also the account of Margot Miles in her book *The Old Tennant* pp. 70–1).

3   Bruce Reyburn, an anthropologist with long experience of working with Warumungu people (see note 10 for Chapter One), possesses a close knowledge of both Spencer and Gillen's work and Stanner's. Reyburn finds in Stanner's Tennant

Creek notebooks some inconclusive puzzling over exceptions and anomalies in expected rules of social organisation. The puzzling went nowhere, Reyburn suggests, for several reasons: Stanner (unlike Spencer and Gillen) had arrived as an unknown individual and was therefore not given the red-carpet treatment; by 1934 the Warumungu people 'had learned the survival value of not allowing their practice to be particularly visible'; and Stanner 'at this stage of his life' couldn't see the 'model' of social organisation that the Warumungu had in *their* heads because he was locked in 'the conceptual prisonhouse of the Anglo-Australian orthodoxy freshly imposed on him by Radcliffe-Brown at Sydney University' (Reyburn, June 1993). My own less-informed hunch is that the escape route beginning to form in Stanner's mind 'at this stage of his life' lay in understanding relations between black and white as well as relations within the Aboriginal social order (see pages 104–6), and that the two kinds of puzzle merged in a later 'stage of his life' (see pages 125–8).

4   The means by which the Warumungu were dispossessed of their 'Reserve' (and the last of their good land) are detailed in Nash (1984).

5   Stanner uses the phrase in concluding the first of his 1968 Boyer Lectures (Stanner, 1991, p. 16). See also note 39 for this chapter.

6   For a lucid summary of the intellectual and institutional ups and downs of the discipline, see Peterson (1990) and, in greater detail, McGregor (1997).

7   For the South Australian viewpoint, and the history of the Board for Anthropological Research, see Jones (1987) and Peterson (1990).

8   Tindale (1941) *passim* illustrates the view that the 'half-castes' were a 'problem', a view thoroughly analysed by McGregor (1997).

9   Stanner in the *International Encyclopedia of the Social Sciences,* 1968, quoted by Beckett and Hinkson (2008). See also the *Australian Dictionary of Biography* entry for Radcliffe-Brown.

10   Quoted in Peterson (1990) p. 12.

11   See Peterson (1990).

12   Elkin was a controversial figure as well as a substantial one. For differing views of the man and his work, see Wise (1985), Berndt (1956) and Berndt and Berndt (1965).

13   Elkin (June 1956).

14   This paragraph quotes from and summarises Elkin (July 1952).

15   See McGregor (1997), particularly pp. 115–20 and 251–9, and Rowse (2017) pp. 170–3.

16   Rowse (2017) pp. 93–97.

17   For a summary of those events, see the entry on Dhakiyarr Wirrpanda in the *Australian Dictionary of Biography.*

18   Elkin's remarks quoted in this paragraph are from Elkin (July 1952, pp. 213–4).

19   'Our tendency has been to reduce Aboriginal life far too much to kinship, section, marriage and ritual formulae, but, useful though such formulae be for the general understanding of that life, we do need descriptions which will reveal the natives for what they are, human personalities with their desires, loves, fears, hates, delights, and so on … We anthropologists, therefore, must take care lest, as a result of our scientific urge to systematize whatever we study, we abet this

dehumanization of a living people.' (McGregor, 1997, pp. 214–15, quoting Elkin's
1935 article 'Anthropology in Australia, Past and Present'.) Elkin increasingly saw
this as a fundamental problem rather than just a 'tendency'. Radcliffe-Brown's
mistake, Elkin argued, lay in seeing culture as an 'epiphenomenon of social
structure' rather than 'a process through time' (Elkin, December 1958, p. 166).

20   Elkin and his discipline had a complicated and often unsympathetic relationship
     with women, both black and white. As noted earlier – see note 13 for Chapter
     One – anthropology was notoriously what old black men told old white men.
     White women, who would have had the access to the world of Aboriginal women
     that white men did not, faced obstacles at every turn, in getting into university,
     in academic prejudice and condescension, in joining the paid workforce, and in
     travelling alone, particularly in the frontier zone. It was not until the 1930s that
     women appeared in anthropology in significant numbers and they, like their
     very few predecessors, had a hard time. 'In the first half of this [the twentieth]
     century the few women who studied Australian Aborigines were woefully treated
     by the establishment. Phyllis Kaberry left Australia, Ursula McConnell retired
     into private life ... both Olive Pink and Daisy Bates were denied an income from
     their work and the satisfaction of publication; they were thus forced into poverty
     outside society's mainstream, gaining a reputation for eccentricity that added
     to their isolation' (Isobel White, quoted by Marie de Lepervanche in Marcus,
     1993, p. 6). Female anthropologists typically understood more clearly than their
     male colleagues that to do anthropology was to enter into a relationship with
     Aboriginal people which entailed responsibilities, including keeping the secret
     secret. The first substantial study of women in Aboriginal society, Phyllis Kaberry's
     Aboriginal Woman: Sacred and Profane, was published in 1939. In his review for
     Oceania, Stanner recognised it as a breakthrough, reporting that Kaberry makes
     out 'Aboriginal woman' to be '"a complex social personality, having her own
     prerogatives"; a "competent, self-reliant and independent" person; often a really
     striking personality; sometimes exercising a notable influence on the affairs of her
     group; always taking a place of right and privilege as well as duty and obligation
     in the spiritual and secular life of her community; and very much like Moliere's
     woman who always had her revenge ready' (Stanner, March 1941).

21   Kaberry's book and Stanner's review illustrate the intimacy of the world of
     Australian anthropology and Elkin's control of it: Elkin had supervised both
     Kaberry and Stanner, and had organised funding for their field work; Stanner and
     Kaberry both did their doctorates under Malinowski in London in the mid to
     late 1930s; Elkin contributed an introduction to Kaberry's book, and as editor of
     Oceania it was he who selected Stanner to write the review.

22   Nash (1984) p. 6.

23   *The Sydney Morning Herald*, 12 July 1932.

24   Idriess (1961) p. 147: Idriess was one of a number of 'adventurers' whose stories
     and reports provided a mix of insight into and mythology about the frontier zone
     for southern consumption. Notable among them were Ernestine Hill (1940), Bill
     Harney (1957, 1961) and Xavier Herbert (1938). Idriess did much to create the 'Flynn

of the Inland' cult; his book of that title (1932) was reprinted thirteen times before a new edition was published in 1951, and a further memorial edition in 1956. Harney and Herbert moved in and out of the orbit of frontier officialdom and anthropology; Herbert had a more penetrating understanding of frontier race relations than the other frontier writers. See also entries on Idriess, Harney, Hill and Herbert in the *Australian Dictionary of Biography*, and discussion of their work by Dewar (1997).

25 *The Telegraph* (Brisbane), 15 August 1936.

26 'The twelve months between July, 1935 and June, 1936, saw the consolidation of the township. The non-Aboriginal population of the field at March, 1936, was given as 533, of which only 92 were women. The Clinic/Hospital commenced about July, the school in November. Three constables were now keeping an eye on the place. Courts were held regularly. Sporting activities were in full swing. Churches were setting up and a second hospital replaced the former on 6 June 1936. As a result of town pressure, a bore was sunk at the Tennant Creek and found water on 10 November 1935, to give the people a slightly better water supply. There were three pubs. All this was under the benevolent eyes of [mining] Wardens Bell, Stuttard and Owen'. Clark (May 1984) p. 14.

27 *The Advertiser* (Adelaide), 4 May 1936. The story was widely syndicated, with minor variations. In some Zulu was 'King' but in others he was 'first man' to 'King Billy'. The fullest account of the events was given in the *Argus* of 10 August.

28 *The Sydney Morning Herald*, 5 August 1936.

29 Quoted in Nash (1984) p. 9.

30 The Warumungu avoided the worst of the Territory's violence, but by almost any other measure both their experience and the Europeans' conduct were appalling. See Wright (1997), particularly Chapter 2, 'In the steps of Stuart'.

31 McGregor (1997) p. 216. Elkin once startled his colleagues by publishing in the leading scholarly journal of which he was editor his own review (barely camouflaged as a 'Book Notice') of his own book. In one of many 'personal recollections' published over the years, he used the vertical pronoun thirty-four times in eight pages; another came in at sixty-nine times in seventeen pages, a slightly higher per-page rate (Elkin, September 1957, October 1958). It should also be said that Elkin was an exceptionally productive scholar. A bibliography of his work (in Berndt and Berndt, 1965) runs to fifteen pages in very small type.

32 Tindale (November 1941).

33 McGregor (1997) *passim*.

34 Stanner (1968) p. 15.

35 'The Northern Territory as it exists to-day', began the report of an inquiry set up by the Commonwealth in 1937, 'is a national problem, a national obligation ... and a detriment to ourselves'. Since the takeover in 1911 (the report continued) the Commonwealth's expenditure had exceeded fifteen million pounds, all for a negligible population and financial return (Northern Territory Investigation Committee, 1937, p. xi). By 'population' the committee meant 'non-Aboriginal population', of course. As the decades passed, both population and revenue increased many times over but never kept up with public expenditure.

36   'I was at work in Kenya: and the new stimulus came from such works as
      McMillan's *Warning From the West Indies* and Ley's *Last Chance in Kenya,* from
      talking to men like L.S.B. Leakey and Jomo Kenyatta, from the strength of the
      African protest, and from the dawning insight that Kenya was a Land of Cloud
      Cuckoo that could not long endure.' Stanner (1968) pp. 16–7.

37   Stanner (1939) p. 17.

38   Elkin (1939) p. 23.

39   Hinkson (2010) gives this role to Stanner's initial field work in the Daly River
      region in 1932. There he encountered not the 'traditional' Aboriginal society he
      had expected but the 'rotting frontier' of white–black relations. The Tennant
      Creek episode came the following year. Stanner described both experiences but
      says of Tennant that 'I was upset, more so than in 1932, so the yeast was working'.

Chapter Four: 1958

1   Along with many of my post-frontier kind, I found it hard to swallow the idea
      that the regime within which Aboriginal people lived was to a significant degree
      negotiated by them. All I could see when I began to learn about the place in
      which I'd lived as a kid was the exploitation, the brutal control, the apartheid.
      What came flooding back were those memories of Aboriginal men standing on
      the back of a truck rigged up for cattle, the dark faces and ragged dress of the
      people sitting on the other side of the running track on sports day, the kids filing
      across in front of the screen at the Pioneer Picture Theatre to the benches reserved
      for them on the far side. That all this belonged to a negotiated arrangement, a
      de facto deal, was hard to see, and to admit to. Many historians encountered the
      same difficulty. In the mid-1980s Rowse saw a 'Liberal-managerial' tradition which
      did not investigate how Aboriginal people understood their relationship with
      the Europeans, and an 'ethnographic' tradition which did. The latter argued that
      Aboriginal people 'applied a model of exchange' to their dealings with the whites,
      a conclusion which since has since won general acceptance (Rowse, August 1988,
      p. 57). See also note 10 for this chapter.

2   The mission began its life under the control of the Aborigines Inland Mission
      (AIM) – not to be confused with John Flynn's Australian Inland Mission – and the
      loose oversight of the Territory administration. Facilities were gradually expanded
      until 1951, when the Territory administration assumed full control and funding
      responsibility, and improvement accelerated. A patrol officer's report provides a
      detailed description of the mission at its fullest development: Average numbers
      during 1953: 49 Aged and Infirm, 85 Able Bodied, 41 children at school, 26 under
      school age. Total 201. Buildings: Superintendent's Residence, School Teacher's
      Residence, Mission House, Native Dining Room, Native Kitchen, School,
      (Sidney Williams hut 80' x 20', gravel floor), Store Number 1, Store Number 2,
      Meat Store, Clinic, Native Huts (5 of same, 10' x 12' with 9' walls, mud brick,
      occupied by 5 married natives employed on the Settlement. Of 'Adobe Brick
      Construction': two stores, 6 native dwellings, ablution block, 4 lavs, a partition

in the school. Meals (for children, workers, hospital patients, other natives at discretion of the Superintendent: breakfast: porridge. Lunch: stews or baked meal including tinned or fresh veg. Evening: rice, tinned or stewed fruit. Yeast bread, butter, jam, or cheese plus tea with milk and sugar at all meals.' Report by Patrol Officer Lovegrove for the year ended December 1953, dated 3 February 1954, National Archives Darwin, Series E 738 Item GE 98 Controlling Agency 7114. Davison (1985) gives a full account of the character and workings of the mission; the judge in a major legal case discussed in Chapter 9 went into some detail in his description of the mission – see O'Loughlin (2000) paras 363–511.

3   Haebich (2000, pp. 620–30) includes maps showing the location of institutions by state and territory and a chronology; Rowse (2017, pp. 25–7) provides a chronology of remote missions. Neither records the Phillip Creek mission.

4   On these conversations, see Chapter Ten.

5   National Archives Darwin, Series E748, Item ED10, Controlling Agency 7114, A/g Patrol Officer Kitching to A/g District Welfare Officer, 19 April 1955.

6   The removal of the children was later made notorious by the 'Cubillo case', discussed in Chapter Nine.

7   Interview with Merv Pattemore, 4 September 2005.

8   Historian Peter Read combined with Engineer Jack to give an account of Jack's life and of the Warlpiri before and after Coniston, including recollections by Jack and others of the long trek north (Read and Japaljarri 1978). Both Nat Williams and Engineer Jack appear in several contemporary and subsequent accounts of the mission and 'the old days'.

9   'The sphere of influence of the Settlement in respect of those natives who are employed on cattle stations and return to the Settlement on "walkabout" includes many stations on the Barkly Tablelands as far east as the Queensland border and south to Wauchope. Activities of Phillip Creek natives employed in the droving industry extends from the Western Australian border to the Queensland border as far south as Alice Springs. The sphere of influence could also include Hooker Creek native settlement, as natives walk from there to Phillip Creek and back during favourable seasons. The majority of natives employed from this Settlement regard it as their country and their home.' Report by Patrol Officer Lovegrove for the year ended December 1953, dated 3 February 1954, National Archives Darwin, Series E 738, Item GE 98, Controlling Agency 7114.

10 See Commonwealth Conciliation and Arbitration Commission (1966) for a careful, if somewhat idealised, account of these relationships. McGrath's 'Born in the Cattle' (1987) is often cited as a turning point in scholarly perception of a complex relationships between white and black rather than a simple exploitation and oppression of one by the other. See also Rowse (August 1988) Chapter 7, 'Working with Cattle' in Broome (2019), Riddett's participant-observer account (1991) and note 1 for this chapter.

11 Some Aboriginal women did stock work (and some of those were the sexual partners of white drovers), and some Aboriginal men worked around the homestead as gardeners and handymen.

12   On the nature, extent and role of violence and intimidation on the stations, see
      Broome (2019) pp. 132–7.

13   Gillen (1968) entry for 20 September 1901, p. 267.

14   Gladstone was a prominent British politician, Kruger an Afrikaner leader in the
      Boer Wars, Paterson the great romancer of the Australian bush and its (white) men.

15   See particularly the ABC's *Missus of Banka Banka* (Australian Broadcasting
      Commission, 1970).

16   These meetings are described in Chapter Ten. See also an obituary for Mrs Fitz at
      www.papak.com.au/uploads/pdfs/K.Fitz.pdf, accessed 21 December 2020.

17   An 1882 report by the Territory's chief of police noted that many of the women
      who worked on the pastoral stations had been obtained by 'running them
      down' and forcibly taking them to stations some distance from their family, a
      practice which, he believed, had been introduced from western Queensland
      (Reid, 1990, p. 159).

18   'Conditions at Banka Banka are in direct contrast to those usually found on
      stations in this district,' reported the district welfare officer in 1964. 'Employees are
      well fed and clothed and are not overworked. all [sic] persons capable of working
      are found jobs and some not capable of wor [sic], such as May who was crippled
      by Polio, are found light tasks. However, Mrs. Ward believes in everybody getting
      a little rather than the good workers getting good wages and the rest nothing. All
      workers receive the minimum rates laid down under the Employment Ordinance.'
      National Archives Darwin, series NTAC 1976/5, Item 1963/469, Controlling
      Agency 7114, Title: Banka Banka station 1941–64.

19   Kathleen was one of six children, all 'half-caste', that is, of mixed descent. Her
      older brother and three older sisters were all taken, the girls to a 'home' in Darwin,
      the boy to the notorious 'Bungalow', formerly the Alice Springs telegraph station.
      Kathleen and her younger sister subsequently escaped the same fate by hiding in
      the spinifex, terrified, as a cop on horseback rode up and down looking for them.

20   'Over a great number of years in North Queensland I met many elderly
      Aborigines [who] had stories to tell of their life of arduous labour in all the major
      rural industries – mining, farming, grazing and pearling,' wrote Henry Reynolds
      in 1999 (p. 230). 'After only a limited amount of research I came to realise that
      such men and women could be found in every town and community in north and
      central Australia.' Reynolds lays out his case in detail in his *Black Pioneers: How
      Aboriginal and Islander People Helped Build Australia*.

21   Edmunds (1995) p. 25.

22   For details, see Summers (2000) pp. 28, 32.

23   See Hall (June 1980), Rowse (2017) pp. 201–6.

24   See Booth and Ford (2016).

25   Taking the girls swimming was not the superintendent's only infraction. On
      Sunday, 8 July 1951 he rang the Tennant Creek police to report that 'a lubra
      (Kathleen) had been forcibly removed from the mission by abo. Snowy'. (This
      'Kathleen' was not Kathleen Fitz, by the way.) Two days later Senior Sergeant
      Graham 'returned to the station at 8pm bringing female aboriginal "Kathleen"'.

Further investigation would be undertaken, the station journal notes ominously, 'in re allegations related by Kathleen to S/Sgt Graham'. Another two days on and the superintendent had been charged with 'sexual intercourse with Aboriginal female Kathleen'. The following day the case was heard, and he was on his way to Alice Springs for six months with hard labour. The superintendent had obviously assumed that the police would do his bidding, not realising that times had changed: the police were hardly even-handed in the use of their powers, but they were no longer at the exclusive disposal of the Europeans, albeit within the continuing framework of 'protection'. Northern Territory Archives Service, Police Station – Tennant Creek, F 303 Police journals, 1933–1969, Volume 01/01/1949 – 30/09/1951.

26   Hasluck (1942); see particularly the introduction and the epilogue.
27   Elkin (1943).
28   Much has been written about Hasluck and his life and career. For starting points, see the entry on Hasluck in the *Australian Dictionary of Biography*; Geoffrey Bolton's 2014 biography; Stannage, Saunders and Nile (eds, 1998), especially chapters by Haebich, Rowse and Brett; Rowse (ed., 2005); and Hasluck's autobiographical writings (1977, 1988).
29   Bolton (2014, p. 247) records the exchange.
30   This version is from a 1963 national conference (Hasluck, August 1963); it was little changed from the first of his national conferences, convened in 1951 (Bolton, 2014, p. 246).
31   Commonwealth Office of Education (1953), quoted in Rademaker (January 2019).
32   Long (March 1967) p. 195.
33   See Northern Territory of Australia (May 1957) and Bolton (2014). On the extraordinary level of control exercised over wards, and its perverse consequences, see Summers (2000) pp. 33–4.
34   The people had to be moved, the government said, because Phillip Creek didn't have enough water to support them. Although the water supply was indeed inadequate, it had been inadequate for the new town of Tennant Creek in the 1930s also. The solution then had been to shift the water, not the town – water was carted from Seven Mile until the 1960s. It should also be noted that 'Seven Mile' had been the Warumungu's best water source for millennia until the *papulanyi* assumed ownership when they sited the telegraph station there in 1871.
35   Warrabri had everything that whitefellas valued – airstrip, power station, police station, sports field, ablution blocks, bakery, a workshop – but very few of the things that its inhabitants cared about. It was an unhappy place at the outset, and remained so. 'The Warlpiri and the Warramunga ... have after three generations of institutionalization, become established inmates of the settlement,' an anthropologist reported in the late 1970s. 'There is little real work at Warrabri: gambling and alcohol are endemic.' (Bell and Ditton, 1980, p. 31.)
36   Stanner (1958) p. 52.
37   See Walker (1986), Harrison (n.d.), Gray (2008) p. 31.
38   Quoted by Sutton (2008) pp. 180–1.

39   See Stanner's essays from the 1950s and 1960s in Stanner (1979b), and
      commentaries on Stanner's work in this period by Beckett, Hinkson, Sutton,
      Keen and Peterson, all in Hinkson and Beckett (eds, 2008).
40   Morphy (2008) p. 137.
41   Morphy (2008) p. 243.
42   Stanner (1991) p. 17.
43   Stanner (1958). Stanner's Presidential Address was published as 'Continuity and
      change among the Aborigines' in Stanner (1979b). Specific references are as
      follows: a view of Aboriginal society as an intricate, unchanging structure, fragile
      to the touch (p. 47); various European things (p. 42); have we truly understood
      the process (p. 46); they do not know how (p. 50); if one tried to invent (p. 59); we
      struggle to comprehend (p. 43); the Noble Friend of the Aborigines (p. 52). Several
      anthropologists were by this time increasingly critical of 'assimilation', particularly
      as expressed by Hasluck and in his policies, but Stanner was the first to condemn
      it outright in each and all of its various forms, and to see its genesis and authority
      in the fundamentals of the discipline. See Rowse (1998).
44   This most powerful of Stanner's insights into the presumptuousness of assimilation
      owes much to his experience in Kenya, where he reviewed one of the great farces
      of colonialism, the Tanganyika groundnut scheme, which took for granted that
      African people would willingly turn themselves into an agricultural proletariat.
      Stanner was particularly irritated by the 'delusional tendency to explain various
      kinds of difficulties as due to African laziness, ignorance or torpor. The strongest
      tendency … in natives as in ourselves, is to remain as they have been, not to
      become other than they are and have been' (Hinkson, 2008, p. 54).
45   Hasluck's remarks as reported here are from Rowse (1998a, p. 37). Elkin, by now
      retired but still a power in the land, seems to have engineered Hasluck's appearance
      and his own role as discussant. Elkin attacked Hasluck's version of assimilation with
      enough venom to cause a stir among the academics and for the fuss to be noted
      in the local (Perth) press. Elkin's motives perhaps included payback for Hasluck's
      failure to include him in his policy-making circle; he may also have sniffed the
      wind and decided that Hasluck was turning 'assimilation' into a dirty word.
46   See McGregor (1997) pp. 250–9. On the anthropologists and assimilation, see
      Rowse (1998a).
47   During one of his trips north, Stanner undertook an Indiana Jones–like expedition
      in search of rock-art galleries in the Fitzmaurice River region, superbly described
      by anthropologist Melinda Hinkson (Hinkson, 2008). She suggests (p. 102) that
      Stanner was in search of something transcendent in Aboriginal high culture that lay
      beyond the grasp of intellectual analysis. Stanner himself once recorded a boyhood
      experience which bears a striking correspondence to – and perhaps relationship
      with – the near-mystical experience of the Yamberin galleries: while playing on a
      beach with some mates (Stanner's note records) he went exploring by himself and
      came across something which 'made me catch my breath'. 'I ran [back] to the beach
      shouting "a cave, a cave!" In a minute we were all back, enraptured by the cave's
      smoke-blackened roof and walls, the charcoal under the floor, the shells and stones

that may perhaps have been handled by the Port Jackson tribes of other days. I never forgot that incident … I was captive long before the time came when my work took me for long periods into the Far North and the Red Centre.' 'Reflective Journeyings' (unpublished manuscript, 1952), MS 3752, Series 1, Item 137 of the Stanner Collection, AIATSIS, by kind permission of Mrs Patricia Stanner.

48 Bolton (2014) p. 235.

49 Historian Judith Brett says that Hasluck was formed by a 'sense of escape' from his past (Brett, 1998, p. 194), which helps explain his image of 'assimilation' as tens of thousands of individual journeys, each culminating in that moment 'when the aboriginal enters the community'. Several Stanner scholars have suggested that Stanner's sense of apartness took him in the opposite direction, toward identification with Aboriginal people.

50 See, for example, the debate between Rowse (1996) and Partington (1997).

51 Stanner (1991) p. 49.

52 Stanner's prescience came with a strong sense of history and an ear to the ground. 'Racial strife' in the form of violent resistance to the Europeans was there from the very beginning and continued for 150 years. The frontier clashes were often followed by sporadic 'political' action that included strikes, walk-offs and protests. Political activity intensified in the 1920s and 1930s with the formation of associations and representative bodies. A lull during and immediately after the war did not last; by the mid-1950s Hasluck professed himself worried by the growth of 'race consciousness among the Aboriginal people'. (Attwood, 2003, *passim*; Hasluck is quoted on p. 199). Stanner understood the forces generating 'race consciousness' and its hostility to assimilation; Hasluck didn't.

Chapter Five: 1967

1 See Commonwealth Conciliation and Arbitration Commission (1966).

2 'When I received my brief early in 1965, I was already forty-two, about to become a QC, with some record as a participant in public debate and probably widely accepted as a "socially aware" person. Yet my knowledge of Aborigines, of Aboriginal history, or what we regard today as Aboriginal issues – let alone Aborigines on cattle stations – was for all practical purposes zero … There was nothing exceptional about my ignorance in 1965. It was shared by all eight professionals whom the machinery of industrial arbitration had assembled to process the pay claim'. 'We were,' Wootten concluded succinctly, 'products of the Silence.' (Wootten, December 2016.)

3 For a description of the kind of realities encountered by Wootten, see Reynolds (1999) pp. 227–42.

4 Commonwealth Conciliation and Arbitration Commission (1966) p. 669. The commissioners, unlike most observers of the day, did at least realise that there was a problem in treating Aboriginal people as though they were or might soon become just everyday Australians. Its difficulty in knowing what to do about this half-grasped reality was not simply intellectual. 'Anything we do must be

limited by our jurisdiction,' they said. 'Although what we do in the exercise of our powers may result in social changes, and may result in aborigines moving from one kind of life to another, we are not social engineers nor can we deal with the whole spectrum of aboriginal life. We can do no more than to attempt to achieve a just result in an industrial situation. We will not ignore the consequences of our acts, including what may happen to aborigines employed on the stations, but we cannot attempt to mould a policy of social welfare for these people in a way a Government can' (Commonwealth Conciliation and Arbitration Commission 1966, p. 656). They were 'social engineers', of course, and perhaps Pontius Pilates also. They could have asked the government, during or after their hearings, to consider the matter; indeed, the employers' representatives could have asked them to do so. All were floundering, products not just of the silence, as Wootten said – see note 2 above – but of assimilationism and the meaning and role it gave to 'equality'.

5   See Stanner (March 1967) for a detailed overview of the demand for, and conditions of, Aboriginal labour on the stations in the years leading up to the equal wages case. On the rapidly changing situation after the case, see the thoughtful and comprehensive Gibb report (December 1972).

6   According to *The Situation of Aborigines on Pastoral Properties in the Northern Territory* (Gibb, December 1972, pp. 42–3), stock work 'no longer carries the unique status it did … there is a restlessness and desire to visit other places; there is some evidence of declining interest in work, reliance on "bludging", addiction to alcohol, petrol sniffing, car stealing, and other delinquencies'.

7   On one of my trips north I travelled with an old friend who had grown up on Argadargada, a station several hundred kilometres north-east of Alice Springs, on the Queensland border. We went with two old Alyawarre people who had once lived on Argadargada to visit what had been the 'blacks' camp' at the back of the homestead, and were joined there by the manager's wife. The two old Aboriginal people stared at the bare ground, still dotted with rusted tins and broken glass, once their home. The manager's wife had been quiet and, it turned out, puzzled. Did Aborigines live here once? she asked.

8   For the national picture, see Broome (2019) pp. 147–8.

9   See Lea (1989a) pp. 34–45, 52–7.

10   Details of changes in size and composition are set out in Lea (1989b, pp. 196–7), Brady (1988, p. 1) and d'Abbs, Togni and Crundall (June 1996, p. 66).

11   *Tennant and District Times* (May 1984).

12   See Lea (1989a) pp. 32–3.

13   Quoted by Edmunds (1995) p. 19.

14   Edmunds (1995) pp. 21–3. On camps and housing in the 1960s and 1970s as a problem across the country, see Heppell (ed., 1979).

15   Edmunds (1995) p. 25.

16   For an introduction to these remarkable people, see entries in the *Australian Dictionary of Biography* for Dhakiyarr Wirrpanda, Wonggu, Donald Thomson and David Burrumarra.

17 For an excellent summary, see www.sbs.com.au/nitv/explainer/yirrkala-bark-petitions, accessed 23 November 2020.

18 Often spoken of as the first Aboriginal strike, the Gurindji action had many antecedents, including the remarkable Pindan events in Western Australia in the 1940s – see Broome (2019) pp. 141–4. What *was* new was the attention generated by the Gurindji strike – and by its consequences.

19 See Stanner (March 1967).

20 Wootten (December 2016).

21 There has been much discussion about what the 'yes' vote meant, given that the propositions put were narrowly technical and of ambiguous import (see Gardiner-Garden, 1996–97). Those propositions were, however, strongly supported in a campaign led by Aboriginal people, and widely understood at that time as delivering 'equality'. It seems reasonable to conclude that that, or that general sentiment, was what people voted for. See Rowse (2017) pp. 260–1 and Broome (2019) pp. 221–2.

22 Hasluck was briefly (1963–64) the defence minister before getting external affairs, where he stayed until 1969; he was then the governor-general until he retired in 1974.

23 The establishment of the CAA is detailed in Dexter (2015, pp. 15–19) and Coombs (1981, pp. 268–70). On the changing ideological and political context, see Rowse (2000) Chapter 1. Dexter's question to the prime minister provided the title for his book (*Pandora's Box*); the title for Rowse's book (*Obliged to Be Difficult*) comes from Coombs' warning to the prime minister that if he proved to be less than 'dinkum', he (Coombs) would feel 'obliged to be difficult' (Dexter, 2015, p. 16).

24 See Bolton (2014) p. 4 and Dexter (2016) pp. 18–19.

25 In her 'W.E.H. Stanner and the historians', Ann Curthoys notes that 'these were probably the most famous Boyer Lectures ever given from their inception in 1959 to the present'. She provides a long list of examples of their impact on historians and others (Curthoys, 2008, p. 234), an impact I am equipped by experience to understand.

Chapter Six: 1971

1 References are as follows: 'I went overland to central Australia' (p. 15); 'to escape from a style of thinking that unconsciously ratified that order of life as natural and unalterable' (pp. 16–17); 'three hundred centuries, of human affairs in this country' (p. 41); 'flowering of intellectual interest in the widest possible world of human customs' (pp. 33–7); 'in places now six or seven generations deep' (p. 26); he trawled through one account of Australia's history after another (pp. 22–4). The very familiar quotation is from page 25. Several historians, including Curthoys, have complained that Stanner was a bit hard on their discipline (Curthoys, 2008, *passim*). Curthoys also provides (pp. 243–5) a long list of popular authors of the 1950s who wrote about Aboriginal people and/or black–white relations, suggesting that Stanner exaggerated the depth of the 'silence'.

2   On the development of Stanner's thinking between his 1958 presidential address
      and the Boyers in 1968, see Curthoys (2008) pp. 239–40.

3   Australian anthropology's finest hour came at much the same moment as another
      of its recurring crises. Condemned as an instrument of colonialism by Aboriginal
      and other activists, and by a number of anthropologists themselves, the discipline
      lost morale and direction. Anthropologists had struggled so long and hard to
      see the beam in their discipline's eye that now they lost sight of a courageous,
      even heroic, struggle by the tiny minority to which they belonged against an
      intimidating majority (Cowlishaw, 2015).

4   Stanner (1968) p. 27.

5   In her 'W.E.H. Stanner and the historians' (2008), Curthoys cites antecedents
      to Stanner's 'great Australian silence' thesis, and argues (p. 235) that 'Stanner's
      brilliant and now iconic phrase "the great Australian silence" and the analysis that
      went with it have come to stand in for a much more complex process of social
      and cultural change', change driven at least as much by 'Aboriginal people, voices,
      and politics' as by Stanner's work. It remains the case, however, that neither the
      antecedents cited by Curthoys nor anyone else had really grasped the fact and
      significance of the silence.

6   See note 28 for Chapter Seven.

7   The term 'dismantled' is from a passing remark by Hal Wootten about
      Aboriginal leader Noel Pearson, who (Wootten said) had been 'educated in the
      white community at a time when the Silence was being dismantled' (Wootten,
      December 2016). I have borrowed and made extensive use of the term because
      it encapsulates conclusions reached about the character and durability of
      'the silence'.

8   For contemporaries, it would hardly need to have been said that a clever history
      graduate of that time was a Melbourne graduate – or that Australian history
      graduates who went to Oxford had come from Melbourne. The University
      of Melbourne history department was regarded as the most influential social
      science department in the country for two or more decades following the war;
      among its many luminaries were the two giants of the discipline, Manning Clark
      and Geoffrey Blainey, whose work is discussed in Chapter Nine. For more on
      Mulvaney and his exceptional contribution to Australian archaeology, history and
      public life, see Bonyhady and Griffiths (eds, 1996).

9   Serle (1973). A collection of documents on 'Modern Australia' published in the
      same year contained just four references to Aboriginal people; a 'new' history of
      Australia published a year later spent just five of its 550 pages on Aboriginal people
      and relevant issues (McGrath and Markus, 1987, p. 119).

10   They were among the first of many lawyers to work in a previously hidden
      world and who went on to play an important role in the campaigns of the great
      Aboriginal refusal. For Woodward, the Aboriginal cause was one among several;
      Wootten, a distinguished lawyer and legal academic, nevertheless regarded himself
      from that time on 'more as an activist than a scholar' (personal communication).
      For background on the origins of the case, see Wright (January 2021).

11   See Langton (1996b) for a detailed account of the struggle within and over the institute's relationship with Aboriginal people, and Mulvaney (1986). On the origins of the institute, and Stanner's role, see Mulvaney in Hinkson and Beckett (2008).

12   Woodward (2005) p. 98.

13   Stanner (1979) p. 280.

14   My account of 'Blackburn' digests, paraphrases and quotes from Stanner's 'The Yirrkala Land Case' (Stanner, 1979b). No other account of the case that I came across is even close to Stanner's for its grasp of the large drama surrounding the case or for its sense of the theatre of the case. Stanner gave his account behind closed doors after the last of the hearings but before the decision was handed down. References are as follows: Stanner's heart sank (pp. 283, 284); 'a most unsettling attack on the laws of property' (p. 280); he had been shown what were in effect the clan's title deeds (p. 280); a very impressive case (pp. 281–6); 'an argument of very great weight and interest' (p. 287). Stanner made further comment on the case a couple of years later, in his second presidential address to the anthropologists, published under the title 'Fictions, Nettles and Freedoms' in his collected essays (Stanner, 1972, 1979b). Other sources used include Blackburn (1971), Williams (1986, 2008), Woodward (2005), Rowse (1998b) and National Museum of Australia, 'A Legal Challenge', www.nma.gov.au/explore/features/indigenous-rights/land-rights/yirrkala, accessed 18 November 2019.

15   Woodward (2005) p. 106.

16   The Aborigines 'must be the only primates known to science who had to go to law to learn that they did not really need either eco-systems or territories' (Stanner, 1972/1979b, p. 303). A colleague recalled (Williams, 2008, p. 212) that Stanner had been 'haunted' by Blackburn's decision.

17   Stanner (1972/1979b) p. 304.

18   Both Coombs and Stanner were public figures with well-documented places in Australia's history. Dexter's contribution, to the work of the CAA particularly, also deserves to be remembered. See Brennan's funeral homily for Dexter (Brennan, May 2018) and Dexter's prodigious documentation (2015) of the CAA's work.

19   The Methodist Church was an early champion of Aboriginal peoples' demand after the war to be seen as a people. The church's 'Four Major Issues in Assimilation' (1963) was a bellwether in the decisive shift in 'progressive' white opinion against assimilation. 'Equality,' the church's statement said, 'does not imply similarity.'

20   The CAA was a victim of its own success, increasingly seen by newly empowered Aboriginal activists as an instrument of old white men, and embroiled in turf wars between agencies scrambling for a piece of the 'Aboriginal affairs' action. The Fraser government eventually acted on the council's own recommendation that it be 'stood down' (Dexter, 2015, pp. 438–40).

21   Woodward (2005) p. 139. One such trap was of Woodward's own creation, although laid with Stanner's assistance. Stanner and Woodward had got along famously on the 'Blackburn' case, and Woodward's report was influenced by Stanner's view that the basic land-owning unit throughout Australia was the patrilineal clan. That in

turn derived from Radcliffe-Brown, and more distantly from Spencer and Gillen's fixed-in-aspic account of traditional – that is, 'uncontaminated' – Aboriginal society. But as recorded by Deborah Bird Rose, an anthropologist involved in many applications subsequently made under the Act, claim after claim showed that neither 'ownership' nor many other elements of Aboriginal society were fixed in aspic, as indeed Stanner himself had done much to establish. His long struggle 'to escape from a style of thinking that unconsciously ratified that order of life as natural and unalterable' was never quite completed. Fortunately, the first Aboriginal land commissioner, John Toohey, took a different view. Toohey came to the position with experience in the WA Aboriginal Legal Service and in advocacy for Aboriginal people, and he established the rule that the 'traditional owners' would not be taken as those who were, in current fact, acknowledged by Aboriginal people to be 'owners'. Toohey's approach served, argues Rose (1996, p. 45), '[to] demolish the tyranny of anthropological models of land tenure'.

22   Malcolm Fraser and Ian Viner took the Coalition closer to bipartisanship in Aboriginal affairs than had been achieved since Stanner and Hasluck commenced hostilities in the late 1950s – and closer than any time since.

Chapter Seven: 1985

1   Northern Territory Department of Aboriginal Affairs report, quoted by Edmunds (1995) p. 24.
2   Town clerk's evidence to the Land Claim Tribunal, 30 March 1985, p. 2492.
3   Goodchild (February 1984) pp. 110–16.
4   Brady (1988) pp. 2–3.
5   Christen (2009) reports that by 2006 Julalikari had an annual budget of $12 million (six times that of the town council), paid half of all council rates, and was the biggest employer in the Barkly region. Christen also provides (pp. 83–5) a capsule history of the development of these organisations.
6   For Christen's lively account of her time in Tennant, see Christen (2009), particularly the preface and Chapter 1.
7   Brady (1988) p. 21.
8   Wright (1997) p. 153 and Boffa, George and Tsey (1994) p. 360.
9   d'Abbs, Togni and Crundall (1996) p. 36.
10   Brady (1988) p. 22.
11   See note 24 for this chapter.
12   Sources of evidence reported in this and the following paragraph are as follows: Tennant had 1.8 per cent of the Territory's population but 3.2 per cent of its per capita grog consumption (Wright, 1997, p. 153); the Territory's own national record (Boffa, George and Tsey, 1994, p. 360); an adult population of 2400 was served by (d'Abbs, Togni and Crundall, 1996, p. 66); in just one typical year (d'Abbs, Togni and Crundall, 1996, p. 36); readings of .124, .216, .230, .248 and .318 (Brady, 1988, p. 67); coronial enquires into a total of 100 deaths found one-third of them to be alcohol-related (Brady, 1988, p. 68); illness and death came from (Brady, 1988,

p. 72); the hospital recorded 261 'alcohol-related presentations' (d'Abbs, Togni and Crundall, 1996, pp. 20–4); an inkling of the scale of the problem (d'Abbs, Togni and Crundall, 1996, pp. 62–4).

13 To claim land was not a small thing. The process proper couldn't get under way until the claimants had established a prima facie case that they were 'traditional owners' of the land in question – that is, 'a local descent group of Aboriginals who have common spiritual affiliations to a site on the land, being affiliations that place the group under a primary spiritual responsibility for that site and for the land, and who are entitled by Aboriginal tradition to forage over that land' (Rose, 1996, p. 40). That involved preparing a 'claim book', which often ran to hundreds of pages, based on interviews with the claimants themselves and others, Aboriginal and non-Aboriginal, and documents of many kinds, official and otherwise, and detailed maps. Then the claim had to be filed, a commissioner and staff assigned, and a legal juggernaut set in motion. On-site visits gathered evidence on matters ranging from foraging and land management practices to life histories of members of the claimant group. In 'sit-down' hearings, claimants, experts and anyone affected by the claim would be questioned and cross-examined on genealogies, kinship, current living arrangements, future plans, possible impacts of the claim, and more (Rose, 1996, p. 43). Then months might pass while the commissioner and staff prepared a report with recommendations to the minister on which, if any, claims might be accepted. More months or even years might pass while the minister considered the recommendations. Then, at last, came the formalities of ownership transfer (Nash, 1999). For a chronology of the Warumungu claim, see note 32 for this chapter.

14 Reynolds (2003).

15 Stanner (1979b) p. 115.

16 This passage is from pages 3464–5 of the transcript of hearings in the Warumungu claim.

17 Much of the credit for this and for other innovations belongs to the first head of the commission, John Toohey. Toohey is introduced in note 21 for Chapter Six; he reappears as one of the six High Court judges responsible for historic *Mabo* decision (see Chapter Eight).

18 Nash (1999).

19 Rose (1996) pp. 50–1.

20 Quoted by Edmunds (1995) p. 115. For a detailed account of the struggle over the rock, see Edmunds, pp. 105–16.

21 Miles (1988) p. 5.

22 In the course of recollections recorded in 1987, retired policeman Tony Lynch mentions in passing and without comment 'six big trace chains' that were 'sent up', presumably by police HQ, for use on Aboriginal people. The whites got handcuffs. Northern Territory Archives Service, NTRS 226 TS 480, p. 262.

23 Edith Graham Nakamarra recalled that 'them old people used to walk in the road, break a branch and wipe their footprints from the dirt so the miners wouldn't see their tracks. Them kids would hide and the old ladies told them to run in front. The old ladies used to wear emu feathers on their feet so their tracks wouldn't show.'

24 Miles' tales disguise as much as they disclose, perhaps advisedly in at least one
    case. A gun fight on Tennant's main street, which serves as colour for Miles, was
    reported in the following terms by retired policeman Tony Lynch: 'There was this
    duel in front of the hotel, a gun duel, and this chap was shot, but before it took
    place, Barney O'Leary and a couple of others (they were decent citizens there) –
    Cameron [a police officer] was having an affair with a girl that worked at the hotel
    and had arrived from Adelaide, and he was in her bedroom when Barney O'Leary
    came and knocked on the door and he said, "You'd better come out, Frank, there's
    going to be some gun play out here. You'd better come out and quieten them
    down." Well Cameron didn't come out of the room and the gun play took place.'
    Lynch also reported that Cameron was dismissed from the force but stayed on
    in Tennant to work a mining lease. Northern Territory Archives Service, Series
    NTRS 226 TS 480, p. 246.
25 Two researchers who reviewed documents in the local museum that were 'used in
    the late 1970s to compile a general history of Tennant Creek' found that 'in one
    case the author had written to a pastoralist to ask "do you want to delete this?"'
    The passage in question referred to the role of Aboriginal people on the property.
    'The final published version [the researchers go on to say] indicates the pastoralist
    chose to exercise their power of veto.' (Gill, Paterson and Kennedy, 2005)
26 Miles (1988) p. 111.
27 Tuxworth (1978) p. 55.
28 The town inherited silence as well as contributed to it. John McDouall Stuart's
    journal spoke of an attack, unprovoked. Newspapers and colonial governments
    talked about the 'outrage' of the Barrow Creek events, as committed by the
    Kaytetye, not the white vigilantes. The consequences of the great cattle invasion
    of the 1880s were either not reported to or were covered up by the government
    in far-off Adelaide. Two famous anthropologists wrote compellingly of the times
    before the white men, but spoke *sotto voce* on what happened when the white
    men arrived. The national government told reporters that the dispossession of the
    Warumungu was merely a transfer of a native reserve from one place to another,
    suitable in every way, a fabrication which the newspapers duly published. Nor did
    enforcement end with the 'bad old days'. In the late 1950s a youthful Fay Gale was
    collecting evidence for her PhD that showed that official claims about Aboriginal
    children benefiting from being removed from their families were false, and she said
    so in a radio interview. 'Immediately following the news report I received a phone
    call at home from the then Head of the Welfare Branch of the Northern Territory,'
    she later recalled. 'He severely reprimanded me, told me I did not know what I
    was talking about and said that he prohibited me from entering the Northern
    Territory. I realised afterwards, when I calmed down and stopped shaking, that of
    course he could not stop me from going to the Territory. But I soon realised that
    he could stop me from visiting any of the missions or institutions or having access
    to any people in the field or any records.' Gale had to delete the Territory from her
    study, leaving South Australian events and evidence only (Gale, 1998, p. 6).
29 Stanner (1991) p. 25.

30   The *Tennant & District Times* published many letters from residents heaping scorn
      and derision on all involved in the Warumungu campaign. 'I have never heard of the
      Warumungu people paying homage to a rock,' wrote one. 'No doubt some "expert"
      will come up with a story that it is a "sacred" eagle or goanna egg. It is pathetic to see
      innocent people so manipulated and confused.' (Quoted in Edmunds, 1995, p. 110.)
      White anger descended into bathos when several townspeople appeared before the
      commissioner. A Mrs Little told Mr Justice Maurice that the bat cave to which her
      children sometimes rode of a weekend 'was almost like a sacred site to them'; her
      husband said much the same thing about the pistol club members' reverent attitude
      toward a rock that was a feature of their shooting range (Edmunds, 1995, pp. 59–60).

31   The image is borrowed from Bongiorno (January 2019).

32   The Warumungu claim was lodged on 20 November 1978, the first hearing was held
      on 1 November 1982, and the enquiry wound up on 19 August 1987. The report was
      sent to the minister on 8 July 1988, and the minister handed title to the claimants
      on 23 May 1991, thirteen years after they lodged the claim (Maurice, 1988, pp. 3–15;
      Media release, Hon. Robert Tickner, accessed at parlinfo.aph.gov.au, 29 March 2019.)

33   Maurice (1988) p. viii.

34   For chronologies of the NT government's manoeuvres, see Maurice (1988)
      Chapter 1, and Nash (2016).

35   For a detailed account of the changing relationships within the town and between
      the town and the Territory government, see Edmunds (1995) Chapter 2.

36   Aboriginal Land Commissioner, 30 March 1985, p. 2485 and following.

37   Maurice (1988). References are as follows: congratulating the 'general population'
      (p. viii); he recommended (pp. 238–40); savaged the Northern Territory
      government (p. viii); caught *in delecto* (p. vii).

38   I visited Alpurrurulam (aka Lake Nash) with Erika Calder to show the people
      there photographs taken all those years ago by Erika's mother, Daphne. It was a
      poignant experience, not least for the affection and esteem in which Daphne and
      Sam were held. Many, men and women alike, asked after them, not in the usual
      formulaic way but to hear what had become of them and how they were getting
      on. See also note 7 for Chapter Five.

39   Dexter records that the suggestion was Stanner's, passed on to Whitlam by
      Coombs (Dexter, 2008, p. 83).

40   Curthoys (2003) includes this among several insights into about the emotions and
      rationalisations underlying Australia's 'national history'. Other, less respectable
      elements of the Territorians' sense of themselves are vigorously promoted
      elsewhere. The Darwin-based *NT News* recently (16 April 2019) filled a front page
      with the headline 'Dildo found on Dick Ward Drive en route to Fanny Bay',
      together with a photograph of the item in question.

41   See Bell and Ditton (1980).

42   Claim transcript, p. 981.

43   Rose (1996) p. 44. For a chronological listing of the many hundreds of land claims
      made under the 1976 legislation, see the annual reports of the Aboriginal Land
      Commissioner.

44   Brett (June 2020, pp. 42–3) documents the origins and implications of the miners' analysis.

Chapter Eight: 1992

1   Interview with Fay Gale, 3 September 2003.

2   Both Mulvaney's *The Prehistory of Australia* (1969) and Rowley's *The Destruction of Aboriginal Society* (1970) reported thinking, research and rethinking begun long before their publications. See, for example, Mulvaney (1958) and Rowley (1962).

3   Serle (1973).

4   See Reynolds (1999) p. 91, and a personal communication from Reynolds to Attwood, reported in Attwood (1996) p. xv.

5   Thomas Kuhn's *The Structure of Scientific Revolutions* (1962) gave the term 'paradigm' its contemporary meaning as a bundle of concepts, interests and assumptions within which 'normal science' is conducted unless and until a new paradigm emerges, typically formulated by those working at the boundaries of the dominant paradigm – Stanner, for example – where they find phenomena that don't 'fit'. Abruptly, the old paradigm is abandoned in favour of the new. 'The study of nineteenth-century Aboriginal–European contact has suddenly become one of the most thoroughly researched fields in Australian history,' say McGrath and Markus in their 1987 survey of the literature (p. 120). I should add that one of many debates triggered by Kuhn's work concerns whether and how it can be applied to the 'soft' social sciences.

6   La Nauze (1959) p. 1.

7   Reynolds (1999) p. 87.

8   Reynolds' semi-autobiographical *Why Weren't We Told?* (1999) records the process: he arrived in Townsville in 1965; was encouraged in a growing interest in race relations by Stanner's 'brilliant' Boyers in 1968 (p. 91); decided in late 1969 or thereabouts to shift his research focus 'from Tasmania to Queensland, from class to race, from convicts and free settlers to Aborigines' (p. 90); gave his first seminar on the history of race relations in May 1970 (p. 92); and published a collection of documents on Aboriginal–settler relations in 1972. The landmark *The Other Side of the Frontier* began life as an academic article published in 1976, emerged in 1981, after a good deal of indecision (described in Reynolds, 2006, pp. 2–3) about its focus and shape, as an in-house publication by his university department in 1981, and was first published commercially the following year, seventeen years after he took up his appointment. See also Reynolds (2009).

9   Mulvaney and White (1980).

10   'The book was written by John Molony, professor of history at the Australian National University, who also chaired the taskforce of the Authority that advised on the Bicentennial history program. Molony took his brief "to write on the land and its white peopling" and said very little about Aboriginal history – other than an apologetic "sorry mate" – on the grounds that "I am not one of them" and therefore could not tell their story' (Macintyre, 2004, p. 113).

11   Millis (1988) p. 131.

12 'Revisionist accounts of Aboriginal history are now fashionable, but their writers seem to commemorate examples of confrontation with more eagerness than they describe the processes of accommodation. They still tend to judge patriotism and heroism in terms of traditional masculine roles, and praise martial fervour more than endurance.' (Barwick, 1985, p. 221.)

13 See Reynolds (1999) pp. 247–8.

14 Mulvaney (1986) p. 56. Mulvaney quotes and endorses Barwick's criticisms (1985).

15 Peterson (1987) p. 115; McGrath and Markus (1987) pp. 119–120, in Borchardt (1987) 119–29

16 Reynolds (2006) p. 6.

17 Reynolds (2006) p. 6.

18 Macintyre (2004) p. 97. The Bicentennial controversy generated a considerable literature at the time and since. This account is drawn from a special edition of *Australian Historical Studies* (Jansen and Macintyre, eds, October 1988), particularly Spearritt's contribution to that volume, Macintyre (2004) and Shaw (ed., 1988).

19 Jupp, in Shaw (1988) p. 76.

20 *Quadrant* (October 1984) p. 6, quoting a 1981 article by Armstrong in *Ethnic News Review*.

21 For accounts of this enormous undertaking, see McDonagh (1987), chapters in Shaw (ed., 1988) by Jupp, Gilbert and Inglis, and chapters by Aveling, Rowse and Lee in Janson and Macintyre (eds, 1988). On the counter-history, *A People's History of Australia since 1788*, see Burgmann and Lee in Janson and Macintyre (eds, 1988).

22 See Broome (2019) pp. 225–35.

23 Reynolds (1984) p. 19.

24 Reynolds (1984) p. 19.

25 Morgan (May 1984) p. 25.

26 'Speech to a dinner marking Ray Evans' retirement from the HR Nicholls Society', n.d., archive.hrnicholls.com.au/copeman2010/morgan-speech.php, accessed 9 March 2020.

27 In fact, around 90 per cent of mining in the Territory in 1983/84 was on Aboriginal land (Broome, 20019, p. 256).

28 Broome (2019) p. 242. Broome reports (p. 243) polls showing that over the course of the campaign, opposition to land rights ballooned from a small minority to a big majority.

29 The table is reproduced in Spearritt (1988) pp. 9–10.

30 Broome (2019) pp. 242–3.

31 See Spearritt (October 1988) p. 12.

32 Broome (2019) p. 271; McIntyre (2004) p. 113.

33 See Foley (May 1997).

34 This account is based on Loos and Mabo (2013), which in its most recent edition is not always easy to follow, containing as it does a foreword, a preface and a prologue, three distinct parts ('A Personal Perspective', 'Koiki Mabo's Story' and 'The Final Years') and an appendix. The foreword is by Marcia Langton; other sections are

mainly by Noel Loos, often drawing extensively on conversations and encounters with Mabo; the appendix is by Mabo. These various sections overlap frequently, and move back and forth between times, places and events. A chronology of Mabo's life (pp. xxxvi–xl) helps orient the reader, as does Langton's brief survey of the history of the Murray Islands (pp. xiii–xiv) and Loos' account of Mabo's life there as a child and a young man (pp. 27–47). Mabo's meeting, friendship and collaboration with Loos (and Henry Reynolds) is reported on pp. 10–13. Reynolds (1999, pp. 24–92, 185–203) covers some of the same ground and gives it context.

35 One history of Queensland's race relations carries the subtitle 'A history of exclusion, exploitation and extermination' (Evans, Saunders and Cronin, 1988).

36 Reynolds (1999) gives a detailed account (pp. 24–92) of his arrival in Townsville, his experience there as an activist, and its impact on his scholarly work. His friendship with Eddie Mabo and his consequent discovery of the centrality of land and the law in the history of race relations are described on pages 185–203. Specific references are as follows: Townsville was 'dry, scruffy, violent' (p. 28); a history lesson of the most powerful kind (pp. 39–40); the university as a post-frontier enclave (p. 47); they didn't know whether they should tell him (pp. 187–8); Mabo was 'consumed' by land rights (p. 192). See also Reynolds (2009).

37 Reynolds (1999) p. 187.

38 The term was coined in the 1920s by the Italian communist Antonio Gramsci to distinguish intellectuals who worked for and with 'subaltern' groups from 'traditional' intellectuals affiliated with the established social order. Gramsci is favoured as a hate figure by contemporary right-wing intellectuals, for whom he is the source of a baleful 'cultural marxism'.

39 Reynolds (1987). Specific page references are as follows: warnings to other colonial powers, not a claim to ownership (pp. 10–11); British law was accommodating of very different forms of title (p. 20); discovery had delivered not just sovereignty but ownership (pp. viii, 176); it was an amazing achievement (p. 2); fierce resistance by the colonists (pp. 150–1); in English humanitarian circles (pp. 150–1); native title was forgotten or ignored (pp. 152, 155); the Privy Council found (pp. 3–4).

40 Reynolds (1987) p. xii.

41 Reynolds (1987) p. 151.

42 For a summary of both scholarly and legal analyses, see Curthoys, Genovese and Reilly (2008), particularly Chapter 2.

43 'The judges may have been attracted to Reynolds' distinctive style of reasoning. Among the current generation of historians writing about Aboriginal Australia, Reynolds is exceptional, not only for his influence, but for the confidence – epistemological as well as political – of his advocacy. He assumes the stance of a legal and historical positivist, appealing directly to his primary sources, without reference to the views of other historians and seldom dwelling on the ambiguities or contradictions between his authorities. He piles example on example until the sceptic's resistance is worn down.' Davison (2003) p. 59.

44 Broome (1996) quoted by Curthoys, Genovese and Reilly (2008) p. 72. See also note 2 for Chapter Five.

45   The Royal Commission into Aboriginal Deaths in Custody overlapped the *Mabo* claim. Announced in August 1987, it made headlines throughout the Bicentennial and reported in five volumes three and a half years after its appointment. Speaking to a distinguished legal audience on the twentieth anniversary of the report, one of the commissioners, Hal Wootten, recalled, 'In just six weeks between 24 June 1987 and 6 August 1987 there were five Aboriginal deaths in custody, all by hanging, and four in police cells. This followed 11 deaths earlier in the year, five by hanging.' (Wootten, November 2011). The commission was another landmark, but it took the upheavals of the Black Lives Matter movement to remind white Australia that many of the commission's recommendations have lapsed and that there have been well over 475 Aboriginal deaths in custody since the recommendations were made.

46   Reynolds' view of *Mabo* and its implications is summarised in *Why Weren't We Told?* (1999), pp. 185–225. For another view, including commentary on Reynolds, see Curthoys, Genovese and Reilly (2008) Chapter 2.

47   Reynolds (1999) pp. 202–3.

48   What became *Mabo* began with *Mabo v Queensland* in the Queensland Supreme Court. In October 1982 an attempt to reach agreement on a statement of facts failed. In 1985 the Queensland government passed an Act to extinguish native title retrospectively. In February 1987 a High Court request that the Supreme Court of Queensland determine the facts was held over until the High Court ruled on a challenge to the legislation. The High Court found that the legislation was invalid. The Supreme Court returned to hear statements on the facts and delivered its judgement in November 1990. In May 1991 hearings commenced in the High Court, which delivered its judgement on 3 June 1992 (Loos and Mabo, 2013, pp. xxxix–xl).

49   One such scratch, not often referred to, was Eddie Mabo's attitude to Aboriginal people. He told Noel Loos that it was 'traditional' for Islanders to regard Aborigines as not 'culturally advanced' and 'lesser beings mainly because they don't know the art of cultivation and they don't live in central villages like we did, and they don't have a religion' (Rowse, 2017, p. 335).

50   Loos, in Loos and Mabo (2013) p. 21.

51   On these points we can take Stanner's word for it. He was 'told by an unimpeachable authority' that he was one of the 'two last men' to have attended an important sacred/secret ceremony performed performed in 1935, and that '[I] was regarded also as one who had "stood up" for blackfellows about land rights.' Stanner's companion on the trip was Arthur Palmer, a young white man then employed by the Northern Land Council. Palmer had met Stanner not long before, 'an old man, enfeebled by encroaching Parkinson's with a frail voice'. But when the Daly was mentioned (Palmer recalled) 'he seemed to change gear, his eyes would sparkle, his wavering voice would strengthen and for several hours at a time would discuss in animated fashion his field work in the thirties and the current state of affairs'. The two men, the old and the young, the patron and the acolyte, worked closely together over the three or four years left to Stanner. In an appreciation of Stanner written after his death, Palmer recalled the partnership,

and quotes from Stanner's 'Big Sunday at Peppiminarti', an unpublished write-up of notes made at the time (and the source of the quotes above). Like so many others, Palmer found that 'the more I got to know Bill Stanner the warmer I felt toward him'. He was, Palmer says, 'a giant'. In a *To Whom It May Concern* we also have Stanner's view of Palmer: 'a young man of high intelligence, pleasing personality, and of considerable force. His sympathies with the Aborigines are plain and his rapport with them [is] excellent … He is a good bush companion [and] a brilliant photographer.' Among Palmer's many photographs of Stanner, I found one to be particularly moving, of the old man with Parkinson's, bare-chested, cane resting against his chair, surrounded by the people of Peppiminarti and with them intent upon a ceremonial performance out of sight of the camera. Arthur Palmer's photographs, his appreciation of Stanner, and Stanner's reference for Palmer were provided by Arthur Beau Palmer. Stanner's 'Big Sunday at Peppiminarti' (1979) is in the Stanner Collection of the Australian Institute for Aboriginal and Islander Studies (AIATSIS).

52   Keating's remark was reported in *The Sydney Morning Herald*, 27 August 2014.

53   Just one paragraph from Broome's excellent summary of the *Mabo* controversy suggests the all-in complexity and bitterness of the conflict: 'Behind the scenes, federal and state bureaucrats, miners, pastoralists and Aboriginal leaders engaged in complex, tortuous and tough negotiations. There were constant reports over fifteen months that created bewilderment about the intricacies of land laws and titles. The federal opposition was paralysed into inaction by internal divisions over Mabo. The federal government's position paper in May 1993 recommended tribunals to adjudicate claims, proposals over compensation, and the validation of titles issued since 1975, but left uncertain by the *Racial Discrimination Act (1975)*. Aboriginal negotiator Noel Pearson called it a "slimy document". This stung Prime Minister Paul Keating, who saw Mabo legislation as creating a moral basis for reconciliation as well as establishing land rights. The federal government's attempt to forge a national approach was rejected by the conservative-governed states, led by Victoria and Western Australia, which rejected federal tribunals, Aboriginal vetoes over development, and a proposal that native title would revive after mining and pastoral leases expired.' (Broome, 2019, p. 287.)

54   Parliamentary Library Publications Archive (2002).

55   Keating (1992): at Kokoda, www.keating.org.au/shop/item/anzac-day---25-april-1992; at Redfern, antar.org.au/sites/default/files/paul_keating_speech_transcript.pdf; at the tomb of the Unknown Soldier, https://www.awm.gov.au/commemoration/speeches/keating-remembrance-day-1993, all accessed 8 December 2020.

Chapter Nine: 2000

1   Stanner and Hasluck went to their graves unrepentant. I could wish that I had written 'less circumspectly', Stanner said, not long before his death 1981 (Stanner, 1979b, p. ix). Hasluck conceded in his last book only that 'we did not see clearly

the ways in which the individual is bound by membership of a family or group' (Hasluck, 1988, p. 130). As Rowse points out in his devastating review of the book (Rowse, August 1989), Hasluck's half-concession is buried in hundreds of pages of reiteration and justification of the philosophy and practice of assimilation.

2   Blainey was born writing history and it looks as though he'll die doing it. On the eve of his ninetieth birthday and after more than fifty books, Blainey published a volume of autobiography, with more promised. At school his favourite pastime was poring over old newspaper files; his first article in a learned journal was published when he was an undergraduate. At just twenty years of age he set off for the remote west coast of Tasmania to research what would become his first book, commissioned by a mining company, at a time when hardly anyone wrote on commission (or about mining). Perhaps that experience was as formative for the young Blainey as Townsville was for the young Reynolds? Perhaps if he'd been commissioned by Peko Mines to go to Tennant Creek as a twenty-year-old, rather than to Tasmania by the Mount Lyell Mining and Railway Company, his history (and ours) would have been different? Blainey wrote another five books about mining and the miners and remained close to the industry throughout his extraordinary career. See Blainey (2019), Macintyre (2004), particularly Chapter 5, Markus and Ricklefs (eds, 1985), Gare, Bolton and Stannage (eds, 2003) and Allsop (2020).

3   Macintyre (2004) p. 80. I saw this Blainey at one remove. I gave my then elderly father a copy of Blainey's *Black Kettle and Full Moon*, a charming miscellany of everyday life as once lived. Ever the stickler, my father wrote to Blainey via his publisher with some minor point of correction; Blainey replied promptly with handwritten thanks. For an account of a less happy encounter with Blainey, see Bongiorno (2020).

4   On the causes espoused by Blainey, see Macintyre (2004). Under the pressure of intense public debate, Blainey's language sometimes went beyond strident to abusive, snide and wild-eyed. In one 1997 article, for example, he claimed that the 'black armband view, while pretending to be anti-racist, is intent on permanently dividing Australians on the basis of race', referred to 'that black armband tribunal, the High Court', and asserted that as long as the black armband view continued to justify black racism 'then Australia's future as a legitimate nation is in doubt' (*The Bulletin*, 8 April 1997).

5   'To some extent my generation was reared on the Three Cheers view of history,' Blainey said. 'This patriotic view of our past had a long run. It saw Australian history as largely a success. While the convict era was a source of shame or unease, nearly everything that came after was believed to be pretty good. [Now] there is a rival view, which I call the Black Armband view of history. In recent years it has assailed the optimistic view of history. The black armbands were quietly worn in official circles in 1988, the bicentennial year ... The multicultural folk busily preached their message that until they arrived much of Australian history was a disgrace. The past treatment of Aborigines, of Chinese, of Kanakas, of non-British migrants, of women, the very old, the very young, and the poor was singled out, sometimes legitimately, sometimes not ... The Black Armband view of history

might well represent the swing of the pendulum from a position that had been too favourable, too self-congratulatory, to an opposite extreme that is even more unreal and decidedly jaundiced.' (Blainey, July–August 1993, p. 11.)

6   For a detailed account of the relationship between the views of Blainey and Howard, see McKenna (November 1997) *passim*.

7   Blainey's teacher then colleague and friend Manning Clark regretted late in life that he'd had his eye so firmly fixed on the white man. 'My story began with the coming of civilization to a country where previously there was barbarism,' he wrote. 'In my mind's eye the First Fleet was a Noah's Ark of civilization.' (Quoted in Curthoys, 2008, p. 237.) The recovered story brought Clark to see his own work and Australia's history in a new light, but not Blainey. Writing in the afterglow of Australia Day in 1988, Blainey reported that the most moving event was the one that the high officials hadn't really wanted, 'the arrival at the narrow throat of Sydney Heads of the First Fleet Re-enactment after crossing the world as homage to a voyage undertaken in 1788' (*The Australian*, 30 January 1988). It is the romance of the sails coming through the heads to found a new country that stayed with him, not the sails he had depicted in *Triumph of the Nomads* as symbols of a gale that would blow out countless campfires and silence hundreds of languages, stripping ancient Aboriginal names from nearly every valley and headland.

8   See Carment (2007).

9   O'Loughlin (August 2000) discusses these events and evidence for them; see particularly paragraphs 435–511.

10   O'Loughlin (August 2000) paragraph 2.

11   Taking children and/or institutionalising them had a long history. In 1814, just twenty-six years after the First Fleet arrived in Sydney Cove, Governor Lachlan Macquarie establish the Native Institution at Parramatta for the purpose of 'Educating, and bringing up to Habits of Industry and Decency, the Youth of both Sexes' (McGregor, 1997, p. 11). South Australia was even quicker off the mark. In 1844, just eight years after its founding as a colony, it made its protector the legal guardian of all part-Aboriginal children. The first appointee was of the view that children were capable of being civilised if removed from their parents (Reid, 1990, p. 7). By the time Spencer recommended to similar effect in 1913, he was following a catalogue of precedents. Another fifty years on, the Northern Territory's administrator wrote to his minister, Paul Hasluck, to recommend against removing children younger than four; the minister instructed that no age limit need be stated: 'The younger the child is at the time of removal the better for the child' (Bolton, 2014, p. 251).

12   O'Loughlin (August 2000) paragraphs 15–23.

13   *The Sydney Morning Herald*, 20 November 1999.

14   Hal Wootten pointed out that 'governments present sums spent on resisting Aboriginal claims in the public accounts totals supposedly spent for the benefit of Aboriginals' (Wootten, 2003, p. 49). That the government's agenda went beyond seeing that the Commonwealth's legitimate interests were appropriately defended

is suggested by its choice of Roddy Meagher QC to lead its legal team. Meagher was well known as ostentatiously Tory and a trenchant critic of the High Court's performance in *Mabo*. In accepting the *Cubillo* brief he left himself open to the charge of pursuing a personal agenda: his father had been deeply involved in the administration of Aboriginal lives in Victoria in ways that had damaged his reputation. See Manne (April 2001) pp. 86–93 and Wootten (2003) p. 36.

15   *The Age*, 7 August 1999.

16   Wilson (1997).

17   Manne (April 2001) pp. 5–6.

18   This account follows Bongiorno (January 2019), which discusses the government's thinking as revealed in just-opened cabinet papers, and Robert Manne's participant-observer history (April 2001). Manne is open to the charge levelled against Roddy Meagher (see note 14 above): that he was pursuing revenge, or at least vindication, against his former colleagues at *Quadrant*. One difference is that Manne wasn't on the government payroll; another is that he was speaking in the public realm, not a court of law; yet another is that he was candid in disclosing his involvement and interests; a fourth is that his passionate engagement with the issue preceded his resignation – it was, indeed, the reason for it. We can add that Meagher was using power against the powerless; Manne used it to deliver a masterly analysis of the *Bringing Them Home* report, the *Cubillo* case, the stance taken by the Howard government, the role of the right-wing intelligentsia, and the relationships between all of these.

19   It allocated a less-than-generous $63 million over four years for counselling and family link-up services, family support, language maintenance programs, and archival and history projects (Broome, 2019, p. 310).

20   Bongiorno (January 2019).

21   Wilson (1997) pp. 266–75. For discussions of the charge, and accounts of the furious controversy that followed, see McGregor (2004) and Reynolds (2001).

22   See Manne (April 2001) pp. 24–31.

23   P.P. McGuiness, *The Sydney Morning Herald*, 27 November 1999.

24   O'Loughlin (August 2000) paragraph 1.

25   Some of those taken from Phillip Creek by cadet welfare officer Les Penhall and Retta Dixon superintendent Amelia Shankleton later returned as adults to live out their lives in Tennant Creek. Lorna Nelson was among those who did not. Eight years old when she arrived at Retta Dixon, she was eighteen when she left. She married and made her life in Darwin. At the time of the court case she had been caring for two grandchildren for more than a decade; they had been abandoned by their mother and their father, her drug-addicted son. *Bringing Them Home*'s grim evidence about the impact of removal was recently extended through studies by the Australian Institute of Health and Welfare (August 2018, June 2019) on the life experience of those removed and of their children. The studies found that in just about every area of life – health, socio-economic status, housing, justice – both generations had an even harder time than other Aboriginal children. Mrs Cubillo was often interviewed about the case, for the account by Curthoys, Genovese and

Reilly (2008, see particularly pp. 135, 136, 165), by Radio National ('Awaye!', 28 January 2005) and by several newspapers. We were not orphans, she insisted. She did not regret the court case. It wasn't about the money. 'I agreed to go to court because I wanted the story to be told.' Lorna returned to the old Phillip Creek site several times; it always made her 'emotional' (*The Australian*, 4 June 2004). In 2004 she was there with eleven others who had been on that fateful truck together, with a crowd of around two hundred people, for the unveiling of a plaque mounted on a modest cairn amidst the scattered remnants of the mission's buildings. (*Land Rights News*, July 2004). Mrs Cubillo was also in the public gallery for the prime minister's Apology to the Stolen Generations (*ABC Premium News*, 11 February 2008).

26   'The judgement, not surprisingly, provoked immense public and scholarly criticism and comment from those with faith in law's redemptive constitutionalism. In a broad sense, the responsive scholarship to the judgement ... challenges law to review its historical blindness to Indigenous experiences under settler colonialism ... The blindness of the law, in particular the application of the rules of evidence, to the applicants' personal histories [is] a product of the law's assertion of its own sovereignty.' (Curthoys, Genovese and Reilly, 2008, p. 135.)

27   Read (2002) pp. 53–60.

28   For a summary of McGrath's evidence and report, see Curthoys, Genovese and Reilly (2008) pp. 150–1.

29   'Her opinion, based on that survey [of documentary evidence] and her own knowledge of the history of Aboriginal and white relations, was that there was disquiet and sometimes deep concern about the general policy and practice of removal of Aboriginal children from their families. I accept Dr McGrath's opinion.' (O'Loughlin, August 2000, paragraph 232.)

30   See particularly Curthoys, Genovese and Reilly (2008), and McCalman and McGrath (eds, 2003). Other volumes discussing problems of evidence and truth published around the same time include Toussaint (ed., 2004), and Gray and Paul (eds, 2002). McCalman and McGrath write (p. 4) that 'many humanities scholars jump at the opportunity' to appear as an expert witness, 'but after a brutal "blooding" in the witness box they rarely repeat the experience ... If lawyers are serious about getting the best proof and getting as close as they can to the truth, we believe they should consider better ways to work with humanist experts.'

31   Curthoys, Genovese and Reilly (2008) p. 137.

32   Wootten (2003) pp. 33, 38.

33   *Quadrant*, vol. 44, no. 11, November 2000.

34   *The Killing of History* (Windschuttle 1994): The book's subtitle named the killers: *How a Discipline Is Being Murdered by Literary Critics and Social Theorists*. Windschuttle had an important point, but for political and ideological reasons he made it the *only* point.

35   Windschuttle (2009): '*no* Stolen Generations' (p. 26, among many others); 'never condone' (p. 12).

36   Much rhetoric (and the term 'history wars') was imported from the United States. Disagreement turned into acrimony in the mid-1980s and then open warfare

from the mid-1990s to around 2005, followed by low-level skirmishing. The 'wars' are reported, analysed and conducted in McKenna (1997), Manne (April 2001), Manne (ed., 2003), Macintyre (2004), Dawson (ed. 2004), Windschuttle, Jones and Evans (eds 2009) and McKenna (2018).

37   Cubillo was not the first or the last of the Stolen Generation cases, but it was the most substantial and significant. Its failure followed others and foreshadowed more, the sole success arising from a very unusual combination of circumstances. For a chronology of Stolen Generations litigation, see Cunneen and Grix (2003).

38   In 2015, a number of years after my audit, the City of Sydney commissioned a monument which took half a step in the right direction by honouring Indigenous servicemen and women. See Ceridwen Dovey's response to Mark McKenna's Quarterly Essay, *Moment of Truth: History and Australia's Future* (2018).

39   See monumentaustralia.org.au, accessed 19 May 2020. Monument Australia is 'a self-funded, non-profit organisation, dedicated to recording monuments throughout Australia'. Its volunteer-generated profiles are in most cases detailed right down to geographical coordinates.

40   The long-unnoticed imbalance is increasingly being remarked upon. Two scholars recently took pride in 'tracking down the only known sculpture of a WWI Indigenous soldier' (Murray and Howes, 5 June 2019); a journalist found that in the immediate environs of Parliament House in Canberra there are more sculptures of kelpies than of Indigenous people (or of women) (Rob Harris, *The Sydney Morning Herald*, 23 March 2021); and an audit of another form of commemoration, the *Australian Dictionary of Biography*, reported that just 210 of nearly 13,000 entries were of Aboriginal and Torres Strait Islander people (Allbrook, 1 November 2017). Noticed less often is that, in this as in other areas, 'the silence' involves active silencing. Such Aboriginal monuments as have been erected have often been defaced, damaged or even dynamited (Read, 2008). Most shocking was the damage to Eddie Mabo's gravestone in Townsville just hours after its unveiling. Painted red swastikas and the word 'Abo' notwithstanding, Townsville police declined to suggest that the attack was racist, preferring instead to 'keep an open mind' and to treat the case as one of vandalism and damage to property (*The Australian*, 4 June 1995).

41   See http://placesofpride.awm.gov.au/#:~:text=Places%20of%20Pride%2C%20 the%20National,war%20memorial%20across%20the%20country, accessed 19 May 2020.

42   Successive Coalition governments have taken up where Howard left off. In 2016 historian Romain Fathi estimated that during the centenary of the First World War, Australia would spend 'at the very least, *75 times* more on commemorative activities per dead soldier than France', and that 'Australia *alone* will probably spend more ... than Germany, Russia, Belgium, France, the United Kingdom, the United States, Italy, Bulgaria, Greece, Serbia and Romania combined' (Fathi, April 2016, emphases in the original). In Flanders an extravagant new memorial and centre was constructed; in Australia, more and yet more markers and memorials, including a comprehensive suite of them on a site overlooking

Albany's magnificent King George Sound, on which see pages 231–2 of the afterword. Another half a billion dollars was found so that the Australian War Memorial could commemorate conflicts in Afghanistan and Iraq and peacekeeping missions in Timor-Leste and Solomon Islands. The journal of the Honest History Association (http://honesthistory.net.au/wp/) and Paul Daley's many articles in *The Guardian* provide points of entry to this and related debates. Among the Morrison government's contributions has been $48 million allocated to commemorating Lieutenant Cook 'taking possession' of Australia, including funding for a replica of the *Endeavour* to circumnavigate the continent, perhaps to make good Cook's failure to do so himself.

43   Reconciliation Place, as it eventually appeared, avoided any representation of conflict, of responsibility or of consequences; see Read (2008) p. 43. Reconciliation Place is described in Batten (2004) pp. 111–13.

44   Pearson (November 1996).

45   Many of Pearson's essays, including those discussed here, were collected and published as *Up from the Mission* (2009). For a sympathetic introduction to Pearson and his ideas, see Altman's review of the book (August 2009).

46   Pearson (October 2001). Pearson was not the first to notice and to try to understand the problem, although he quickly became by far the most prominent. A white anthropologist (and one-time student of Stanner), Peter Sutton, made a very similar case in a September 2000 paper; in the published version of that paper in 2001, he thanked a who's who of anthropology and the Aboriginal intelligentsia for assisting in the preparation of the paper, and credits Colin Tatz with having raised its central questions as early as 1990. The 'social deterioration' problem and its relationship with 'Aboriginal policy' and politics was in the air. Sutton's later book *The Politics of Suffering* (2009) prompted a sharp debate, but within relatively limited circles; for a particularly telling contribution, see Hinkson (August 2009). My own view is that, here as elsewhere, Sutton owed much to Stanner's cast of mind, and that the Boyers (the last lecture particularly) warned about the intractability of the difficulties experienced by many Aboriginal people and the blind naivety of much white goodwill.

47   See Pearson's Ben Chifley Memorial Lecture (August 2000), Dr Charles Perkins Memorial Oration (October 2001), fifth Annual Hawke Lecture (November 2002), Sir Ninian Stephen Lecture (March 2003), speech to the High Court Centenary Conference (October 2003) and AMA Oration (May 2004). All can be found at www.gooriweb.org/pearson.html, accessed 25 June 2019.

48   In a June 2005 interview on ABC TV's *Insiders*, Pearson declared a speech by Howard on 'symbolic' and 'practical' reconciliation, delivered a few days previously, to be of 'tectonic' significance. He lamented 'that both the Indigenous leadership and the media generally overlooked the importance of that speech'. (Pearson, June 2005).

49   A selection, from Gooriweb's 'The Pearson Dossier': 'Shift in the right direction', 'Moved by Pearson's passion', 'Pearson sparked a revolution that emboldened PM to act', 'Costello embraces Pearson's radical reforms', 'ALP backs "tough love"

approach', 'Aboriginal leaders join attacks on Pearson', 'Pearson labelled arrogant and ignorant', 'Clash of cultures: Aboriginal leader rejects Pearson as "new messiah"', 'Noel Pearson "drunk with power"', and 'Telling whites what they want to hear'. See www.gooriweb.org/pearson.html, accessed 25 June 2019.

50   See www.smh.com.au/national/apology-by-john-howard-actor-20080209-gds08v. html, accessed 14 December 2020. My favourite among many signs of these times: a racehorse named Johnny Say Sorry. The humourless guardians of the racing industry required that the name be changed forthwith on the grounds that it was a political statement (*The Age*, 26 November 2001).

51   Quoted in Broome (2019) p. 344.

52   That this confusion has been a constant in Australia's history is argued at various points throughout this book. That it remains widespread is suggested by a speech given by Prime Minister Kevin Rudd in August 2009, not long after his Apology, to launch Thomas Keneally's *Australians: Origins to Eureka*. Keneally's book showed that our national story makes a terrific read, the prime minister said, even if it doesn't include 'wars, revolution [or] bloodshed'. The author must have been puzzled at this point – his book is not shy about the bloody realities of the frontiers – and completely flummoxed as the prime minister proceeded to criticise those who 'refused to confront hard truths about our past'. Perhaps the prime minister's earlier formulation about wars and bloodshed was a mere slip, an irony? No, it was not. He returned to the point and made it all over again: do not doubt, Rudd insisted, that ours is a great story even if there are no 'rivers of blood shed in pursuit of contested wars for our nation's future' (https://pmtranscripts.pmc.gov. au/release/transcript-16778). This was the delusion expressed in almost identical terms by the ANZAAS president during the historians' gathering back in 1959 (see note 6 for Chapter Eight).

Chapter Ten: 2005

1   Haynes (1998) p. xiv.

2   Two surveys from the late 1990s – Dewar's *In Search of the Never-Never: Looking for Australia in Northern Territory Writing* (1997) and Haynes' *Seeking the Centre: The Australian Desert in Literature, Art and Film* (1998) – suggest the sheer volume of cultural production inspired by 'the Outback', 'the Never-Never' and 'the Red Centre'; much has been added since.

3   The local school couldn't handle them (*The Australian*, 13 August 2002), their expulsion (*The Weekend Australian*, 5–6 April 2003), child bonuses being blown (*The Weekend Australian*, 24–25 July 2004), 'getting smashed is a way of life' (*The Bulletin*, 8 February 2005), the house block offered for sale at a dollar (*The Sydney Morning Herald*, 20 October 2004). Tennant's notoriety rose to a dreadful crescendo in 2018 with revelations of the rape of a toddler, and a subsequent visit to the town by Prime Minister Malcolm Turnbull.

4   The Northern Institute, Charles Darwin University (2013) p. 1. Life on welfare is inherently debilitating, as Noel Pearson and many others have pointed out, but

its administration compounded the problem. In his evidence to the land claim commissioner, the town clerk reported that by the mid-1980s there were fifteen or sixteen governmental agencies operating in (and on) Tennant Creek. Transcript of evidence of Bruce McRae, 30 March 1985, p. 2489.

5   Anyinginyi Health Aboriginal Corporation (October 2016). 'Children of the Barkly', Submission to the Royal Commission into the Protection and Detention of Children in the Northern Territory.

6   The Northern Institute (2013), p. 15.

7   Banners promoting the shows included 'Strip and Prawn', '17 Strips in 2 Hours', and 'Blow Out with a Blow Job' (Boffa, George and Tsey, December 1994).

8   Wright (1997) pp. 255–6.

9   d'Abbs, Togni and Crundall (June 1996) p. 12. See also Wright's 1997 account of these events, and particularly of their social and historical context.

10 For logs of publications related to the Warumungu/Tennant Creek, see Nash (2016) and Nash (2020).

11 Maurice (1988) p. xx.

12 The curator was an academically trained social historian. Writing about her work on the exhibition (Kelham, 2008), she betrays a consciousness of Aboriginal people in and around the town in the 1930s, the period covered in the exhibition, and 'sympathy' for them, but little or no understanding of relationships between black and white other than those between individuals. Kelham worried about the absence of 'Aboriginal voices' (p. 59), and 'as a mark of respect for Tennant's contemporary Indigenous population' (p. 59) used the term 'Aboriginal' in the exhibition where her witnesses of the 1930s would have said 'nigger'; the legal system of the 1930s is said to have 'disadvantaged' the Warumungu (p. 61); black and white are described as leading 'disparate' lives (p. 62). The upshot is described in the introduction to Kelham's article (p. 56): 'When asked to create a social history exhibition in a small mining town, out of "depressingly ugly" objects, the author of this paper struggled to find ways to use objects to teach, stimulate and entertain. This paper looks at the results: ways in which personal accounts of the past have been incorporated into regional museum exhibitions in central Australia as a means of authenticating new historical research, enhancing object meaning, making emotional connections with the past and encouraging new audiences to visit museums. Oral history quotes painted on walls and shovel heads; talking photo albums, digitised multi-media presentations which combine audio, photographic and other images with print: through disparate ways, the author and the museum sought to give objects meaning for their audience.' In short, the medium completely dominated the message.

13 They included a Kreisler short-wave radio that my father had got Uncle Jack to send up so that he could keep up with ABC News on shortwave. Kids notice the strangest things – I recognised the radio from a missing bit of the 'K'.

14 'History' refers here to evidence-based written accounts of the past, 'public history' to other ways of marking and remembering, usually more 'popular' ones. The 'heritage' boom of the 1970s and 1980s prompted an interest by

scholarly historians in public history and the closely related issues of memory and commemoration (including who remembers and forgets what and why) sufficient to give birth to a sub-discipline. Its arrival in Australia in the early 1990s was marked by a special edition of the history discipline's top journal, *Australian Historical Studies*, and a new journal, *Public History Review*.

15   The entry for Tennant Creek in US encyclopedia *Encarta* in 2003 suggests how successful the town has been in having its account of itself expunge others: 'Tennant Creek lies far inland, at the centre of the Northern Territory's richest mineral reserves. [It] is on the Stuart Highway but in fact is 11 km (7 mi) south of the creek itself, which was discovered in 1860 and named after John Tennant of Port Lincoln, South Australia. [It is] the main town of a cattle ranching area. The region became the site of an Overland Telegraph Station in 1872 (now a museum), but it was not until the 1930s and the nation's "Last Great Gold Rush" that Tennant Creek became properly established as a settlement … Local legend says that a wagon loaded with beer and with timber for the construction of a new hotel further north broke down in Tennant Creek in the 1930s. The wagoners decided to stay where they were, drink the beer, and open a hotel in Tennant Creek instead. Gold was subsequently discovered nearby and a small gold rush began. The 1950s saw the discovery of other mineral reserves around Tennant Creek. Silver and copper are today extracted locally. Population (1991) 3,480.'

16   The event was reported in *Land Rights News* (July 2004).

17   Christen (2009, pp. 232–60) records the genesis and development of Nyinkka Nyunyu.

18   Much of the credit, or blame, for Tennant Creek's public history goes to Mrs Hilda Tuxworth and her son Ian. Mrs Tuxworth's efforts included collecting a mass of documentation, deposited in an informal archive housed in the old hospital dispensary building, and a formal collection held by the University of Queensland; recording interviews for the NT government's oral history program; and writing and publishing a modest history of the town (Tuxworth, 1978). Ian Tuxworth was the local member of the Territory's legislative assembly, and a minister in conservative governments from the late 1970s to the mid-1980s, including briefly as chief minister (see Chapter Seven). His two big contributions to the telling of Tennant's story (and to the Territory's history campaign) were the Battery Hill complex and the old telegraph station. The larger movement of which the Tuxworths' activities were part is described in Carment (2007).

19   The architects worked to and for an Aboriginal-owned company, and consulted widely as to the design – see www.stephenlumbarchitect.com/nyinkka-nyunyu-art-cultural-centre. That they still didn't get it right is suggested by the letting in 2020 of an $8 million tender for a revamp, including improved entry, retail space, artist studios, office space and amenities, and 'an enhanced visitor experience' (*Tennant & District Times*, 20 November 2020).

20   See Plate 47, 'Young Warrumungu woman. Tennant Creek, 1901', in Batty, Allen and Morton (2005).

21   Williams (2015).

22   When I subsequently read Kimberly Christen's *Aboriginal Business* (2009), I
      realised that in 2006 I had been enrolled in something like a package tour, the
      same tour guides, much the same cast, Nyinkka Nyunyu as base camp and tour
      operator. Christen spent much more time with the people I met than I did, and
      was very much better equipped to understand what was going on. Christen also
      found that even though the Warumungu people concerned have had to deal with
      a procession of inquisitive whitefellas for most of their lives, they did so with
      patience and courtesy. I have drawn frequently on Christen's work.

23   Fifteen years after I met those seven people, all have passed away.

24   Edith and Rose were proud of their father/grandfather for the way he managed
      the difficulties faced by many 'black trackers'. They told me that he was still kindly
      remembered by many *wumparrani* for the way he was often able to protect people
      unfairly pursued by *papulanyi* law, including Warlpiri people fleeing from police
      and vigilantes after the Coniston massacres in 1928. 'My dad used to tell us about
      the old days,' Edith said. 'People came up from west got shot, a lot of people got
      shot out at the Pebbles all way up to Attack Creek. *Papulanyi* would chase them
      with horses. Dad helped them, those poor buggers, Warlpiri mob. He hid them in
      a cave so rangers couldn't track them.' See also note 30 for Chapter One.

25   See Chapter Four, in particular note 19.

26   Both Jean McCarthy and Day Day Frank have since passed away.

27   Debts accumulated in reaching this conclusion are to Stanner (1968) for his
      formulation 'the story of the unacknowledged relations between two racial groups
      within a single field of life'; to Henry Reynolds, particularly in *This Whispering in
      Our Hearts* (1998), for grasping the relationship between conscience and material
      wants; and to Tim Rowse (2017) for showing how much in Australia's history can
      only be understood as flowing from relations between frontier and post-frontier.
      On Reynolds' debt to Stanner, see note 8 for Chapter Eight; Rowse's *Indigenous
      and Other Australians since 1901* is organised around Stanner's 'relations between
      two racial groups within a single field of life'.

Afterword

1   Among the scholars, the anthropologists – first to arrive on the scene – were also
      the first to leave. Deserving to retire with full honours, anthropology was unfairly
      accused – and often accused itself – of doing the intellectual dirty work of empire.
      A discipline that had struggled to comprehend the Aboriginal universe when just
      about everyone else was ignoring it now spent much of its energy on introspection
      and on providing technical services to land claims processes. The law followed.
      After *Cubillo*, the lawyers, like the anthropologists, became heavily involved in
      the administration of relations between white and black rather than in revealing
      or changing them. Something similar can be said about the historians too. Many
      are still hard at work on recovering the story, but in its detail. Important findings
      have been made, notably about the sophistication of pre-European material
      culture (recorded in Bill Gammage's *The Biggest Estate on Earth* in 2011 and, more

contentiously, in Bruce Pascoe's *Dark Emu* in 2014), and about the extent and
character of armed conflict (by Ørsted-Jensen and Evans in 2014). But even these
are not revelations of the kind that made the historians the chief exposers of the
silence, putting them on front pages in the 1970s and 1980s and again during the
history wars. The passionate construction of a new paradigm has given way to
academic industry within it.

On the other side of that bitter frontier, the pundits and polemicists switched
their attention to new outrages, as committed by the climate scientists particularly.
Among the history warriors, only Blainey has shown any sign of changing his
mind and then only to take with one hand much of what he gave by the other.
The story as he first told it, in *Triumph of the Nomads*, no longer ends with the
sails of doom. In 2015 and 2016 Blainey published *The Story of Australia's People* in
two volumes, the first subtitled *The Rise and Fall of Ancient Australia*, the second
The Rise and Rise of a New Australia. He concludes that assimilation might be an
unfashionable word but it nonetheless 'goes on and on', and he distorts Stanner to
suggest that Aboriginal people have long voted with their feet to join white society,
representing him (Blainey, 2016, p. 296) as saying that some migrations were so
long-lasting that he doubted that all Aborigines had a deep, persisting affinity with
their 'clan country'. Stanner's views were both different from and more complex
than Blainey claims: 'There is a real, and an intense, bond between an Aboriginal
and the ancestral estate he shares with other clansmen,' Stanner told his colleagues,
to try to get them to see 'change' as well as 'continuity'. 'I have seen a man,
revisiting his homeland after an absence, fall on the ground, dig his fingers in the
soil, and say: "O, my country." But he *had* been away, voluntarily; and he was soon
to go away *again* voluntarily. Country is a high interest with a high value; rich
sentiments cluster around it; but there are other interests; all are relative, and any
can be displaced. If the bond between person and clan-estate were always and in all
circumstances of the all-absorbing kind it has sometimes been represented to be,
then migrations of the kind I have described could not have occurred.' (Stanner,
1958, 1979, p. 49, emphases in the original.) As for the puzzle of how purportedly
irresistible assimilation relates to the rise of a self-conscious Aboriginal people,
Blainey's solution is to not mention it. Like Hasluck eighty-odd years ago, Blainey's
last line of defence is to claim a moral equivalence between black and white. 'Both
sides,' he said recently, 'deserve blame and praise.' (Blainey, *The Weekend Australian*,
26 August 2017.) His most recent (2020) book is *Captain Cook's Epic Voyage*. Good
grief! as Charlie Brown might have said.

2   Rachel Perkins' online directory The Black Book listed more than 2700
Indigenous organisations and individuals working in ninety-five professions in the
arts, media and cultural industries – and that was published fifteen years ago (*The
Australian Financial Review*, 23–24 July 2005).

3   On discussions and negotiations at state and territory level, see Hobbs (2019).

4   The meeting of Catholic school principals referred to in this paragraph was at
Ballarat in 2019; the struggles over public history on Botany Bay are described
in McKenna (2018) pp. 46–61; the documentaries on Adam Goodes are *The*

Australian Dream and *The Final Quarter.* The prime minister's words: '*Yanggu gulanyin ngalawiri, dhunayi, Ngunawal dhawra. Wanggarra lijinyin mariny bulan bugarabang.* Today, Mr Speaker, we are meeting together on Ngunawal Country and we acknowledge and pay our respects to their Elders.' (Turnbull, 2020, p. 560.) Turnbull's subsequent curt dismissal of the call for a Voice to Parliament illustrates how words often substitute for action. On the Tasmanian developments, which will see an Aboriginal elder lay a wreath on Anzac Day to commemorate those who died in the frontier wars and the creation of a new 'frontier conflict memorial and commemoration', see Reynolds (April 2021).

5   The Statement's objectives and priorities have been formulated in different ways, most commonly as demands for a constitutionally recognised 'Voice to Parliament', and a truth-telling process, both to be overseen by a Makarrata Commission. See https://ulurustatement.org/faqs, accessed 2 February 2021. The Statement, along with predecessors stretching back to the Bark Petitions of 1963 and beyond, is running into opposition led by conservative federal governments. See McKenna (2018) and Rowse (February 2021a).

6   In asking this question (and many others) I have followed Rowse's lead – see particularly 'The moral complexity of truth-telling' (Rowse, February 2021b).

7   For a detailed discussion, see Chapter One, pages 25–6.

8   Henry Reynolds was among the first to insist on the role of conscience in shaping our history, and perhaps the most persistent in making the point over and again. See note 27 for Chapter Ten.

9   By 2020 the AIATSIS (Australian Institute of Aboriginal and Torres Strait Islanders) library contained 120,625 print items. Of these, 18,445 were histories, including 412 'general' histories, 750 'oral histories', 1959 biographies and 270 autobiographies. Articles, speeches and so on would run to much larger totals.

10   See Kemp, Owen and Barnes (December 2020).

11   See note 52 for Chapter Nine.

12   For a brief survey of the 'statue wars', see Carlson (June 2020).

13   There is no such thing as 'cancel culture', only those who wish to accuse others of belonging to it (and who manage to overlook the frequent vandalism of those few statues and other markers that honour Aboriginal people). There *is* anger among many people in a number of countries who have been excluded from public life, which unfortunately appears sometimes as a kind of censoriousness and self-righteousness, forcefully analysed by commentator Waleed Aly (November 2020). An inquiry chaired by a senior conservative figure, Dr David Kemp, recently (and sensibly) pointed out that the excluded in Australia would be less inclined to disfigure historical markers if the markers told more of their story (Australian Heritage Council, March 2018). However, this doesn't address, for example, the offensiveness to Aboriginal and Torres Strait Islander people of living in a town named for a violent racist and slaver. There are many ways for the present to respond to the leavings of the past, but sometimes the only decent thing to do is to cancel them. On damage to Indigenous memorials, see note 40 for Chapter Nine.

14   Among these communities I must list Melrose, the town where I first noticed
     the silence of public history (see Foster and Nettelbeck, 2012). See also Milliken
     (May 2019), McKenna (2018) and Batten and Batten (2008) for accounts of
     reconciliation debates, ceremonies and markers relating to Dubbo, Botany Bay
     and Kurnell, Coniston, and Myall Creek. On the reconciliation at Myall Creek
     and of the Wirrpanda and McColl families, see www.abc.net.au/news/2018-06-10/
     myall-creek-massacre-memorial-a-symbol-of-reconciliation/9845158 and https://
     independentaustralia.net/australia/australia-display/wukidi-the-reconcilation-of-
     mccoll-and-wirrpanda,7975 (Dhakiyarr Wirrpanda killed Constable McColl in
     Arnhem Land in 1933 after being shot at by McColl, an incident mentioned on
     p. 78 in Chapter Three.) Perth's new museum reflects the close involvement of
     Indigenous groups from initial conception to final form (Wong, November 2019).
15   The Heritage Commission was a statutory body established in the 1970s to
     document and protect Australia's natural and cultural heritage. The websites
     referred to are the Australian Heritage Database, www.environment.gov.au/
     heritage/publications/australian-heritage-database; Monument Australia, www.
     monumentaustralia.org.au; the University of Newcastle's colonial massacres map,
     https://c21ch.newcastle.edu.au/colonialmassacres/map.php; and the AWM's
     register of war memorials, https://placesofpride.awm.gov.au.
16   For a short overview of the AWM's relations with its critics, see my article 'Saving
     the war memorial from itself', https://insidestory.org.au/saving-the-war-memorial-
     from-itself, accessed 20 February 2021.
17   See note 52 for Chapter Nine.
18   There have been many proposals to establish a museum or similar specialising in
     Aboriginal history and/or the history of relations between Aboriginal peoples and
     the rest of us. Among the first was Stanner's 1965 sketch for a 'Gallery of Southern
     Man'; among the most recent is Henry Reynolds' call for 'a new national museum
     dedicated to the frontier wars and supported with the same level of funding
     that is received by the War Memorial' (February 2021) and Mark McKenna's
     suggestion (February 2021) that a 'national museum that showcased Indigenous
     cultures and languages and acknowledged the frontier wars' might be a better
     use of public resources than yet more expenditure on the AWM. An important
     complication for any solution: deciding where and how to represent the frontier
     wars is a straightforward matter, but deciding who should be commemorated and
     how is not.
19   For details on this and other points made in this paragraph, see my article 'Saving
     the war memorial from itself', https://insidestory.org.au/saving-the-war-memorial-
     from-itself, accessed February 20, 2021.
20   Among them, a former head of the Defence Force (*The Age*, 11 November 2020),
     a former head of the AWM itself (*The New Daily*, 14 July 2020) and the former
     head of the AWM's history section, who founded the journal *Honest History* after
     resigning his post.
21   In these matters the Labor Party has a history of highs and lows stretching back to
     the Bark Petitions. Keating, and perhaps specifically his Redfern speech, was the

highest of its highs. It is now at its lowest low – it recently sent a junior shadow
minister to sit on the platform for the announcement of the half-billion-dollar
grant to the AWM for wildly disproportionate commemoration of conflicts that
are trivial compared to the frontier wars. Indigenous leaders might look for an
undertaking from the Opposition that a Labor government would put the AWM
in the hands of a senior cabinet minister who, perhaps via a high-level review, will
review its Act, reduce or eliminate its dependence on non-public funding, and
appoint a new council charged with returning the memorial to its stated mission.

22   What would make it possible for a foreign minister, in this case Marise Payne,
      to criticise the Chinese government for its enforced assimilation of the Uighers
      without betraying even a flicker of recognition that she spoke for a country (and
      a political party) that had only recently stopped trying to enforce assimilation?
      And what to make of one of her predecessors as foreign minister, Alexander
      Downer, bragging about his family of 'nation-builders', apparently oblivious to
      the work of the family's patriarch in 'opening up the north'? Or of a 2009 political
      biography of Sir John Downer (by a former Labor premier) that makes no
      mention of Downer's role in that 'opening up'? And of the University of Adelaide's
      inauguration in 2012 of a biennial 'Sir John Downer Oration'?

23   I have borrowed the term from Inglis (1998); the caps are mine.

BIBLIOGRAPHY

PRIMARY SOURCES

National Archives of Australia (NAA) Land Claim Exhibits

Nash, David Land Claim Book, August 1980 (Exhibit 14, Warlmanpa, Warlpiri, Mudbura and Warumungu Claim, NAA Series E1477, Item LC26/14).

Sutton Peter, Nash David and Morel Petronella, Anthropologists' Report May 1993 (Muckaty Pastoral Company Land Claim, NAA Series E1471, Item LC135/NLC 2).

NAA Land Claim Transcripts (Warumungu Claim)

Kathleen Fitz and others (Series E1471, Item LC496, 071-1000).

Jack Kijkari (Series E1471, Item LC495, 879-91).

Topsy Nelson Napurrula (Series E1471, Item LC22/494, 669-75).

Lucky Graham, Edith Graham, Day Day Frank and others (Series E1471, Item LC492, 452-512).

Jimmy Frank and Ross Williams (Series E1471, Item LC490, 176-216).

Bunny Napurrula (Series E1471, Item LC22/516, 3286-96).

Jimmy Frank (Series E1471, Item LC22/515, 3213).

Jimmy Frank, Day Day Frank, Lucky Graham, Kathleen Fitz (Series E1471, 1-914, various).

Billy Boy, Jimmy Jones (Series E1471, Item LC22/517, 3460-90).

Bruce McRae (Series E1471, Item LC22/508, 2463-2575).

David Nash (Series E1471, Item LC22/522, 3895-3900).

See also 'Land Claim Reports' in 'Published Sources' (below).

National Archives of Australia (Darwin)

The Northern Territory's Native Affairs Branch maintained a file on each of the stations visited by its patrol officer, on each patrol officer, and on the Phillip Creek settlement, all now held in the National Archives of Australia (Darwin). Files used were:

Rockhampton Downs Station (Series F1/0, Item 1966/802).
Banka Banka Station (Series NTAC 1976/5, Item 1963/469).
Report by Patrol Officer Lovegrove for the year ended December 1953, dated 3 February 1954 (Series E738, Item GE98, Controlling Agency 7114).
PO Sweeney (Series F1/0, Item 1943/65).
PO Harney (Series F1/0, Item 1944/275).
Phillip Creek – Review Reports (Series E738, Item GE98).
Phillip Creek – Education (Series E748, Item ED10).

NORTHERN TERRITORY ARCHIVES SERVICE

Police Station: Tennant Creek, F303 Police journals 1933–1969, Volume 01/01/1949–30/09/1951.
Transcripts of interviews with Kevan Weaber (TS 351), Bill Fullwood (TS 431), Tony Lynch (TS 480), Harry Giese (TS 755), Alf Chittock and Peter Gunner (TS 787), Murphy Japanangka (TS 862).

AUTHOR INTERVIEWS AND PERSONAL COMMUNICATIONS

Personal communication from Hal Wootten, 17 June 2020.
Author interviews:
Fay Gale, Adelaide, 3 September 2003.
Merv Pattemore, Darwin, 3 September 2005.
Edith Graham Nakamarra, Tennant Creek, 24 August 2005.
Jimmy Jones Jampin, Tennant Creek, 25 August 2005.
Rosie Thompson Nakamarra, Tennant Creek, 26 August 2005.
Bunny Napurrula, Tennant Creek, 29 August 2005.
Therese Patterson Napurrula, Tennant Creek, 29 August 2005.
Judy Nixon Nakamarra, Tennant Creek, 29 August 2005.
Kathleen Fitz Napanangka, Tennant Creek, 30 August 2005.
Notes were made in the course of all author interviews and expanded/corrected immediately after the interviews if required.

OTHER UNPUBLISHED SOURCES

Anyinginyi Health Aboriginal Corporation (October 2016) 'Children of the Barkly', Submission to the Royal Commission into the Protection and Detention of Children in the Northern Territory, https://webarchive.nla.gov.au/awa/20181010003025/https://childdetentionnt.royalcommission.gov.au/submissions/Pages/default.aspx, accessed 10 October 2018.
'Discovering Tennant Creek' tourist map keyed for a walking tour (with 30 points of interest) and a 'Mural Drive' (22 points of interest).
Nyinkka Nyunyu Information Series: no. 1 *Wanjjal payinti* Bush TVs; no. 2 *Punttu Warumungu* skin relationships; no. 3 *Mayi* Bush Tucker recipes; no. 4 Wapparr Language; no. 5 *Wurrmulalkki* Returned Histories.

Priest, Charles A.V. (1986) 'Northern Territory Recollections', 'Earlier Northern Territory Recollections', 'Further Northern Territory Recollections', 'Still Further Northern Territory Recollections'; typescripts held in the State Library of Victoria.

Priest, Charles A.V. (1987) 'Tennant Creek recollections (with a South Australian Interlude)', typescript held in the State Library of Victoria.

Spencer, Baldwin (1901–02) Journal, 1 July 1901 – 11 February 1902, Mitchell Library MSS 29/3 (CY Reel 62, Record identifier 9arW6Xan).

Stanner, W.E.H. (1952) 'Reflective Journeyings', MS 3752 Item 137, Stanner Collection, Australian Institute for Aboriginal and Torres Strait Islander Studies.

PUBLISHED SOURCES

Aboriginal Oral Histories, Biographies and Autobiographies: See in Sources (below): Crugnale (comp.) (1995); Davenport, Johnson and Yuwali (2005); Henty-Gebert (2005); Hercus and Sutton (eds) (1986); Koch (ed.) and Koch (transl.) (1993); Lester (1993); Lowe and Pike (1990): Merlan (comp.) (1996); Nash (1984, 2016, 2016a, 2016b); Read and Read (1991); Richards, Hudson and Lowe (eds) (2002); Rubuntja and Green (2002); Tuxworth (1978); Vaarzon-Morel (ed.) (1995).

Key Published Sources on Tennant Creek and the Warumungu: See in Sources (below): Boffa, George and Tsey (December 1994); Brady (1988); Carment (1991, 1998); Christen (2009); d'Abbs, Togni and Crundall (June 1996); Davison (1985); Edmunds (1995); Goodchild Research Studies (February 1984); Grant (1991); Kilmartin and Matches (June 1995); Lea (1989a, 1989b); Miles (1988); The Northern Institute, Charles Darwin University (2013); Pearce (1984); *Tennant & District Times* (1984).

Australian Dictionary of Biography **entries:** Blackburn, Sir Richard Arthur; Cubadgee, Dick; Dhakiyarr Wirrpanda; Downer, Sir John William; Elkin, Adolphus Peter; Fison, Lorimer; Gillen, Francis James; Gunn, Jeannie; Horn, William Austin; Howitt, Alfred William; Lindsay, David; Lingiari, Vincent; Mabo, Edward Koiki; Radcliffe-Brown, Alfred Reginald; Rowley, Charles Dunford; Spencer, Sir Walter Baldwin; Stanner, William Edward; Stirling, Sir Edward Charles; Stuart, John McDouall; Tindale, Norman Barnett; Todd, Sir Charles; Tuxworth, Hilda Elsie; Willshire, William Henry; Windeyer, Richard.

Land Claim Reports: The Aboriginal Land Commissioner published the final report for each concluded claim; all are listed in the commissioner's annual reports. Reports used include:

 Warlmanpa, Warlpiri, Mudbura and Warumungu Land Claim (Report 11, 1981).

 Keytej, Warlpiri and Warlmanpa Land Claim (Report 14, 1982).

 Warumungu Land Claim (Report 31, 1988).

 McLaren Creek Land Claim Report (Report 32, 1990).

 Warlmanpa [Muckaty PL] (Report 51, 1997).

SOURCES

Abbott, C.L.A. (1950) *Australia's Frontier Province*, Angus & Robertson, Sydney.

Administrator (Northern Territory) (November 1915) *Report of the Administrator for the Year 1914–1915*, Commonwealth of Australia, Canberra.

Afianos, C. (ed.) (1984) *The Tennant & District Times: 50 Golden Years*, The *Tennant & District Times* commemorative issue in conjunction with the 'Back to Tennant Creek' celebrations, May 1984.

Allbrook, Malcolm (November 2017) 'Indigenous lives, the "cult of forgetfulness" and the *Australian Dictionary of Biography*', *The Conversation*, 1 November 2017, https://theconversation.com/indigenous-lives-the-cult-of-forgetfulness-and-the-australian-dictionary-of-biography-86302.

Allsop, Richard (2020) *Geoffrey Blainey: Writer, Historian, Controversialist*, Monash University Press, Clayton.

Altman, Jon (August 2009) 'The Boy from Hope Vale' (review of Noel Pearson's *Up from the Mission*), *Australian Book Review*, no. 313, July–August 2009.

Aly, Waleed (November 2020) 'Woke politics and power', *The Monthly*.

Anonymous (1904) 'The Australian Blackfellow under the microscope' (review of Spencer and Gillen's *The Northern Tribes of Central Australia*), *Life*, 15 October 1904.

Anthony, Thalia and Harry Blagg (June 2020) 'Enforcing assimilation, dismantling Aboriginal families: a history of police violence in Australia', *The Conversation*, 19 June 2020, https://theconversation.com/enforcing-assimilation-dismantling-aboriginal-families-a-history-of-police-violence-in-australia-140637.

Attwood, Bain (ed.) (1996) *In the Age of Mabo: History, Aborigines and Australia*, Allen & Unwin, St. Leonards.

—— (2003) *Rights for Aborigines*, Allen & Unwin, Crows Nest.

—— (2005) *Telling the Truth about Aboriginal History*, Allen & Unwin, Crows Nest.

Attwood, Bain and Stephen Foster (eds) (2003) *Frontier Conflict: The Australian Experience*, National Museum of Australia, Canberra.

Attwood, Bain and Tom Griffiths (eds) (2009) *Frontier, Race, Nation: Henry Reynolds and Australian History*, Australian Scholarly Publishing, Melbourne.

Austin, Tony (1997) *Never Trust a Government Man: Northern Territory Aboriginal Policy 1911–1939*, Northern Territory University Press, Darwin.

Austin, Tony and Suzanne Parry (eds) (1998) *Connection and Disconnection: Encounters between Settlers and Indigenous People in the Northern Territory*, Northern Territory University Press, Darwin.

Australian Broadcasting Commission (1970) 'Missus of Banka Banka', *A Big Country*, TV series.

Australian Heritage Council (March 2018) *Protection of Australia's Commemorative Places and Monuments*, Commonwealth of Australia, Canberra.

Australian Institute of Health and Welfare (August 2018) *Aboriginal and Torres Strait Islander Stolen Generations and Descendants: Numbers, Demographic Characteristics and Selected Outcomes*, Cat. no. IHW 195, AIHW, Canberra.

Australian Institute of Health and Welfare (June 2019) *Children Living in Households with Members of the Stolen Generations*, Cat. no. IHW 214, AIHW, Canberra.

Baker, Ken (1985) 'The Bicentenary: celebration or apology?', *IPA Review*, vol. 38, no. 4, Summer 1985.

Baker, Ken (ed.) (1985) *The Land Rights Debate: Selected Documents*, Institute of Public Affairs, Melbourne.

——(1988) *A Treaty with the Aborigines?*, Institute of Public Affairs, Melbourne.

Barwick, Diane E. (1985) 'This most resolute lady: a biographical puzzle', in Barwick, Beckett and Reay (eds) (1985).

Barwick, Diane E., Jeremy Beckett and Marie Reay (eds) (1985) *Metaphors of Interpretation: Essays in Honour of W.E.H. Stanner*, ANU Press, Canberra.

Batten, Bronwyn (2004) 'Monuments, memorials and the presentation of Australia's Indigenous past', *Public History Review*, no. 11.

Batten, Bronwyn and Paul Batten (2008) 'Memorialising the past: is there an "Aboriginal" way?', *Public History Review*, no. 15.

Batty, Philip, Lindy Allen and John Morton (eds) (2005) *The Photographs of Baldwin Spencer*, Miegunyah Press and the Museum of Victoria, Carlton and Melbourne.

Batty, Philip (ed.) (2006) *Colliding Worlds: First Contact in the Western Desert 1932–1984*, Museum of Victoria, Melbourne.

Batty, Philip and Jason Gibson (2014) 'Reconstructing the Spencer and Gillen Collection online: museums, Indigenous perspectives and the production of cultural knowledge in the digital age', https://www.researchgate.net/publication/280053960, accessed 14 February 2021.

Beckett, Jeremy and Melinda Hinkson (2008) '"Going more than half way to meet them": on the life and legacy of W.E.H. Stanner', in Hinkson and Beckett (eds) (2008).

Bell, Diane (1983) *Daughters of the Dreaming*, Allen & Unwin, Sydney.

Bell, Diane and Pam Ditton (1980) *Law, the Old and the New: Aboriginal Women in Central Australia Speak Out*, published for Central Australian Aboriginal Legal Aid Service by *Aboriginal History*, Canberra.

Berndt, Ronald M. (1956) 'Professor A.P. Elkin – an appreciation', *The Australian Journal of Anthropology*, vol. 5, no. 3.

Berndt, Ronald M. and Catherine H. Berndt (eds) (1965) *Aboriginal Man in Australia: Essays in Honour of Emeritus Professor A.P. Elkin*, Angus & Robertson, Sydney.

—— (1979) *Aborigines of the West: Their Past and Their Present*, UWA Press, Crawley.

Berndt, Ronald M. and Catherine H. Berndt (1987) *End of an Era: Aboriginal Labour in the Northern Territory*, AIATSIS, Canberra.

—— (1999) *The World of the First Australians: Aboriginal Traditional Life: Past and Present*, Aboriginal Studies Press, Canberra.

Berndt, Ronald M. and Robert Tonkinson (eds) (1988) *Social Anthropology and Australian Aboriginal Studies: A Contemporary Overview*, Aboriginal Studies Press, Canberra.

Birtles, Dora (1946) *The Overlanders*, Shakespeare Head, London and Sydney.

Blackburn, Julia (1997) *Daisy Bates in the Desert*, Vintage, London.

Blackburn, Kevin (2002) 'Mapping Aboriginal nations: the "nation" concept of late nineteenth century anthropologists in Australia', *Aboriginal History*, vol. 26.

Blackburn, Mr Justice (1971) *Milirrpum and Others v Nabalco Pty Ltd and the Commonwealth of Australia: Reasons for Judgement*, Federal Law Reports (FLR Vol. 17-10).

Blainey, Geoffrey (1982) *Triumph of the Nomads: A History of Ancient Australia* (revised edition) Macmillan, South Melbourne.

—— (July–August 1993) 'Drawing up a balance sheet of our history', *Quadrant*.

—— (February 2015) 'I can see parts of our history with fresh eyes', *The Australian*, 21 February 2015.

—— (2015) *The Story of Australia's People: The Rise and Fall of Ancient Australia*, Viking, Melbourne.

—— (2016) *The Story of Australia's People: The Rise and Rise of a New Australia*, Viking, Melbourne.

—— (August 2017) 'Let's reclaim history instead of distorting it', *The Weekend Australian*, 26 August 2017.

—— (2019) *Before I Forget*, Hamish Hamilton, Melbourne.

Boffa, Jon, Chris George and Komla Tsey (December 1994) 'Sex, alcohol and violence: a community collaborative action against striptease shows', *Australian Journal of Public Health*, vol. 18, no. 4, pp. 359–66.

Bolger, Audrey (1991) *Aboriginal Women and Violence: A Report for the Criminology Research Council and the Northern Territory Commissioner of Police*, North Australia Research Unit, Australian National University, Darwin.

Bolton, Geoffrey (2014) *Paul Hasluck: A Life*, UWA Publishing, Crawley.

Bongiorno, Frank (2015) *The Eighties*, Black Inc., Collingwood.

—— (September 2017) 'The statue wars: can we hold more than one idea in our heads at the same time?' *Inside Story*, 4 September 2017.

—— (January 2019) 'Bringing them home: cabinet papers 1996–97', *Inside Story*, 1 January 2019.

—— (2020) 'Review of *Geoffrey Blainey: Writer, Historian, Controversialist*', *Australian Historical Studies*, vol. 51, no. 2, pp. 229–30.

Bonyhady, Tim and Tom Griffiths (1996) *Prehistory to Politics: John Mulvaney, the Humanities and the Public Intellectual*, Melbourne University Press, Carlton South.

Booth, Katharine and Lisa Ford (2016) '*Ross v Chambers*: assimilation law and policy in the Northern Territory', *Aboriginal History*, no. 40, January 2016.

Borchardt, D.H. (ed.) (1987) *Australians: A Guide to Sources*, vol. 7 in *The Australians Historical Library*, Fairfax, Syme and Weldon, Broadway.

Bottoms, Timothy (2013) *Conspiracy of Silence: Queensland's Frontier Killing Times*, Allen & Unwin, Crows Nest.

Bowern, Claire (March 2018) 'The origins of Pama-Nyungan, Australia's largest family of Aboriginal languages', *The Conversation*, 13 March 2018.

Brady, Maggie (1988) *Where the Beer Truck Stopped: Drinking in a Northern Australian Town*, North Australia Research Unit, Australian National University, Casuarina.

Brennan, Frank (April 2018) 'Public servant to the First Australians: funeral homily for Barrie Dexter CBE', *Eureka Street*, 26 April 2018.

Brett, Judith (1998) 'Limited politics', in Stannage, Saunders and Nile (eds) (1998).
—— (June 2020) *The Coal Curse: Resources, Climate and Australia's Future*, Quarterly Essay 78, Black Inc., Carlton.
Broome, Richard (2019) *Aboriginal Australians: A History since 1788* (fifth edition) Allen & Unwin, Crows Nest.
Buchanan, Gordon (1933) *Packhorse and Waterhole: With the First Overlanders to the Kimberleys*, Angus & Robertson, Sydney.
Burgmann, Verity and Jenny Lee (eds) (1988) *A Most Valuable Acquisition: Volume One of A People's History of Australia since 1788*, McPhee Gribble, Melbourne.
Carlson, Bronwyn (June 2020) 'Taking a wrecking ball to monuments – contemporary art can ask what really needs tearing down', *The Conversation*, 12 June 2020, https://theconversation.com/friday-essay-taking-a-wrecking-ball-to-monuments-contemporary-art-can-ask-what-really-needs-tearing-down-140437, accessed 2 February 2021.
Carment, David (1987) 'The Tuxworth government: a political history', Occasional Paper no. 1, University College of the Northern Territory, Darwin.
—— (1991) 'Australia's depression gold rush: Tennant Creek 1932–1936', Occasional Paper no. 5, Northern Territory University, Darwin.
—— (1998) 'The dispossession of the Warumungu: encounters on a Northern Australian mining frontier', in Austin and Parry (eds) (1998).
—— (2001) *A Past Displayed: Public Memory and Cultural Resource Management in Australia's Northern Territory*, Northern Territory University Press, Darwin.
—— (2004) 'History, identity and politics: Australian Historical Association presidential address 2004', *History Australia*, vol. 2, no. 1, 2005.
—— (2007) *Territorianism: Politics and Identity in Australia's Northern Territory 1978–2001*, Australian Scholarly Publishing, Melbourne.
Carment, David and Helen J. Wilson (eds) (1996) *Northern Territory Dictionary of Biography: Vol. 3*, Northern Territory University Press, Darwin.
Chatwin, Bruce (1987) *The Songlines*, Picador, London.
Chauvel, Charles and Elsa (1959) *Walkabout*, W.H. Allen, London.
Christen, Kimberly (2009) *Aboriginal Business: Alliances in a Remote Australian Town*, Aboriginal Studies Press, Canberra.
Clark, Anna (August 2018) 'The "great Australian silence" 50 years on', *The Conversation*, 3 August 2018, https://theconversation.com/friday-essay-the-great-australian-silence-50-years-on-100737, accessed 5 September 2018.
Clarke, John (July 2000) 'Apology by John Howard, actor', transcript in *The Sydney Morning Herald*, 9 February 2008, https://www.smh.com.au/national/apology-by-john-howard-actor-20080209-gds08v.html.
Cohen, Barry (May 1984) 'Environmental, protection legislation and its impact on resource industries: speech by the Minister for Home Affairs and Environment, Mr Barry Cohen MP, to the Australian Mining Industry Council, in Canberra, 2 May', *Australian Foreign Affairs Record*, no. 55.
Commonwealth Conciliation and Arbitration Commission (1966) *The Cattle Station Industry (Northern Territory) Award, 1951: Variation*, Fair Work

Commission, https://www.fwc.gov.au/documents/documents/education/resources/1966cattleindustry.pdf.

Coombs, H.C. 'Nugget' (1981) *Trial Balance: Issues of My Working Life*, Macmillan, South Melbourne.

Cowlishaw, Gillian (August 2015) 'Friend or foe? Anthropology's encounter with Aborigines', *Inside Story*, 19 August 2015, https://insidestory.org.au/friend-or-foe-anthropologys-encounter-with-aborigines, accessed 2 February 2021.

Cross, Jack (2011) *Great Central State: The Foundation of the Northern Territory*, Wakefield Press, Mile End, South Australia.

Crotty, Martin and Paul Sendziuk (March 2018) *The State of the Discipline: University History in Australia and New Zealand: A Report to the Australian Historical Association Executive*, https://www.theaha.org.au/wp-content/uploads/2018/10/The-State-of-the-Discipline_University-History-in-Australia-and-NZ-2018.pdf, accessed 15 November 2019.

Crugnale, Jordan (comp.) (1995) *Footprints Across Our Land: Short Stories by Senior Western Desert Women*, Magabala Books, Broome.

Cunneen, Chris and Julia Grix (2003) 'Chronology of the Stolen Generations litigation 1993–2003', *Indigenous Law Bulletin*, vol. 5, issue 23.

Curthoys, Ann (2002) *Freedom Ride: A Freedom Rider Remembers*, Allen & Unwin Crows Nest.

—— (2003) 'Constructing national histories', in Attwood and Foster (eds) (2003).

—— (2008) 'W.E.H. Stanner and the historians', in Hinkson and Beckett (eds) (2008).

Curthoys, Ann and Ann Genovese (2003) 'Evidence and narrative: history and the law', in McCalman and McGrath (eds) (2003).

Curthoys, Ann, Ann Genovese and Alexander Reilly (2008) *Rights and Redemption: History, Law and Indigenous People*, UNSW Press, Coogee.

d'Abbs, Peter, Samantha Togni and Ian Crundall (June 1996) *The Tennant Creek Liquor Licensing Trial, August 1995 – February 1996: An Evaluation*, revised edition, Menzies School of Health Research, Darwin.

Davenport, Sue, Peter Johnson and Yuwali (2005) *Cleared Out: First Contact in the Western Desert*, Aboriginal Studies Press, Canberra.

Davis, S.L. and J.R.V. Prescott (1992) *Aboriginal Frontiers and Boundaries in Australia*, Melbourne University Press, Carlton.

Davison, Graeme (2000) *The Use and Abuse of Australian History*, Allen & Unwin, St Leonards.

—— (2003) 'History on the witness stand: interrogating the past', in McCalman and McGrath (eds) (2003).

Davison, Graeme, John Hirst and Stuart Macintyre (1998) *The Oxford Companion to Australian History*, Oxford University Press, Melbourne.

Davison, Patricia (1985) *The Manga-Manda Settlement, Phillip Creek: An Historical Reconstruction from Written, Oral and Material Evidence*, Material Culture Unit, James Cook University of North Queensland, Townsville.

Dawson, John (2004) *Washout: On the Academic Response to* The Fabrication of Aboriginal History, Macleay Press, Sydney.

Day, David (1996) *Claiming a Continent: A History of Australia*, Angus & Robertson, Pymble.

Dewar, Mickey (1992) *The 'Black War' in Arnhem Land: Missionaries and the Yolngu 1908–1940*, North Australia Research Unit, Australian National University, Darwin.

—— (1997) *In Search of the Never-Never: Looking for Australia in Northern Territory Writing*, Northern Territory University Press, Casuarina.

—— (2012) 'Finding a past we can live with', Eric Johnston lecture, Northern Territory Library, https://ntl.nt.gov.au/eric-johnston-lecture, accessed 3 September 2019.

Dexter, Barrie (2008) 'Stanner: reluctant bureaucrat', in Hinkson and Beckett (eds) (2008).

—— (2015) *Pandora's Box: The Council for Aboriginal Affairs, 1967–1976*, Keeaira Press, Southport.

Donovan, P.F. (1984) *At the Other End of Australia: The Commonwealth and the Northern Territory 1911–1978*, University of Queensland Press, St Lucia.

Dow, Coral (2002) 'Mabo: ten years on', Parliamentary Research Service E-Brief, 23 May 2002 https://www.aph.gov.au/About_Parliament/Parliamentary_Departments/Parliamentary_Library/Publications_Archive/archive/mabo, accessed 3 December 2020.

Dreyfus, Mark (2003) 'Historians in court', in McCalman and McGrath (eds) (2003).

Duncan, Tim (1988–89) 'History as a kangaroo court', *IPA Review*, December 1998 – February 1989.

Durack, Mary (1959) *Kings in Grass Castles*, Constable, London.

Edmunds, Mary (1995) *Frontiers: Discourses of Development in Tennant Creek*, Aboriginal Studies Press, Canberra.

Elkin A.P. (September 1934) 'Anthropology and the future of the Australian Aborigines', *Oceania*, vol. 5, no. 1.

—— (1938) *The Australian Aborigines: How to Understand Them*, Angus & Robertson, Sydney.

—— (September 1939) 'Anthropology in Australia, 1939', *Oceania*, vol. 10, no. 1.

—— (1943) 'Native Policy in Australia', review of Hasluck's *Black Australians* and Foxcroft's *Australian Native Policy, Historical Studies Australia and New Zealand*, vol. 2, no. 8.

—— (July 1952) 'Australian Aboriginal and white relations: a personal record', *Royal Australian History Society Journal*, vol. 48, part 3.

—— (1955) 'Anthropology: its study and use in Australia', *International Social Science Bulletin*, vol. 8, no. 2.

—— (June 1956) 'A.R. Radcliffe-Brown, 1880–1955', *Oceania*, vol. 26, no. 4.

—— (September 1957) 'Aboriginal policy 1930–1950: some personal recollections', *Quadrant*, vol. 1, no. 4.

—— (October 1958) 'Anthropology in Australia: one chapter', *Mankind*, vol. 5, issue 6.

—— (December 1958) 'Review of Radcliffe-Brown's *A Natural Science of Society*', *Oceania*, vol. 29, no. 2.

—— (November 1974) 'Book notice', *Oceania*, vol. 45, no. 2.

—— (1979) 'Aboriginal–European relations in Western Australia: an historical and personal record', in Berndt and Berndt (eds) (1979).

Evans, Raymond (2014) 'The debatable land', a review of the *Cambridge History of Australia: Volume 1 and Volume 2, History Australia,* vol. 11, no. 2.

Evans, Raymond, Kay Saunders and Kathryn Cronin (1988) *Race Relations in Colonial Queensland: A History of Exclusion, Exploitation and Extermination,* University of Queensland Press, St Lucia.

Evans, Raymond, and Robert Ørsted-Jensen (2014) '"I cannot say the numbers that were killed": assessing violent mortality on the Queensland frontier', available at SSRN: https://papers.ssrn.com/sol3/papers.cfm?abstract_id=2467836.

Fathi, Romain (April 2016) 'Is Australia spending too much on the "Anzac centenary"? A comparison with France', *Honest History,* 14 April 2016.

—— (April 2021) 'Crowds at dawn services have plummeted in recent years. It's time to reinvent Anzac Day', *The Conversation,* 21 April 2021.

Flannery, Tim (ed.) (2009) *Watkin Tench's 1788,* Text Publishing, Melbourne.

Fogarty, John and Jacinta Dwyer (2012) 'The first Aboriginal land rights case', in Helen Sykes (ed.) *More or Less: Democracy and New Media,* available at www.futureleaders.com.au/book_chapters/pdf/More-or-Less/John-Fogarty_Jacinta-Dwyer.pdf, accessed 1 September 2019.

Foley, Gary (May 1997) '*The Sydney Morning Herald* and representation of the 1988 Bicentennial', www.kooriweb.org/foley/essays/pdf_essays/the%20smh%20and%20 1988.pdf, accessed November 2019.

—— (n.d.) 'The Noel Pearson dossier', Gooriweb, https://www.gooriweb.org/pearson. html, accessed 3 December 2020.

Foster, Robert and Amanda Nettelbeck (2012) *Out of the Silence: the History and Memory of South Australia's Frontier Wars,* Wakefield Press, Mile End.

Furphy, Samuel (2013) *Edward M. Curr and the Tide of History,* ANU Press, Canberra.

Gale, Fay (1999) 'Shared space – divided cultures: Australia today', Cunningham Lecture, Occasional Paper Series 1/1999, Academy of the Social Sciences in Australia.

Gammage, Bill (2013) *The Biggest Estate on Earth,* Allen & Unwin, Crows Nest.

Gardiner-Garden, John (1993) 'The Mabo debate: a chronology', Parliamentary Research Service, Background Paper No. 23, Department of the Parliamentary Library, Canberra.

—— (1996–97) 'The origin of Commonwealth involvement in Indigenous Affairs and the 1967 referendum', Information and Research Services, Background Paper No. 11, Department of the Parliamentary Library, Canberra.

Gare, Deborah, Geoffrey Bolton, Stuart Macintyre and Tom Stannage (eds) (2003) *The Fuss that Never Ended: The Life and Work of Geoffrey Blainey,* Melbourne University Press, Carlton South.

Gibb, C.A. (Chair) (December 1972) *The Situation of Aborigines on Pastoral Properties in the Northern Territory: Parliamentary Paper No. 62,* report of the committee of review, Commonwealth of Australia, Canberra.

Giese, Harry (1990) 'Planning a program for Aborigines in the 1950s', Occasional Paper no. 16, Northern Territory Library Service, Darwin.

Gill, N., A. Paterson and M. Kennedy (2001) '"Murphy, do you want to delete this?" Hidden histories and hidden landscapes in the Murchison and Davenport Ranges', in Ward and Muckle (eds) (2001).

Gillen, Francis (1968) *Gillen's Diary: The Camp Jottings of F.J. Gillen on the Spencer and Gillen Expedition Across Australia 1901–1902*, Libraries Board of South Australia, Adelaide.

Gillen, Robert S. (ed.) (1995) *F.J. Gillen's First Diary 1875: Adelaide to Alice Springs, March to June*, Wakefield Press, Kent Town.

Gleeson, Jane and Michaela Richards (1985) *Mataranka and the Daly, Two Studies in the History of Settlement in the Northern Territory*, North Australia Research Unit, Australian National University, Darwin.

Goodchild Research Studies (February 1984) *Tennant Tomorrow: Prospects and Strategies for Economic Development and Population Growth*, Tennant Creek Town Council, Tennant Creek.

Goot, Murray and Tim Rowse (2007) *Divided Nation? Indigenous Affairs and the Imagined Public*, Melbourne University Press, Carlton.

Grant, Archibald Wesley (1991) 'Culture Shock: Tennant Creek', *Journal of Northern Territory History*, no. 2.

Gray, Geoffrey (2008) '"A chance to be of some use to my country": Stanner during World War II', in Hinkson and Beckett (eds) (2008).

Griffiths, Billy (2018) *Deep Time Dreaming: Uncovering Ancient Australia*, Black Inc., Carlton.

Griffiths, Tom (July 2006) 'The frontier fallen', *Eureka Street*, 5 July 2006, https://www.eurekastreet.com.au/article/the-frontier-fallen, accessed 18 June 2016.

Haebich, Anna (1998) 'The formative years: Paul Hasluck and Aboriginal issues during the 1930s', in Stannage, Saunders and Nile (1998).

—— (2000) *Broken Circles: Fragmenting Indigenous Families 1800–2000*, Fremantle Arts Centre Press, Fremantle.

Haines, A.B. (1932) 'At Tennant's Creek', *Walkabout*, 1 June 1932.

Hall, Robert (June 1980) 'Aborigines, the army and the Second World War in northern Australia', *Aboriginal History*, vol. 4, no. 1.

Hardman, William and John McDouall Stuart (1975) *Explorations in Australia: The Journals of John McDouall Stuart During the Years 1858, 1859, 1860, 1861 & 1862 When He Fixed the Centre of the Continent and Successfully Crossed it from Sea to Sea*, Libraries Board of South Australia, Adelaide.

Harney, W.E. 'Bill' (1957) *Life among the Aborigines*, Robert Hale, London.

—— (1961) *Grief, Gaiety and Aborigines*, Robert Hale, London.

Harrison, Des (n.d.) '2/1st North Australia Observer Unit', The Australian Light Horse Association, https://www.lighthorse.org.au/2-1st-north-australia-observer-unit, accessed 21 June 2004.

Hartwig, M.C. (1960) *The Coniston Killings*, BA (Hons) thesis, University of Adelaide.

—— (1965) *The Progress of White Settlement in the Alice Springs District and Its Effects upon the Aboriginal Inhabitants, 1860–1894*, PhD thesis, University of Adelaide.

Hasluck, Paul (1942) *Black Australians: A Survey of Native Policy in Western Australia,*

1829–1897, Melbourne University Press, Melbourne.

—— (August 1963) Statement in the House of Representatives by the Minister for Territories, 14 August 1963 (published as 'Assimilation in Action').

—— (1977) *Mucking About: An Autobiography*, Melbourne University Press, Carlton.

—— (1988) *Shades of Darkness: Aboriginal Affairs 1925–1965*, Melbourne University Press, Carlton.

Haynes, Roslynn D. (1998) *Seeking the Centre: The Australian Desert in Literature, Art and Film*, Cambridge University Press, London, Melbourne.

Henty-Gebert, Claire (2005) *Paint Me Black: Memories of Croker Island and Other Journeys*, Aboriginal Studies Press, Canberra.

Hercus, Luise and Peter Sutton (eds) (1986) *This Is What Happened: Historical Narratives by Aborigines*, Australian Institute of Aboriginal Studies, Canberra.

Heppell, Michael (ed.) (1979) *A Black Reality: Aboriginal Camps and Housing in Remote Australia*, Australian Institute of Aboriginal Studies, Canberra.

Herbert, Xavier (1938) *Capricornia*, Publicist Publishing, Sydney.

Hiatt, L.R. (ed.) (1975) *Australian Aboriginal Mythology: Essays in Honour of W.E.H. Stanner*, Australian Aboriginal Studies no. 50, Australian Institute of Aboriginal Studies, Canberra.

Hiatt, L.R. (1996) *Arguments about Aborigines: Australia and the Evolution of Social Anthropology*, Cambridge University Press, Cambridge.

Hill, Barry (2002) *Broken Song: T.G.H. Strehlow and Aboriginal possession*, Knopf, Milsons Point.

Hill, Ernestine (1943) *The Great Australian Loneliness*, Robertson & Mullens, Melbourne.

—— (December 1943) 'Where are the Wararmunga?' *Walkabout*, vol. 10, no. 2.

—— (1951) *The Territory*, Angus & Robertson, Pymble.

Hinkson, Melinda (2005) 'The intercultural challenge of Stanner's first fieldwork', *Oceania*, March–June, vol. 75, no. 3.

—— (2008a) 'Stanner and Makerere: on the "insuperable" challenges of practical anthropology in post-war East Africa', in Hinkson and Beckett (2008).

—— (2008b) 'Journey to the source: in pursuit of Fitzmaurice rock art and the high culture', in Hinkson and Beckett (2008).

—— (August 2009) 'The trouble with suffering', review of Sutton's *The Politics of Suffering*, *Arena Magazine*, 1 https://openresearch-repository.anu.edu.au/handle/1885/55607.

—— (2010) 'Thinking with Stanner in the present', *Humanities Research*, vo. 16, no. 2.

Hinkson, Melinda and Jeremy Beckett (eds) (2008) *An Appreciation of Difference: W.E.H. Stanner and Aboriginal Australia*, Aboriginal Studies Press, Canberra.

Hirst, John (1998) 'The Blackening of Our Past', *IPA Review*, December 1998 – February 1989.

Hobbs, Harry (July 2019) 'How the treaty momentum is growing', *Inside Story*, 24 July 2019, https://insidestory.org.au/how-the-treaty-momentum-is-growing, accessed 28 July 2019.

Hunter, Rosemary (1996) 'Aboriginal histories, Australian histories, and the law', in

Attwood (ed.) (1996).

Idriess, Ion (1932) *Flynn of the Inland*, Angus & Robertson, North Ryde.

—— (1947) *Drums of Mer*, Angus & Robertson, Sydney.

—— (1961) *Tracks of Destiny*, Angus & Robertson, Sydney.

Inglis, Ken (1998) *Sacred Places: War Memorials in the Australian Landscape*, Melbourne University Press, Carlton.

Institute of Public Affairs (August–October 1988) 'The anti-development movement is locking up large tracts of Australia' (map), *IPA Review*, no. 40.

James, Barbara (1989) *A Social and Structural History of Four Australian Inland Mission Buildings in the Northern Territory*, National Trust (Northern Territory), Darwin.

Janson, Susan and Stuart Macintyre (eds) (October 1988) *Making the Bicentenary*, special edition of *Australian Historical Studies*, no. 23.

Jones, Philip (1987) 'South Australian anthropological history: the Board for Anthropological Research and its early expeditions', *Records of the South Australian Museum*, vol. 20, no. 1.

—— (December 1995) 'Norman B. Tindale, October 1900 – 19 November 1993, an obituary', *Records of the South Australian Museum*, vol. 28, no. 2.

—— (2007) *Ochre and Rust: Artefacts and Encounters on Australian Frontiers*, Wakefield Press, Mile End.

Jupp, James (1988) 'Editing an encyclopedia of the Australian people', in Shaw (ed.) (1988).

Keating, Paul (1992) 'Redfern speech', 10 December 1992, https://antar.org.au/sites/default/files/paul_keating_speech_transcript.pdf, accessed 4 December 2019.

—— (1993) 'Remembrance Day 1993: commemorative address', Speech at the tomb of the Unknown Soldier, 11 November 1993, https://www.awm.gov.au/commemoration/speeches/keating-remembrance-day-1993, accessed 4 December 2019.

—— (May 2011) 'Lowitja O'Donoghue oration', Don Dunstan Foundation, University of Adelaide, 31 May 2011, https://www.dunstan.org.au/events/lodo-2011, accessed 3 December 2020.

Keen, Ian (2008) '"Religion", "magic", "sign" and "symbol" in Stanner's approach to Aboriginal religions', in Hinkson and Beckett (2008).

Kelham, Megg (2007) 'Discovering local history through museums at the Battery Hill Mining Centre, Tennant Creek: an educational resource for middle-upper primary and lower secondary schools', self-published, Alice Springs.

—— (2008) 'Learning history from the horse's mouth', *Oral History Association of Australia Journal*, issue 30.

Kemp, Deanna, John Owen and Rodger Barnes (December 2020) 'Juukan Gorge enquiry puts Rio Tinto on notice, but without drastic reforms, it could happen again', *The Conversation*, 9 December 2020, https://theconversation.com/juukan-gorge-inquiry-puts-rio-tinto-on-notice-but-without-drastic-reforms-it-could-happen-again-151377, accessed 2 February 2021.

Kerley, William (1987) 'From land rights to separatism', *IPA Review*, vol. 41, no. 3, November 1987 – January 1988.

Kevin, J.C.G. (ed.) (1939) *Some Australians Take Stock*, Longmans, Green, London.

Kidd, Rosalind (2006) *Trustees on Trial: Recovering Stolen Wages*, Aboriginal Studies Press, Canberra.

Kilmartin, Christine and Geoff Matches (June 1995) *Tennant Creek: Living There – Views from Families and Service Providers*, report to the Department of Human Services and Health, Australian Institute of Family Studies, Melbourne.

Kimber, R.G. (1991) *The End of the Bad Old Days: European Settlement in Central Australia, 1871–1894*, State Library of the Northern Territory, Darwin.

Koch, Grace (ed.) and Harold Koch (transl.) (1993) *Kaytetye Country: An Aboriginal History of the Barrow Creek Area*, IAD Press, Alice Springs.

Kuper, Adam (ed.) (1977) *The Social Anthropology of Radcliffe-Brown*, Routledge & Kegan Paul, London.

Lake, Marilyn (ed.) (2006) *Memory, Monuments and Museums: The Past in the Present*, Melbourne University Press in association with the Australian Academy of the Humanities, Carlton.

Land Rights News (July 2004) 'Tears shed at Phillip Creek', Central Land Council.

Langton, Marcia (1993) 'Rum, seduction and death: "Aboriginality" and alcohol', *Oceania*, vol. 63, no. 3.

—— (1996a) 'Foreword' to Loos and Mabo (1996).

—— (1996b) 'The stuff of heritage', in Bonyhady and Griffiths (1996).

—— (March 2011) 'Anthropology, politics and the changing world of Aboriginal Australians', *Anthropological Forum*, vol. 21, no.1.

—— (May 2012) 'Why I continue to be inspired by Pearson', *The Weekend Australian*, 5–6 May 2012.

La Nauze, J.A. (1959) 'The study of Australian history, 1929–1959', *Historical Studies: Australia and New Zealand*, vol. 9, no. 33.

Lea, John (1989a) *Government and the Community in Tennant Creek 1947–1978*, North Australia Research Unit, Australian National University, Darwin.

—— (1989b) 'South of the Berrimah line: government and the Aboriginal community in Katherine and Tennant Creek after World War Two', in Loveday and Webb (eds) (1989).

Lester, Yami (1993) *Yami: The Autobiography of Yami Lester*, IAD Press, Alice Springs.

Long, J.P.M. (1967) 'The administration and the part-Aboriginals of the Northern Territory', *Oceania*, vol. 37, no. 3.

—— (1992) *The Go-Betweens: Patrol Officers in Aboriginal Affairs Administration in the Northern Territory 1936–1974*, North Australia Research Unit, Australian National University, Casuarina, Northern Territory.

Loos, Noel (1982) *Invasion and Resistance: Aboriginal–European Relations on the North Queensland Frontier 1861–1897*, ANU Press, Canberra.

Loos, Noel and Eddie Koiki Mabo (2013) *Edward Koiki Mabo: His Life and Struggle for Land Rights*, University of Queensland Press, St Lucia.

Loveday, Peter and Ann Webb (eds) (1989) *Small Towns in Northern Australia*, North Australia Research Unit, Australian National University, Darwin.

Lowe, Pat with Jimmy Pike (1990) *Jilji: Life in the Great Sandy Desert*, Magabala Books, Broome.

Macintyre, Stuart and Anna Clark (2004) *The History Wars*, revised edition, Melbourne University Press, Carlton.

Manne, Robert (April 2001) *In Denial: The Stolen Generations and the Right*, Quarterly Essay 1, Black Inc., Melbourne.

—— (2004) 'Aboriginal child removal and the question of genocide, 1900–1940', in Moses (ed.) (2004).

Manne, Robert (ed.) (2003) *Whitewash: On Keith Windschuttle's Fabrication of Australian History*, Black Inc., Melbourne.

Marcus, Julie (2001) *The Indomitable Miss Pink: A Life in Anthropology*, UNSW Press. Sydney.

Marcus, Julie (ed.) (1993) *First in Their Field: Women and Australian Anthropology*, Melbourne University Press, Carlton.

Marett, R.R. and T.K. Penniman (1931) *Spencer's Last Journey, Being the Journal of an Expedition to Tierra del Fuego by the Late Sir Baldwin Spencer*, The Clarendon Press, Oxford.

Markus, Andrew (1990) *Governing Savages*, Allen & Unwin, Sydney.

Markus, Andrew and MC Ricklefs (eds) (1985) *Surrender Australia? Essays in the Study and Use of History: Geoffrey Blainey and Asian Immigration*, George Allen & Unwin, Sydney.

Mason, Timothy (1998) 'The anthropologist's bagmen: Frazer, Spencer and Gillen, and the primitive in Australia', *Cultures of the Commonwealth*, no. 5.

Maynard, John (2007) *Fight for Liberty and Freedom: The Origins of Australian Aboriginal Activism*, Aboriginal Studies Press, Canberra.

McCalman, Iain and Ann McGrath (eds) (2003) *Proof & Truth: The Humanist as Expert*, The Australian Academy of the Humanities, Canberra.

McDonagh, Oliver (1987) 'The making of *Australians: A Historical* Library – a personal retrospect', in *Australians: A Historical Library*, vol. 10 *(The Guide and Index)*, https://socialsciences.org.au/library/the-making-of-australians-a-historical-library-a-personal-retrospect, accessed 10 December 2019.

McGuinness, Paddy (2000) 'Aboriginal massacres and stolen children', *Quadrant*, vol. 44, no. 11.

McGrath, Ann (1987a) *'Born in the Cattle': Aborigines in Cattle Country*, Allen & Unwin, Sydney.

—— (1987b) 'History and land rights', *Law and History in Australia*, vol. 3, republished in McCalman and McGrath (eds) (2003).

—— (1987c) '"Stories for country": Aboriginal history, oral history, and land claims', *Oral History Association of Australia Journal*, vol. 9, republished in McCalman and McGrath (eds) (2003).

McGrath, Ann and Andrew Markus (1987) 'European views of Aborigines', in Borchardt (ed.) (1987).

McGregor, Russell (1997) *Imagined Destinies*, Melbourne University Press, Carlton.

—— (2004) 'Governance, not genocide: Aboriginal assimilation in the postwar era', in Moses (ed.) (2004).

—— (August 2009) 'Another nation: Aboriginal activism in the late 1960s and early

1970s', *Australian Historical Studies*, vol. 40, no. 3.

McKay, Graham R. and Bruce A. Sommer (eds) (1999) 'Further applications of linguistics to Aboriginal contexts', Occasional Paper no. 7, Applied Linguistics Association of Australia, Melbourne.

McKenna, Mark (1997) 'Different perspectives on black armband history', Research Paper 5, Department of the Parliamentary Library, 1997–98.

—— (2018) *Moment of Truth: History and Australia's Future*, Quarterly Essay 69, Black Inc., Carlton.

—— (February 2021) 'Australia's haunted house', *The Monthly*.

Meagher, Douglas (2000) 'Not guilty', *Quadrant*, vol. 44, no. 11.

Meggitt, Mervyn J. (1962) *Desert People: A Study of the Walbiri Aborigines of Central Australia*, Angus & Robertson, Sydney.

Memmott, Paul (2010) 'Paddy Woodman', *Australian Aboriginal Studies*, no. 2.

Merlan, Francesca (1978) '"Making people quiet" in the pastoral north – reminiscences of Elsey Station', *Aboriginal History*, vol. 2, no. 1.

Merlan, Francesca (comp.) (1996) *Big River Country: Stories from Elsey Station*, IAD Press, Alice Springs.

Methodist Church (June 1963) 'Four major issues in assimilation: a memorandum issued by the National Missionary Council of Australia', Sydney, https://www.nma.gov.au/__data/assets/pdf_file/0011/698357/four-major-issues-in-assimilation.pdf, accessed 7 October 2020.

Miles, Margot (1988) *The Old Tennant: Stories on Life in Tennant Creek*, self-published.

Milliken, Robert (May 2019) 'The game changer', *Inside Story*, 10 May 2019, https://insidestory.org.au/the-game-changer, accessed 20 May 2019.

Milliss, Roger (1988) 'Contact history: the message of Waterloo Creek', in Shaw (ed.) (1988).

Morgan, Hugh (May 1984) 'Religious traditions, mining and land rights', in Baker (ed.) (1985).

—— (1988) 'The guilt industry', *IPA Review*, vol. 42, no. 1, May–July 1988.

—— (2010) 'Remarks at the dinner marking Ray Evans's retirement from the H.R. Nicholls Society', 7 October 2010, http://archive.hrnicholls.com.au/copeman/copeman2010/morgan-speech.php, accessed 9 March 2020.

Morphy, Howard (1988) 'The resurrection of the Hydra: twenty-five years of research on Aboriginal religion', in Berndt and Tonkinson (eds) (1988).

—— (2008) '"Joyous maggots": the symbolism of Yolngu mortuary rituals', in Hinkson and Beckett (eds) (2008).

Morton, S.R. and D.J. Mulvaney (eds) (1996) *Exploring Central Australia: Society, the Environment and the 1894 Horn Expedition*, Surrey Beatty & Sons, Chipping Norton.

Moses, A. Dirk (ed.) (2004) *Genocide and Settler Society: Frontier Violence and Stolen Indigenous Children in Australian History*, Berghahn Books, New York.

Mulvaney, John (1958) 'The Australian Aborigines 1606–1929: opinion and fieldwork', *Historical Studies*, vol. 8, no. 30.

—— (1986) '"A sense of making history": Australian Aboriginal studies 1961–1986', *Australian Aboriginal Studies*, no. 2.

—— (2003) 'Barrow Creek, northern Australia, 1874', in Attwood and Foster (eds) 2003.

Mulvaney, John and J.H. Calaby (1985) *So Much That Is New: Baldwin Spencer, 1860–1929: A Biography*, Melbourne University Press, Carlton.

Mulvaney, John and Peter White (1980) 'Aboriginal Australians and the Bicentennial history: a progress report', *Australian Archaeology*, no. 11.

Mulvaney, John with Alison Petch and Howard Morphy (1997) *My Dear Spencer: The Letters of F.J. Gillen to Baldwin Spencer*, Hyland House, South Melbourne.

—— (2000) *From the Frontier: Outback Letters to Baldwin Spencer*, Allen & Unwin, Sydney.

Murray, Tom and Hilary Howes (2019) 'How we tracked down the only known sculpture of a WWI Indigenous soldier', *The Conversation*, 5 June 2019.

Myers, Fred R. (1991) *Pintupi Country, Pintupi Self: Sentiment, Place, and Politics Among Western Desert Aborigines*, University of California Press, California.

Nash, Daphne and Paul Memmott (March 2016) 'Housing conditionality, Indigenous lifeworlds and policy outcomes: Tennant Creek case study', Australian Housing and Urban Research Institute at the University of Queensland.

Nash, David (1984) 'The Warumungu's reserves 1892–1962: a case study in dispossession', *Australian Aboriginal Studies*, no. 1.

—— (1999) 'Linguistics and land rights in the NT', in McKay, Graham R. and Bruce A. Sommer (eds) (1999).

—— (2016) 'Warumungu land: a partial history of land title', https://www.anu.edu.au/linguistics/nash/aust/wru/land.html, accessed 29 March 2019.

—— (October 2016a) 'Motion pictures, video, and CD-ROM recordings relating to the Warumungu', https://www.anu.edu.au/linguistics/nash/aust/wru/film.html, accessed 14 October 2019.

—— (October 2016b) 'Warumungu non-linguistic references', https://www.anu.edu.au/linguistics/nash/aust/wru/eth-ref.html, accessed October 2019.

—— (2020) 'References about Warumungu language or references in linguistics works – published and unpublished', https://www.anu.edu.au/linguistics/nash/aust/wru/lx-ref.html, accessed 24 March 2021.

National Museum of Australia, 'Struggle for land rights: Yirrkala 1963–1971', https://www.nma.gov.au/explore/features/indigenous-rights/land-rights/yirrkala, accessed 18 November 2019.

Nettelbeck, Amanda and Robert Foster (2007) *In the Name of the Law: William Willshire and the Policing of the Australian Frontier*, Wakefield Press, Kent Town.

Northern Institute, The (2013) 'The Demography of the Territory's "Midtowns": Tennant Creek', Charles Darwin University, no. 201305, https://www.cdu.edu.au/sites/default/files/the-northern-institute/Mid%20towns_Tennant%20Creek_Final.pdf, accessed 15 January 2021.

Northern Territory of Australia (1915) *Report of the Administrator for the Year 1914–1915*, Government of the Commonwealth of Australia, Government Printer, Victoria.

Northern Territory of Australia (1935) *Report on the Administration of the Northern Territory for the Year Ended 30th June 1934*, Government of the Commonwealth of

Australia, Commonwealth Government Printer, Canberra.

Northern Territory of Australia (May 1957) 'Government Gazette, no. 19B, 13 May'.

Northern Territory Investigation Committee (1937) *Report of the Board of Inquiry Appointed to Inquire into the Land and Land Industries of the Northern Territory Of Australia ('Payne Report')*, Government Printer, South Australia.

O'Byrne, Denis and Robert Walker (1993) *Telegraph Stations of Central Australia: Historical Photographs*, Conservation Commission Northern Territory, Alice Springs.

Ogden, John (2008) *Portraits from a Land Without People: A Pictorial Anthology of Indigenous Australia 1847–2008*, Cyclops Press, Sydney.

O'Loughlin, Mr Justice (August 2000) *Lorna Cubillo and Peter Gunner v The Commonwealth of Australia: Reasons for Judgement*, Federal Court of Australia, Darwin.

Paisley, Fiona (2000) *Loving Protection? Australian Feminism and Aboriginal Women's Rights 1919–1939*, Melbourne University Press, Carlton.

Partington, Geoffrey (1996) *Hasluck versus Coombs: White Politics and Australia's Aborigines*, Quakers Hill Press, Sydney.

—— (1997) 'The Interpretation of Aboriginal Policies: Some Problems – Geoffrey Partington Replies to Tim Rowse', *Meanjin*, vol. 56, no. 2.

Paul, Mandy and Geoffrey Gray (eds) (2002) *Through a Smoky Mirror: History and Native Title,* Aboriginal Studies Press, Canberra.

Pearce, Howard (1984) *Tennant Creek Historic Sites Study: A Report to the National Trust (Northern Territory)*, National Trust of Australia, Darwin.

Pearson, Noel (November 1996) 'An Australian history for all of us', Address to the Chancellor's Club Dinner, University of Western Sydney, 20 November 1996, http://www.kooriweb.org/foley/pearson/uws20nov1996.pdf, accessed 30 November 2020.

—— (August 2000) 'The light on the hill', Ben Chifley Memorial Lecture, Bathurst, 12 August 2000, https://capeyorkpartnership.org.au/speeches/the-light-on-the-hill-ben-chifley-memorial-lecture-noel-pearson, accessed 7 December 2020.

—— (October 2001) 'On the human right to misery, mass incarceration and early death', Dr Charles Perkins Memorial Oration, University of Sydney, 25 October 2001, https://capeyorkpartnership.org.au/speeches/dr-charles-perkins-memorial-oration-noel-pearson, accessed 7 December 2020.

—— (November 2002) 'Indigenous Australia: the social and cultural predicament', fifth annual Hawke Lecture, 3 November 2002, https://www.unisa.edu.au/connect/Hawke-Centre/Annual-Hawke-Lecture/5th-Annual-Hawke-Lecture, accessed 7 December 2020.

—— (March 2003) 'The High Court's abandonment of "the time-honoured methodology of the common law" in its interpretation of Native Title in Mirriuwung Gajerrong and Yorta Yorta', Sir Ninian Stephen Annual Lecture, University of Newcastle, 17 March 2003, https://parlinfo.aph.gov.au/parlInfo/search/display/display.w3p;query=Id%3A%22media%2Fpressrel%2F8ZB96%22, accessed 7 December 2020.

—— (October 2003) 'Land is susceptible of ownership', High Court Centenary Conference, Canberra, 9–11 October 2003, http://gooriweb.org/pearson/hc10oct2003.pdf, accessed 7 December 2020.

—— (2004) 'Land rights and progressive wrongs', *Griffith Review*, no. 2, summer 2003/2004), https://www.griffithreview.com/articles/land-rights-and-progressive-wrongs, accessed 30 November 2020.

—— (May 2004) 'AMA 2004 Oration', Australian Medical Association National Conference, 28 May 2004, www.kooriweb.org/foley/pearson/ama_may2004.pdf, accessed 7 December 2020.

—— (June 2005) 'Pearson backs Howard's approach to Indigenous affairs', *Insiders*, ABC-TV, 5 June 2005, https://www.abc.net.au/insiders/pearson-backs-howards-approach-to-indigenous/1586294, accessed 20 November 2020.

—— (2009) *Up from the Mission: Selected Writings*, Black Inc., Melbourne.

—— (December 2012) 'Keating and the speech we had to have', *The Australian*, 10 December 2012, https://capeyorkpartnership.org.au/media-articles/keating-and-the-speech-we-had-to-have, accessed 3 December 2020.

—— (September 2018) '2018 Hal Wootten Lecture', 6 September 2018, https://capeyorkpartnership.org.au/wp-content/uploads/2018/09/Hal-Wootten-Lecture_Noel-Pearson-6-September-2018.pdf, accessed 3 December 2020.

Peasley, W.J. (1983) *The Last of the Nomads*, Fremantle Arts Centre Press, Fremantle.

Perkins, Rachel and Marcia Langton (eds) (2008) *First Australians: An Illustrated History*, Miegunyah Press, Carlton.

Peterson, Nicolas (1987) 'Aboriginal studies and anthropology', in Borchardt (ed.) (1987).

—— (1990) '"Studying man and man's nature": the history of the institutionalisation of Aboriginal anthropology', *Australian Aboriginal Studies*, no. 2.

—— (2008) '"Too sociological"? Revisiting "Aboriginal territorial organisation"', in Hinkson and Beckett (eds) (2008).

Powell, Alan (2009) *Far Country: A Short History of the Northern Territory*, Melbourne University Press, Carlton.

Pybus, Cassandra (2020) *Truganini: Journey Through the Apocalypse*, Allen & Unwin, Crows Nest, NSW.

Rademaker, Laura (January 2019) 'Why do so few Aussies speak an Australian language?', *The Conversation*, 18 January 2019, https://theconversation.com/why-do-so-few-aussies-speak-an-australian-language-109570, accessed 20 January 2019.

Read, Peter (1999) *A Rape of the Soul So Profound: The Return of the Stolen Generations*, Allen & Unwin, St Leonards.

—— (2002) 'The Stolen Generations, the historian and the court room', *Aboriginal History*, vol. 26.

—— (2008) '"The truth that will set us all free": an uncertain history of memorials to Indigenous Australians', *Public History Review*, vol 15.

Read, Peter and Engineer Jack Japaljarri (1978) 'The price of tobacco: the journey of the Warlmala to Wave Hill, 1928', *Aboriginal History*, vol. 2.

Read, Peter and Jay Read (1991) *Long Time, Olden Time: Aboriginal Accounts of Northern Territory History*, IAD Press, Alice Springs.

Reid, Gordon (1990) *A Picnic with the Natives: Aboriginal-European Relations in the Northern Territory to 1910*, Melbourne University Press, Carlton.

Reyburn, Bruce (June 1993) 'Re: Wrong Way Land Claim Part One',
http://nativenet.uthscsa.edu/archive/nl/9306/0200.html, accessed 10 November 2020.

Reynolds, Henry (ed.) (1972) *Aborigines and Settlers: The Australian Experience, 1788–1939*, Cassell Australia, North Melbourne.

Reynolds, Henry (April 1976) 'The other side of the frontier: early Aboriginal reactions to pastoral settlement in Queensland and Northern New South Wales', *Historical Studies*, vol. 17, no. 66.

—— (1982) *The Other Side of the Frontier: Aboriginal Resistance to the European Invasion of Australia*, Penguin Books, Ringwood.

—— (1984) 'The breaking of the Great Australian Silence: Aborigines in Australian historiography 1955–1983', Trevor Reese Memorial Lecture, University of London, Institute of Commonwealth Studies, Australian Studies Centre, 30 January 1984.

—— (1987) *The Law of the Land*, Penguin, Ringwood.

Reynolds, Henry (comp.) (1989) *Dispossession: Black Australians and White Invaders*, Allen & Unwin, Sydney.

—— (1996) *Aboriginal Sovereignty: Reflections on Race, State and Nation*, Allen & Unwin, St Leonards.

—— (1998) *This Whispering in Our Hearts*, Allen & Unwin, St Leonards.

—— (1999) *Why Weren't We Told? A Personal Search for the Truth about Our History*, Viking, Ringwood.

—— (2000) *Black Pioneers: How Aboriginal and Islander People Helped Build Australia*, Penguin, Ringwood.

—— (2001) *An Indelible Stain? The Question of Genocide in Australia's History*, Penguin, Ringwood.

—— (2003) *The Law of the Land*, third edition, Penguin, Camberwell.

—— (2005) *Nowhere People: How International Race Thinking Shaped Australia's Identity*, Viking, Camberwell.

—— (2009) 'Class, race, nation', in Attwood and Griffiths (eds) (2009).

—— (2013) *Forgotten War*, NewSouth Publishing, Sydney.

—— (September 2017) 'Thinking about memory and monuments', *Pearls and Irritations*, 28 September 2017.

—— (2018) *This Whispering in Our Hearts Revisited*, NewSouth Publishing, Sydney.

—— (2021) *Truth-telling: History, Sovereignty and the Uluru Statement*, NewSouth Publishing, Sydney.

—— (February 2021) 'It's time for a new museum dedicated to the fighters of the frontier wars', *The Conversation*, 19 February 2021, https://theconversation.com/friday-essay-its-time-for-a-new-museum-dedicated-to-the-fighters-of-the-frontier-wars-155299.

—— (April 2021) 'Anzac Day and the frontier wars', *Pearls and Irritations*, 25 April 2021.

Richards, Eirlys, Joyce Hudson and Pat Lowe (eds) (2002) *Out of the Desert: Stories from the Walmajarri Exodus*, Magabala Books, Broome.

Riddett, Lyn Anne (1991) 'Growing up in the pastoral frontier: conception, birth and childhood on cattle stations in the Northern Territory, 1920–1950', and 'Recreation and entertainment on Northern Territory pastoral stations, 1910–1950', Occasional Paper no. 23, State Library of the Northern Territory, Darwin.

Ritter, David (1999) 'Whither the historians? The case for historians in the Native Title process', *Indigenous Law Bulletin*, vol. 4, no. 17.

—— (2008) 'Tilting at doctrine in a changing world: the three editions of Henry Reynolds' *The Law of the Land*', *Journal of Australian Studies*, vol. 32, no. 3.

Roberts, Tony (2005) *Frontier Justice: A History of the Gulf Country to 1900*, University of Queensland Press, St Lucia.

—— (August 2009) 'Black–white relations in the Gulf Country to 1950,' Blackheath History Forum, 29 August 2009, www.abc.net.au/reslib/200909/r436689_2099971. pdf, accessed 16 June 2018.

—— (November 2009) 'The brutal truth: what happened in the Gulf Country', *The Monthly*, https://www.themonthly.com.au/issue/2009/november/1330478364/tony-roberts/brutal-truth, accessed 16 June 2018.

Rose, Deborah Bird (1996) 'Histories and rituals: land claims in the Territory', in Attwood (ed.) (1996).

Rowley, C.D. (June 1962) 'Aborigines and other Australians', *Oceania*, vol. 32, no. 4.

Rowse, Tim (August 1988) 'Paternalism's changing reputation', *Mankind*, vol. 18, no. 2.

—— (August 1989) 'Review of Hasluck's *Shades of Darkness*', *Mankind*, vol. 19, no. 2.

—— (1996) 'Review of Partington's *Hasluck versus Coombs*', *Meanjin*, vol. 55, no. 4.

—— (1998a) 'The modesty of the state: Hasluck and the anthropological critics of assimilation', in Stannage, Saunders and Nile (1998).

—— (1998b) 'Terra Nullius', in Davison, Hirst and Macintyre (1998).

—— (2000) *Obliged To Be Difficult: Nugget Coomb's Legacy in Indigenous Affairs*, Cambridge University Press, Melbourne and New York.

—— (2002a) *Indigenous Futures: Choice and Development for Aboriginal and Torres Strait Island Australia*, UNSW Press, Sydney.

—— (2002b) 'Response to Hal Wootten', *Australian Aboriginal Studies*, no 2.

—— (2004) 'Notes on the history of the Aboriginal population of Australia', in Moses (ed.) (2004).

Rowse, Tim (ed.) (2005) *Contesting Assimilation*, API Network, Perth.

—— (2008) 'After the Dreaming: the Boyer lecturer as social critic', in Hinkson and Beckett (eds) (2008).

—— (2012) *Rethinking Social Justice: From 'Peoples' to 'Populations'*, Aboriginal Studies Press, Canberra.

—— (2017) *Indigenous and Other Australians since 1901*, UNSW Press, Sydney.

—— (February 2021a) 'Is the Voice already being muted?' *Inside Story*, 1 February 2021, https://insidestory.org.au/is-the-voice-already-being-muted, accessed 3 February 2021.

—— (February 2021b) 'The moral complexity of truth-telling', *Inside Story*, 26 February 2021, https://insidestory.org.au/the-moral-complexity-of-truth-telling-tim-rowse.

Rubuntja, Wenten with Jenny Green (2002) *The Town Grew Up Dancing: The Life and Art of Wenten Rubuntja*, Jukurrpa Books, Alice Springs.

Rudd, Kevin (August 2009) 'Launch of first volume of Tom Keneally's *Australians: Origins to Eureka*', National Library of Australia, Canberra, 27 August 2009, https://pmtranscripts.pmc.gov.au/release/transcript-16778, accessed 17 September 2019.

Ryan, Susan (1982) 'The Makarrata: Labor's policy', *Aboriginal Law Bulletin*, no. 37.

Saltré, Frédérik, Corey J.A. Bradshaw and Katharina J. Peters (December 2019) 'Did people or climate kill off the megafauna? Actually, it was both', *The Conversation*, 4 December 2019, https://theconversation.com/did-people-or-climate-kill-off-the-megafauna-actually-it-was-both-127803, accessed 17 May 2020.

Sandall, Roger (2001) *The Culture Cult: Designer Tribalism and Other Essays*, Westview Press, Colorado.

Serle, Geoffrey (1973) 'The state of the profession in Australia', *Australian Historical Studies*, vol. 15, no. 61.

Shaw, Danny (1999) 'Myths and facts about Aborigines and social security', *Indigenous Law Bulletin*, no. 26.

Shaw, George (ed.) (1988) *1988 and All That: New Views of Australia's Past*, University of Queensland Press, St Lucia.

Shiels, H. (ed.) (1963) *Australian Aboriginal Studies*, Oxford University Press, Oxford.

Spearritt, Peter (October 1988) 'Celebration of a nation: the triumph of spectacle', in Janson and Macintyre (eds) (1988).

Spencer, Baldwin (ed.) (1896) *Report on the Work of the Horn Scientific Expedition to Central Australia*, Dulau and Co., London, and Melville, Mullen and Slade, Melbourne.

Spencer, Baldwin (1901) *Guide to the Australian Ethnographicalal Collection in the National Museum of Victoria*, Government Printer, Melbourne.

—— (1904) 'How we wrote our book', *Life*, 15 October 1904.

—— (1913) 'Preliminary report on the Aboriginals of the Northern Territory', *Bulletin of the Northern Territory*, 7 July 1913.

Spencer, Baldwin and Frances Gillen (1899) *The Native Tribes of Central Australia*, Macmillan, London, reprinted 1969, Anthropological Publications reprint, Oosterhout.

—— (1904) *The Northern Tribes of Central Australia*, Macmillan, London, reprinted 1969, Anthropological Publications reprint, Oosterhout, the Netherlands.

—— (1912) *Across Australia*, Macmillan, London.

Stannage, Tom, Kay Saunders and Richard Nile (eds) (1998) *Paul Hasluck in Australian History: Civic Personality and Public Life*, University of Queensland Press, St Lucia.

Stanner, W.E.H. (1939) 'The Aborigines', in Kevin (ed.) (1939).

—— (March 1941) 'Review of *Aboriginal Woman, Sacred and Profane* by Phyllis M. Kaberry', *Oceania*, vol. 11, no. 3.

—— (1958) 'Continuity and change among the Aborigines', presidential address to Section F (Anthropology) ANZAAS, Adelaide, reprinted in Stanner (1979b).

—— (1963) 'Introduction', in Shiels (ed.) (1963).

—— (March 1967) 'Industrial justice in the Never-Never', *The Australian Quarterly*, vol. 39, no. 1, reprinted in Stanner (1979b).

—— (1970) 'The Yirrkala land case: dress-rehearsal', in Stanner (1979b).

—— (1972) ANZAAS presidential address, published as 'Fictions, nettles and freedoms' in Stanner (1979b).

—— (1979a) 'Address by W.E.H. Stanner to celebrate first Institute microfiche publication', *AIAS Newsletter* (new series) no. 12.

—— (1979b) *White Man Got No Dreaming: Essays 1938–1973*, ANU Press, Canberra.

—— (1980) 'Report upon Aborigines and Aborigines' reserve at Tennant's Creek 1934' for the Australian National Research Council, *Australian Institute of Aboriginal Studies Newsletter* (new series), no. 13.

—— (1991) *After the Dreaming: The Boyer Lectures 1968*, ABC Books, Sydney.

Strehlow, T.G.H. (1957) 'Dark and white Australians: talk to a public meeting convened by the South Australian Peace Committee, Adelaide, 6 April 1957', Riall, Melbourne.

—— (1964) *Assimilation Problems: The Aboriginal Viewpoint*, Aborigines Advancement League of South Australia, Adelaide.

Summers, John (2000) *The Parliament of the Commonwealth of Australia and Indigenous Peoples 1901–1967*, Parliament of Australia, Parliamentary Library, Canberra.

Sutton, Peter (2001) 'The politics of suffering: Indigenous policy in Australia since the 1970s', *Anthropological Forum*, vol. 11, no. 2.

—— (2008a) 'Stanner's veil: transcendence and the limits of scientific inquiry', in Hinkson and Beckett (eds) (2008).

—— (2008b) 'Stanner and Aboriginal land use: ecology, economic change and enclosing the commons', in Hinkson and Beckett (eds) (2008).

—— (2009) *The Politics of Suffering: Indigenous Australians and the End of the Liberal Consensus*, Melbourne University Press, Carlton.

Taylor, Peter (1980) *An End to Silence: The Building of the Overland Telegraph Line from Adelaide to Darwin*, Methuen, Sydney.

Tickner, The Hon Robert (May 1991) 'Return of land ends long wait for Warumungu', https://parlinfo.aph.gov.au/parlInfo/search/display/display.w3p;query=Id:%22media/pressrel/HPR04000998%22;src1=sm1, accessed 29 March 2019.

Tindale, Norman B. (November 1941) 'A survey of the half-caste problem in South Australia', *Proceedings of the Royal Geographical Society of Australasia (South Australian Branch)*, no. 42.

—— (1974a) *Aboriginal Tribes of Australia: Their Terrain, Environmental Controls, Distribution, Limits and Proper Names*, ANU Press, Canberra.

—— (1974b) 'Tribal Boundaries in Aboriginal Australia' map, http://archives.samuseum.sa.gov.au/tribalmap, accessed 15 June 2018.

Tonkinson, Robert (1978) *The Mardudjara Aborigines: Living the Dream in Australian Desert*, Holt, Rinehart and Winston, Fort Worth.

Toussaint, Sandy (1999) *Phyllis Kaberry and Me*, Melbourne University Press, Carlton.

Toussaint, Sandy (ed.) (2004) *Crossing Boundaries: Cultural, Legal, Historical and Practice Issues in Native Title*, Melbourne University Press, Carlton.

Treaty '88 Campaign (1988) 'Aboriginal sovereignty: never ceded', reproduced in *Australian Historical Studies*, vol. 23, no. 91.

Turnbull, Malcolm (2020) *A Bigger Picture*, Hardie Grant, Richmond.

Tuxworth, Hilda (1978) *Tennant Creek: Yesterday and Today*, self-published, Darwin.

Van Krieken, Robert (2000) 'From *Milirrpum* to *Mabo*: the High Court, *Terra Nullius* and moral entrepreneurship', *UNSW Law Journal*, vol. 23, no. 1.

Vaarzon-Morel, Petronella (ed.) (1995) *Warlpiri Women's Voices: Our Lives Our History*, IAD Publications, Alice Springs.

Ward, Graeme. and Adrian Muckle (eds) (2001) *The Power of Knowledge, the Resonance of Tradition: Proceedings of the AIATSIS Indigenous Studies Conference*, Aboriginal Studies Press, Canberra.

Walker, Richard and Helen (1986) *Curtin's Cowboys: Australia's Secret Bush Commandos*, Allen & Unwin, Sydney.

Williams, Nancy (1986) *The Yolngu and Their Land: A System of Land Tenure and the Fight for its Recognition*, Australian Institute of Aboriginal Studies, Canberra.

—— (2008) 'Stanner, *Milirrpum* and the Woodward Royal Commission', in Hinkson and Beckett (eds) (2008).

Wilson, Helen J. (1995) *The Heritage of Tennant Creek*, National Trust of Australia (Northern Territory), Darwin.

Wilson, Ronald (1997) *Bringing Them Home: Report of the National Inquiry into the Separation of Aboriginal and Torres Strait Islander Children from Their Families*, Human Rights and Equal Opportunity Commission, Sydney.

Windschuttle, Keith (1994) *The Killing of History: How a Discipline Is Being Murdered by Literary Critics and Social Theorists*, Macleay Press, Sydney.

—— (2002) *The Fabrication of Aboriginal History, Volume 1: Van Diemen's Land 1803–1847*, Macleay Press, Sydney.

—— (2006) 'The return of postmodernism in Aboriginal history', *Quadrant*, April 2006.

—— (2009) *The Fabrication of Aboriginal History, Volume 3: The Stolen Generations 1881–2008*, Macleay Press, Sydney.

Windschuttle, Keith, David Martin Jones and Ray Evans (eds) (2009) *The Howard Era: Essays*. Quadrant Books, Balmain.

Wise, Tigger (1985) *The Self-Made Anthropologist: A Life of A.P. Elkin*, George Allen & Unwin, Sydney.

Wolfe, Patrick (1999) *Settler Colonialism and the Transformation of Anthropology*, Cassell, London and New York.

Wong, Kieran (November 2019) 'Re-imagining a museum of our First Nations', *The Conversation*, 18 November 2019.

Woodward, A.E. (1982) *Report of the Royal Commission into Australian Meat Industry*, Australian Government Printing Service, Canberra.

—— (2005) *One Brief Interval*, Miegunyah Press, Melbourne.

Wootten, Hal (2002) 'Review of *Indigenous Futures: Choice and development for Aboriginal and Islander Australia* by Tim Rowse', *Australian Aboriginal Studies*, no. 2.

—— (2003) 'Conflicting imperatives: pursuing truth in the courts', in McCalman and McGrath (eds) (2003).

—— (November 2011) 'Reflections on the 20th anniversary of the Royal Commission

into Aboriginal Deaths in Custody', *Indigenous Law Bulletin*, vol. 7, no. 27.
—— (December 2016) 'Where were the Aborigines?', *Inside Story*, 19 December 2016, https://insidestory.org.au/where-were-the-aborigines, accessed 20 December 2016.
Wright, Alexis (1997) *Grog War*, Magabala Books, Broome.
Wright, Clare (January 2021) 'Masters of the future or heirs of the past? Mining, history and Indigenous ownership', *The Conversation*, https://theconversation. com/friday-essay-masters-of-the-future-or-heirs-of-the-past-mining-history-and-indigenous-ownership-153879, accessed 30 January 2021.
Young, Michael W. (2004) *Malinowski: Odyssey of an Anthropologist, 1884–1920*, Yale University Press, New Haven and London.
Yunupingu, Mandawuy et al. (1993) *Voices from the Land: Boyer Lectures 1993*, ABC Books, Sydney.

INDEX

Tuxworth, Hilda (*Tennant Creek: Today and Yesterday*) 154–5, 214 *see also* Darwin National Trust
Tuxworth, Ian (Northern Territory Minister for Mines and Energy) 155, 213

Uganda 104
Uluru Statement from the Heart 233, 239, 242
Unaipon, David (inventor and author) 84, 128, 172
United Nations 100
United Nations Security Council 100
United States 136, 137, 140, 173–4, 244
United States Supreme Court 171
University of Adelaide 9, 71
University of Cambridge 129
University of Melbourne 47, 49, 51, 71–2
University of Newcastle 239–40
University of Oxford 49–50, 74, 83, 129
University of Sydney 72, 74, 99, 192
University of Western Australia (UWA) 71, 98
Unmatjera people *see* Anmatyerre people
Urubunna people 43

Vatican, the 34
Vesteys company 93–4, 116–17
Victorian Football League (VFL) 58
Victorian government 77, 79

Wakaja people 15, 115
Walpiri people *see* Warlpiri people
Walunkwa ('water snake') 45–6, 60
Wambaia people *see* Wambaya people
Wambaya people 15, 115, 222, 224
Waramanga people *see* Warumungu people
Ward, Mary (Banka Banka Station) 94–6, 115, 143, 145, 155, 191, 238 *see also* Blue Moon gold mine; Wyndham
Ward, Russel (*The Australian Legend*) 171
Ward, Ted (Banka Banka Station) 94–5 *see also* Blue Moon gold mine; Wyndham
Warlmanpa people 115, 224
Warlpiri Country 93
Warlpiri people 10, 15, 45, 77, 81, 83, 91, 115, 204, 218, 222

Warrabri 'model settlement' (Ali Curung) 102–3, 114, 222
Warramunga people *see* Warumungu people
Warramulla people 81, 84–5
Warumungu Country 21, 27, 31, 45, 91, 93, 96, 102–3, 138, 149
Warumungu land claim 148–53, 155–60, 165, 177, 189, 207, 209, 213, 237, 275 n.13 *see also* Federal Court of Australia; Legislative Assembly of Northern Territory
Warumungu Pabula Housing Association (Julalikari Council) 143–4
Warumungu people xiii, 1–2, 7–10, 15–16, 19–21, 23–4, 28, 43–4, 46, 57, 63, 67, 81–2, 87–96, 102–3, 115, 141–5, 149, 155–7, 174, 214, 236 *see also* Attack Creek; Banka Banka Station; Phillip Creek mission; Tennant Creek
    Aboriginal Land Rights (Northern Territory) Act 1976 141
    ankkul nyinta 152
    bata aurinnia 21
    children taken 82, 185–92, 195, 216
    dispossession and loss 41, 63–4, 68–70, 80–2, 102–3, 115, 154, 157, 160, 180, 186, 236, 261 n.4
    frontiers on all sides 20–1, 23–4, 27, 30–1, 80–2, 102–3, 115, 127, 142, 154, 160, 180, 214, 263 n.30
    the gold miners 45, 57, 66–70, 80–2, 84, 86, 94–6, 106–7, 113, 116, 125, 127, 154–5, 180, 216, 236
    Murramunti ('Thakomara man of white cockatoo totem') 226
    papulanyi ('whitefella') xiii, 21, 24, 30–1, 41, 64, 87, 149, 212, 216, 222, 224, 226–7
    social welfare 206, 208
    state-sponsored terrorism 30, 64, 84
    Warrabri 'model settlement' 102–3, 114, 222
    work in the army 87, 92–3, 97, 104
    work on the stations 93–4, 111–13, 216, 218, 222
    wumparrani ('black' or 'blackfella') xiii, 87, 214
    yarntingi (together) 152

www.ingramcontent.com/pod-product-compliance
Lightning Source LLC
Chambersburg PA
CBHW052120270326
41930CB00012B/2695